für / for Dietz

California

Hillert Ibbeken

California

Impressionen aus dem amerikanischen Westen
Impressions from the American West

Edition Axel Menges

ISBN 978-3-936681-11-6

Reproduktionen/Reproductions: L & N Litho, Waiblingen
Druck und Bindearbeiten/Printing and binding: Everbest Printing Company, Ltd., China

Übersetzung ins Englische/Translation into English: Michael Robinson

Inhalt

Contents

If you're going to Hanapauh …

Die Tische im Flughafenrestaurant von Heathrow waren alle besetzt. Ich war aber hungrig und hatte einen langen Aufenthalt vor mir beim Flug von Berlin nach San Francisco. Also fragte ich ein kultiviert aussehendes Paar, ob ich mich dazusetzen dürfte. Ich durfte. Ihre Unterhaltung auf Deutsch verriet mir, daß sie kein Liebespaar und kein Ehepaar waren, sondern Kollegen, die gemeinsam zu einer Historikertagung nach San Francisco fuhren. Der Mann, etwa mein Alter, sprach sehr artikuliert und hatte eine Art, zu lächeln, die mir bekannt vorkam. Spontan fragte ich ihn: »Sind Sie Armin Wolf?« Er war es. Wir hatten als Klassenkameraden seinerzeit eine Fahrradtour durch Süddeutschland gemacht, Anfang der fünfziger Jahre, und uns danach aus den Augen verloren, weil er woanders Abitur machte. Das ist jetzt mehr als ein halbes Jahrhundert her. Was für ein freundlicher Zufall. Von jener süddeutschen Reise ist mir übrigens wenig in Erinnerung geblieben. Eigenartigerweise aber dies, daß wir zufällig in die Bachwoche in Ansbach hereinschneiten und dort Wilhelm Kempff mit den *Goldbergvariationen* hörten, von denen ich keinen Ton verstand, obwohl ich damals schon ganz gut Cello spielte. Erst viel später, 1985, sollte ich erfahren, daß es eine wunderbare Transkription für Streichtrio von Dimitry Sitkovetsky gibt.

Während des langen Fluges hatte ich dann einen Fensterplatz auf der rechten, der nördlichen Seite, wo die hoch stehende Sonne, die den ganzen Flug begleitete, nicht blendete und ich die Gletscher photographieren konnte, die vom östlichen Grönland ins Meer geschickt werden. Ich bin, oder besser, ich war Geologe und setzte mich, wenn es irgendwie ging, im Flugzeug immer so, daß ich die wichtigen Dinge, über die der Flug geht, gut sehen, photographieren und filmen konnte. Unmittelbar an der grönländischen Küste gibt es noch hohe, schroffe Berge, aber zum Landesinneren hin werden sie immer mehr von Eis eingehüllt und schließlich gänzlich überdeckt. Nur noch die Farbe Weiß ist zu sehen. Hier irgendwo muß Alfred Wegener liegen, der Vater der Theorie der Kontinentalverschiebung, der 1930 auf einer Expedition ins grönländische Inlandeis umgekommen war. Der anschließende Flug über das nördliche Kanada ist etwas langweilig, über Stunden hin immer nur die gleiche glaziale Rumpflandschaft.

Meine Gedanken konnten dahin zurückkehren, wo sie schon Wochen und Monate vor der Reise kreisten, zu der Freude und Spannung, der Angst und Sorge vor dem Jahr, das ich nun als Gastprofessor in Hayward verbringen sollte, einem kleinen College der California State University, südlich von Berkeley und Oakland, gegenüber von San Mateo an der Bucht von San Francisco, in der Bay Area. Ich tauschte mit Detlef Warnke, einem Kollegen dort, der meine Stelle in Berlin für ein Jahr übernahm, einem Deutschen, der schon früh ausgewandert und amerikanischer geworden war als so mancher Amerikaner. Bei einem ersten Kontakt hatte ich mit ihm in Berlin-Spandau den Ort seiner Flak-Stellung gesucht, wo er 1945 als Sechzehnjähriger Deutschland verteidigen mußte.

Als ich ziemlich erschlagen und aufgeregt den Zoll hinter mir hatte, fehlte mein wichtigster Koffer, mit sämtlichen Vorlesungsmanuskripten und Hunderten von Diapositiven. Zwei Tage lang war ich am Boden zerstört, dann kam der Koffer, welche Erlösung. Das war im Juli 1980. Das Fall Quarter fing zwar erst Ende September an, die Zeit wollte ich aber nutzen, um im Lande anzukommen und Englisch zu lernen, genauer, Amerikanisch. Meine Eltern hatten es für richtig befunden, den Knaben auf ein humanistisches Gymnasium zu schicken, mit viel Latein und Griechisch und sehr wenig Englisch. Mit englischer Literatur, namentlich der geologischen, hatte ich keine Probleme, aber Sprechen und besonders Verstehen gingen mehr als schlecht. Ich hatte als junger Student und auch später jahrelang in Italien gearbeitet und sozusagen auf der Straße ziemlich fließend Italienisch gelernt, das wollte ich jetzt hier in Kalifornien wiederholen. Es ging gründlich daneben.

Im Studentenwohnheim waren keine Plätze frei, so saß ich zuerst in diversen Motels und dann in meinem Apartment, Hancock, Crestview no. 10, mit wunderschönem Blick auf die San Mateo Bridge und die Bucht, aber davon lernte ich kein Englisch. Meine Rettung war der Fernseher, besonders aber das Radio. Ich hatte in dem Auto, das ich auch noch kaufen mußte, immer ein kleines Diktiergerät auf dem Nebensitz liegen und hörte pausenlos Radio. Wenn ich etwas nicht verstand, dann sprach ich das auf das Gerät und schaute abends zu Hause im Wörterbuch nach. Mein Lieblingssender war: »This is North California's Radio Concert Hall, KBFC, FM 102.1, San Francisco and KIB Palo Alto«, von einer sonoren, enorm vertrauensvollen Männerstimme gesprochen; sie brachten immer gute Musik und Nachrichten. Ich entsinne mich an eine Sendung über die Fuge bei Mozart, wo ich fast jedes Wort verstand, während ich bei Football-Reportagen nicht ein einziges Wort mitbekam, doch einmal hieß es: »Billy is not the quickest.« Das vergesse ich bezeichnenderweise nie. Besonders wertvoll für das Umgangsenglisch war für mich der *San Francisco Chronicle*, den ich mir hielt und der am Sonnabend oder Sonntag immer ein paar Extraseiten mit Cartoons enthielt, von denen mich besonders Herman by Unger amüsierte, ein Jammer, daß es so etwas in Deutschland nicht gibt, jedenfalls nicht in den großen Tageszeitungen.

Von der amerikanischen Tagespolitik habe ich nicht viel mitbekommen. Jimmy Carter war noch Präsident, ein Dauerbrenner in den Medien waren die Geiseln in Teheran. Zu diesem Problem hatte ich einen besonderen Bezug, weil ich Ende 1978 ein paar Monate im Iran gearbeitet hatte, am östlichen Rand der großen Salzwüste, im Chorassan; das Ende des Schah-Regimes deutete sich an, aber wir waren noch ungeschoren aus dem Land herausgekommen. Das Schicksal der Geiseln konnte ich mir lebhaft vorstellen. Sie kamen erst beim Amtsantritt von Reagan im Januar 1981 frei. Mir fiel damals auf, wie wenig die Amerikaner vom Iran und einem muslimischen Lande verstanden, eigentlich gilt das für fast die ganze außeramerikanische Welt, von der der Durchschnittsamerikaner kaum etwas weiß. So gab es im *San Francisco Chronicle* auch nur wenig über Europa und kaum etwas über Deutschland zu lesen.

Bevor ich einen eigenen Wagen hatte, mietete ich einen, damit erwarb ich meine amerikanische Driver's Licence. Es hieß LeCar und war das kleinste und allerdings auch billigste Auto, in dem ich je gefahren war. Als ich einen Ausflug zur Half Moon Bay machte, hielt neben mir an der Ampel etwas, was man in Deutschland einen Ami-Schlitten nannte, ein riesiges Gefährt, ein Flugzeugträger von Auto, in dem eine farbige Familie saß, Papa, Mama und fünf kleine Kinder, mit rosa Rüschenkleidchen und großen Haarschleifen auf den Köpfchen. Die drängten an die Scheiben, drückten sich die Näschen platt, gestikulierten und deuteten auf mein winziges Auto, so etwas hatten sie noch nie gesehen. Bei der Prüfung mußte ich einen Fahrtest machen, der akribisch protokolliert wurde. Dann sagte der Prüfer: »Bitte wenden Sie hier«. Es war eine breite, unbefahrene Straße. Ich guckte also demonstrativ in den Rückspiegel, schlug nach links ein und wendete LeCar in einem so kleinen Bogen, daß ich schon auf der Fahrbahnmitte in der Gegenrichtung stand. »No Sir«, sagte er, »so nicht, bitte immer schön vor und zurücksetzen.« Also tat ich so, als würde ich einen Flugzeugträger kommandieren und setzte viermal vor und zurück, um dasselbe Ergebnis zu erzielen.

Von meinen Bemühungen, von der Universitätsadministration zu einem vollwertigen Mitglied der Faculty gemacht zu werden, will ich lieber nicht sprechen. Verwaltungen sind eben Verwaltungen, weltweit. Man war allerdings immer sehr freundlich, ich kam schnell dazu, Amerika das »May I help you«-Land zu nennen. Nach einiger Zeit hatte ich endlich auch meine Social Security Number, und am 25. September hielt ich meine erste Vorlesung. Das damals spärlich geführte Tagebuch vermerkt darüber: »Oh Gott«. So war es dann wohl auch.

Aber das änderte sich. Als ich am Ende des übernächsten Quarter, des Spring Quarter – ich hatte eine zweistündige geologische Ozeanographie für Hörer aller Fakultäten gelesen, als ich dort noch mit einigen Studenten schwatzte, nach der letzten Vorlesung – kam eine bildschöne Studentin auf mich zu, eine Mexikanerin, vermute ich, in einer Art weißem Tüllkleid, also nicht in Jeans, machte die Andeutung eines Knickses, strahlte mich an und sagte: »I enjoyed your lecture.« Und fort war sie. Ich schwebte den Rest des Tages.

Die Amerikaner sind sehr freundlich und zugewandt, jedenfalls verglichen mit Deutschland, zumindest damals. Vielleicht sogar ganz besonders Fremden gegenüber. Das überraschte mich vom ersten Tag an. Eine Studentin zeigte mir San Francisco, besonders die Küste, Point Lobos und die Giant Camera am Cliff House. Dort projiziert eine sich drehende Optik auf dem Dach das Szenario ins Innere auf eine große, flach liegende Schale, begleitet von esoterischer Musik. Sie sprach mit dem jungen Mann, einem bärtigen Hippie-Typ, der die Eintrittskarten verkaufte. Die beiden redeten so, als wären sie Bruder und Schwester, die sich seit langem nicht mehr gesehen hätten, mindestens fünf Minuten lang, auf das herzlichste, es gab sonst keine störenden Kunden. »Woher kennst Du den denn?«, fragte ich sie später. »Wen denn?«, fragte sie. »Na, den an der Kasse.« »Den kenne ich nicht«, sagte sie, »nie gesehen.«

Bei einer Wanderung im Lassen Volcanic National Park war ich beim Abstieg meiner Gruppe etwas voraus gegangen und traf, allein, auf einen älteren Mann, der an einem der wenigen Bäume rastete und einen Schuh ausgezogen hatte. Er sagte, glaube ich, nicht einmal »Hallo«, sondern ganz unvermittelt: »Sehen Sie sich das an, was für eine Blase, ich sag noch zu meiner Frau, ich ziehe die neuen Schuhe lieber nicht an, die drücken bestimmt, und nun sehen Sie, hier haben wir die Bescherung.« Als ob ich sein langjähriger Weggenosse und Freund wäre, ich war aber eben ein Wildfremder.

Da meine Familie aus den verschiedensten Gründen nicht mitgekommen war und nur mein ältester Sohn Weihnachten zu mir stieß, der sich aber schnell in eine amerikanische Gastfamilie verabschiedete, da ich also allein war, mußte ich mir für mein soziales Leben etwas einfallen lassen. Ich ging zum Dean des Music Department und bat um ein Cello. Ein reizender Mann, ich bekam es sofort, verbunden mit der Bitte, doch im Uni-Orchester mitzuspielen; es diente mir ein Jahr. Auch einen Spind im Department bekam ich, um das Instrument zu versorgen, und ich konnte in den schalldichten Räumen üben, wann immer ich wollte. Fred, der Institutstechniker und Oboist, warb mich für PATS an, die Palo Alto Telemann Society, ein lockerer Verband von Musikfreunden, die mal bei Anna in Berkeley, bei Irma in San Jose oder Bill in San Francisco Musik machten; zu trinken brachte jeder etwas mit, ganz wie in Australien, BYO, bring your own. Also spielte ich im Uni-Orchester mit, zweimal in der Woche, mittags, zwei Stunden, ein volles Symphonie-Orchester, ein volles Programm, jedes Quarter ein Konzert, ich will hier nicht die Programme aufzählen. Höhepunkt war der Umstand, daß der Bay Area einmal die Cellisten ausgingen und ich gefragt wurde, ob ich im Berkeley Symphony Orchestra, ganz hinten natürlich, die *Transfiguration* von Oliver Messiaen mitspielen wolle, unter dem damals blutjungen Kent Nagano, assistiert vom Komponisten persönlich. Kent Nagano ist heute Chefdirigent des DSO, des Deutschen Symphonie Orchesters Berlin. Das Konzert fand in der damals gerade erst fertiggestellten Davies Symphony Hall in San Francisco statt, im Mai 1981, es beeindruckte mich enorm. Riesenspaß machte mir auch die *Beggar's Opera* von John Gay, die wir, solistisch besetzt, im April in Hayward aufführten; nie werde ich vergessen, wie die kleinen Nutten oben am Bühnenrand den Kontrabassisten unten im Orchestergraben anzumachen versuchten. Während der Aufführung, versteht sich.

Eine herzliche Freundschaft verband mich mit Dieter Bergmann, einem emigrierten Juden, der in Castro Valley eine gynäkologische Praxis betrieb. Er führte ein sehr gastliches Haus mit viel Musik. Er spielte nicht mehr sehr gut Geige, kannte aber die gesamte Literatur und kam überall durch, auch an den schwersten Stellen. Er kochte vorzüglich. »Deshalb kommen alle immer noch gerne zu mir«, pflegte er zu sagen. Leider lebt er nicht mehr.

Auch über ein Mißverständnis muß berichtet werden. Vor dem Konzert kündigte der Dirigent, Denis DeCoteau, ein Dress Rehearsal an. Nun gut, dachte ich, ich weiß, was Dress heißt, ich weiß, was Rehearsal heißt, also werde ich mich konzertgerecht anziehen. Ich bügelte mein einziges weißes Hemd, so gut das ohne Bügeleisen ging, ich zog meinen Anzug an, den ich noch nie gebraucht hatte, weil man die Vorlesungen in Jeans hielt, und ich band mir meine einzige Krawatte um. Als ich zum College hochfuhr, sah ich dicke blaue Wolken, seit Wochen, ja Monaten hatte es nicht geregnet, jetzt kündigte sich ein Unwetter an. Ich mußte über das ganze Uni-Gelände hetzen, weil Faculty Parkplatz und Music Building entgegengesetzt liegen und die Campus Police Falschparkern gegenüber gnadenlos war. Es kam, wie es kommen mußte, der Sturzregen erwischte mich und das Cello voll, das ich ausnahmsweise dabei hatte, weil ich zu Hause noch eine schwere Stelle hatte üben wollen. Durchnäßt kam ich im Music Building an, einem großen Rundbau. Da kam mir Dick, der Kontrabaß entgegen, wie immer in halb zerrissenen Jeans. »Na«, dachte ich, »Dress Rehearsal, der wird sich beeilen müssen.« Dann sah ich Anna, die Trompete, ebenfalls in Jeans, und mehrere andere, kein Kleid, kein Anzug weit und breit. Geistesgegenwärtig spurtete ich zu meinem Spind, zog meine nasse Jacke aus, legte die Krawatte ab und krempelte die Ärmel hoch. Jetzt sah ich wieder normal aus. »Heute gibt es nur ganze Durchgänge«, sagte der Dirigent, »Dress Rehearsal«. Jetzt erst ging mir ein Licht auf, es war eine Generalprobe, so heißt das in Deutschland, das »Dress« haben sich die Musiker vom Theater geholt, hätte ich nur gleich im Wörterbuch nachgeschaut. Was wohl ein amerikanischer Musiker gemacht hätte, wenn er zu einer »Generalprobe« in Deutschland gebeten worden wäre?

Über alldem kam die Geologie nicht zu kurz. Ich war zwar nur wegen der Lehre gekommen, konnte aber sogar ein kleines Projekt starten, ein sedimentologisches. Nördlich des Kopfes der San Mateo Bridge, auf der Hayward-Seite, gab und gibt es alte Salzgärten, die wohl schon von den Spaniern angelegt worden waren. Dort waren weite Becken ausgebaggert worden, um einen öffentlichen Gezeitenpark einrichten zu können. Damals war das Projekt gerade angelaufen, und die ganze Gegend war eingezäunt und abgesperrt. Den Hauptkanal überspannte bereits eine solide, hölzerne Brücke. Dort baute ich zusammen mit Phil, unserem Institutstechniker, eine Tiden-Meßstation; auch die Strömungsgeschwindigkeiten konnte ich messen. Da mir das Volumen des Gezeitengebiets aus vorbildlichen Kartenunterlagen bekannt war, konnte ich den Wasserhaushalt des Gebietes berechnen und anhand der Schwebstoffe in den Wasserproben feststellen, ob neuer Schlick in die Becken eingebracht oder von dort abtransportiert wurde. Das interessierte die Kollegen von der Biologie, die dort ein Parallelprogramm betrieben, um herauszufinden, wie das bislang sterile Gebiet von Flora und Fauna wieder besiedelt würde. Da wir keine selbstaufzeichnenden Geräte hatten, habe ich so manchen Tag und manche Nacht auf der Brücke verbracht, um einen besonders großen Tidenhub auszumessen, und das dauert, der Mond will es so, immer um die zwölf Stunden.

Das Tidal Marsh Project hatte noch einen Nebeneffekt, der mir sehr willkommen war. Howard Cogswell, ein Kollege von der Biologie, bereits nahe dem Retirement, war ein begeisterter Flieger. Er hatte, schon hoch in den Jahren, seinen Pilotenschein gemacht und sich eine kleine, viersitzige Cessna angeschafft, mit der er Luftaufnahmen der Tidal Marsh für sich und seine Kollegen machte. Ich fragte ihn, ob er auch für mich fliegen würde, und so kamen wir zusammen. Im Rückteil der Kabine hatte er ein Loch in den Boden des Flugzeugs bohren lassen, so daß man auch Senkrechtaufnahmen machen konnte. Wir flogen oft und teilten uns die Spritkosten. Immer, wenn wir abhoben, tat er einen lauten Jauchzer vor Freude. Ein toller Kerl. Wir flogen nicht nur über das Wattgebiet von Hayward, sondern über die ganze südliche Bucht, deren vielfach verästelte Priele bei Niedrigwasser bizarre Muster abgeben. Wir flogen auch über die San-Andreas-Störung entlang der Lower and Upper Crystal Springs Reservoirs zur Half Moon Bay, von wo aus man San Francisco liegen sieht, die Metropole mit ihren Hochhäusern und die Golden Gate Bridge. Oder über Palo Alto und die Stanford Ranch mit dem hohen Bibliotheksturm, über die Küstenberge zum Pazifik, zur Año Nuevo Bay. Ich konnte durch das Bodenloch mit beiden Kameras photographieren, sowohl mit der Leica als auch mit der Großbildkamera, von der gleich die Rede sein wird. Nie kehrten wir ohne üppige Photoausbeute zum Hayward Air Terminal zurück.

Im ersten Halbjahr hatte ich sehr viel photographiert, besonders geologische Sujets, mit meiner Leica; Digitalkameras gab es damals noch nicht, ebensowenig übrigens Computer, oder eben nur in den ersten Anfängen, kein Internet, aber auch kaum Kreditkarten, mit denen man heute überall zu seinem Gelde kommt, jedenfalls hatte ich keine. Überhaupt war der Geldverkehr von Berlin nach Hayward sehr mühselig. Ich hatte ein Konto bei der First Interstate Bank in der naiven Annahme eingerichtet, dies sei eine Internationale Bank. Sie bediente aber nur einige Staaten im Westen des Landes. Also, ich hatte viel mit der Leica photographiert, besaß aber in Berlin eine große Linhof-Kamera. Die brachte ich von einem Weihnachtsbesuch in Berlin mit und war nun in der Lage, Kalifornien und die angrenzenden Staaten so richtig zu photographieren, wenig in Farbe, viel in Schwarzweiß. Es konnte dabei nicht ausbleiben, daß ich mit dem Werk von Ansel Adams in Berührung kam, der damals noch lebte. Besonders faszinierte mich sein Zonensystem, das mir den Weg zur theoretischen Photographie eröffnete, mit der ich mich noch viele Jahre beschäftigte. Erst die differenzierte Filterung der Multigrade-Papiere brachte hier die einfache Lösung. Adams hat die Landschaftsphotographie beeinflußt wie kein anderer. Er hatte aber auch das Glück, in einer spektakulären Welt zu Hause zu sein, was die Leistung seiner nachgerade theatralischen Aufnahmen natürlich nicht mindert. Ich mußte bei meinen Aufnahmen die Dinge immer so nehmen, wie sie gerade waren, Geld und Zeit zum Ausharren und Warten auf dramatische Wolken hatte ich nicht.

Der ganze Westen der USA ist geologisches Wunderland. Ich wäre ein Schelm gewesen, wenn ich mir nicht möglichst viel angeschaut hätte. Weite Reisen führten mich in den Yellowstone National Park und nach Mesa Verde, mit allem, was dazwischen liegt, zum Beispiel zum Mount St. Helens, der gerade ausgebrochen war. Meine besondere Liebe gehörte Point Reyes, den weiten Landschaften nordwestlich von San Francisco, die sich von Hayward in einfachen Tagestouren erreichen lassen. Point Reyes habe ich noch jedem meiner Gäste gezeigt. Sehr oft war ich im Yosemite National Park, öfter aber noch im Death Valley, in das ich auch in vielen späteren Jahren immer wieder zurückgekehrt bin. Meine Neigung für das Death Valley wurde 1989 belohnt, als wir einen Monat lang auf dem Hanaupah-Fächer gegenüber Dante's View arbeiteten und ich bis dahin unbekannte Sedimente des vormaligen Lake Manly fand, der hier vor vielen Jahren einmal plätscherte, das »Hanaupah-Fan Shoreline Deposit at Thule Spring«, nach neuester kosmogener Zeitbestimmung vor 145 000 bis 128 000 Jahren abgelagert. Wir wohnten damals in Shoshone, weil Furnace Creek zu teuer war, und mußten jeden Tag die 130 km zum Fächer hin- und zurückfahren, was aber wegen des fehlenden Verkehrs kein Problem war.

Für den geschichtsträchtigen Europäer sind die Landschaften des amerikanischen Westens von eigenartiger Anziehungskraft. Eine Nichte von mir, in Australien aufgewachsen, wurde nach ihrem Haupteindruck von einer Englandreise gefragt. Die Antwort: »Too much history«. Sie hat den Nagel auf den Kopf getroffen. Im amerikanischen Westen gibt es, zumindest im europäischen Sinne, keine History. Es gibt gelegentlich »historical landmarks«, auf denen an irgendein kleines Ereignis erinnert wird, nicht zu vergleichen mit der in Jahrhunderten blutgetränkten Erde Europas. Wenn ich das Leid der europäischen Menschen bedenke, dann nehme ich die Geschichtslosigkeit eines Death Valley gern in Kauf und lächele nicht über die »historical landmarks«.

Vielleicht liegt die Faszination der amerikanischen Landschaften, besonders der Wüstenlandschaften, gerade in dieser Geschichtslosigkeit. In Deutschland, etwa in Brandenburg, lebt die eher schlichte Landschaft von ihrer Geschichte. Hier hat der Große Kurfürst gesiegt, dort hat Napoleons Armee eine Schlacht verloren. Die eigentliche, menschenlose Natur ist unter Äckern, unter Wald und Heide verborgen. Im amerikanischen Westen, in den Wüstenlandschaften, in denen allerdings auch Indianer getötet oder vertrieben wurden, herrscht eine grandiose, menschenlose Natur ohne, im Vergleich zu Europa, nennenswerte Menschengeschichte und ohne menschliche Eingriffe. Hier herrscht die Erdgeschichte, ein Faszinosum besonderer Art. Wer sie lesen kann, ist doppelt beschenkt.

Ich war voller Bangigkeit nach Kalifornien gekommen, weil ich eine sehr hohe Meinung von amerikanischer Forschung und Lehre hatte und Sorge trug, ob ich da werde bestehen können. Mir wurde jedoch bald klar, daß auch hier nur mit Wasser gekocht wird. Dazu eine kleine Geschichte: Wir hatten mit John Cummings, dem leider viel zu früh verstorbenen Geologen, dem wohl originellsten Kollegen, eine Studentenexkursion irgendwohin gemacht, standen an einem Aufschluß am Straßenrand und hatten alle eine Probe von dem dort anstehenden Sandstein abgeschlagen und betrachteten sie mit der Lupe. Ich hatte mein Stück angeleckt und naß gemacht, das mache ich immer, weil ich von meinen italienischen Kalksandsteinen her gewohnt bin, daß man nur so Mikrofossilien sehen kann, etwa Globotruncanen. »Donnerwetter«, sagte Cummings, »Du bist ja wirklich ein echter Profi.« »Wieso das«, fragte ich. Er: »Weil Du die Proben angeleckt hast.« Es stellte sich heraus, daß amerikanische Erdölgeologen die Proben anlecken, um an der sich möglicherweise ins Gestein zurückziehenden Spucke schon im Gelände zu erkennen, ob die Probe eine gewisse Porosität hat, tief unten also als Speichergestein für Öl oder Gas in Frage kommen könnte. Das ist natürlich ein primitiver Gelände-, kein Laborversuch. Ich erklärte ihm meine Methode, von der er so wenig gehört hatte wie ich von seiner, und wir klopften uns auf die Schultern. Das war also 1:1 oder unentschieden ausgegangen. Ganz anders stand und steht es mit der Hochschuldidaktik. Uns war schon als Studenten in den 1950er Jahren aufgefallen, wie haushoch angelsächsische Lehrbücher den deutschsprachigen überlegen waren. Das ist heute etwas besser, aber nur, weil wir die angelsächsische Didaktik weitgehend übernommen haben. Ich schreibe hier aber nur von der Geologie, in anderen Fächern kann ich das nicht beurteilen. Trotzdem stammen die beiden wichtigsten deutschen Lehrbücher *Historische Geologie* und *Allgemeine Geologie* aus dem Spektrum Verlag von amerikanischen Autoren, es sind Übersetzungen der amerikanischen Erstausgaben, 1994 und 1995 erschienen. Es wäre einer umfassenden Analyse der Didaktik wert, festzustellen, woran das liegt. Sie würde sicherlich auch die unterschiedliche Mentalität, ja sogar die Sprachen der deutschen und englischen Menschen umfassen müssen. Das zu leisten ist nicht mein Ding.

Es wird nicht nur heute, 2006, sondern schon lange diskutiert, ob das amerikanische Lehrsystem dem deutschen überlegen sei. Für die Geologie kann ich sagen, daß beide Systeme am Ende gleich gute oder schlechte Geologen produzieren. Aber die Amerikaner studieren schneller, effektiver, und sie haben weniger Studienabbrecher. Das liegt an der starken Verschulung, besonders im Grundstudium, und der ständigen Lern- und Lehrkontrolle. In Hayward wurde jede Lehrveranstaltung geprüft, schon in der Mitte des Quarter, also nach wenigen Wochen konnte der Dozent eine Zwischenprüfung veranstalten, deren Ergebnis ihm zeigte, ob er zu schnell durch den Stoff gegangen war, zu langsam oder ob er gerade richtig lag. Auch jeder Student konnte sich so jederzeit selber einschätzen. Das ist die eine Seite der Medaille. Die andere ist, daß jeder Dozent nach jeder Lehrveranstaltung von den Studenten evaluiert wurde, durch Fragebögen der Faculty-Verwaltung. Das dauerte höchstens eine Viertelstunde, die Bögen wurden schon damals elektronisch ausgewertet. Jeder Lehrer konnte also sehen, wo seine Stärken und Schwächen lagen. Als Gast war ich übrigens von der Bewertung ausgeschlossen. Mein Versuch, das auch in Berlin einzuführen, endete seinerzeit mit einer glatten Bauchlandung. Heute gibt es in einzelnen Fachbereichen einen Uni-Zensus über das Internet. Das zu vertiefen kann aber nicht das Thema dieser kalifornischen Erinnerungen sein.

Wie steht es also um das Fazit dieses wundervollen Jahres? Im Ausland zu leben, war nicht neu für mich. Ich hatte zwanzig Jahre lang in Italien gearbeitet, zwar nicht kontinuierlich, aber doch immer monatelang. Aber so stark beruflich und menschlich eingebunden, das war ich noch nie. Ich nenne drei Themen, die Landschaft, die Menschen, den Beruf. Vielleicht in dieser Reihenfolge.

Gemessen an den eher kleinräumigen Landschaften Mitteleuropas mit ihrer dichten Vegetation sind die Wüstenlandschaften des amerikanischen Westens weit und leer, sie sind versteinert. Ich glaube, es ist diese fast horizontlose Weite, die das Erlebnis der Landschaft bestimmt. Es ist wie eine versteinerte Welt vor ihrer Besitzergreifung durch Pflanze und Tier und durch den Menschen. Eine Art Ur-Landschaft. Jenseits aller Ästhetik ist es für den Geologen eine besonders anziehende Welt, weil er, von Wüstenlack und anderen Verwitterungskrusten abgesehen, einen direkten Zugang zum Objekt seiner Begierde hat.

In den fünfundzwanzig Jahren, die ich seit meinem Aufenthalt in Kalifornien überblicke, hat sich in Deutschland vieles zum Besseren gewandelt, was das ganz simple tägliche Zusammenleben der Menschen ausmacht. Die Leute sind freundlicher, umgänglicher geworden, auch in den Behörden, so daß der Abstand zu Kalifornien nicht mehr so kraß ist wie früher. Im Supermarkt gibt es hierzulande heute schon einmal ein freundliches Wort der Verkäuferin, ein Lächeln. Das war mir in Kalifornien seinerzeit extrem aufgefallen. An der Landstraße hielt ein Polizist den Verkehr auf, weil ein Baum umgefallen war, der gerade weggeräumt wurde. Ich stand als erster in der Autoschlange. Der Polizist gab den Weg mit einer Geste frei und sagte zu mir: »Thank you for your cooperation«. Ich war fassungslos. Ich halte so etwas in Deutschland immer noch für undenkbar.

Meine berufliche Arbeit in Kalifornien ist schwer korrekt zu beurteilen und zu Berlin in ein Verhältnis zu bringen. Ich war ein Gast, fast ein Exot, damit gab es keinerlei Konkurrenzsituation, keinerlei Unter- oder Überordnung mit wem auch immer. Ich hielt die vorgeschriebenen Vorlesungen und Übungen und machte die Exkursionen, wobei ich eigentlich nur mit engagierten Studenten zu tun hatte. Wenn ich im Institut oder Labor etwas brauchte – ich bekam es sofort. Die Zusammenarbeit mit den Kollegen von der Biologie im Tidal Marsh Project war perfekt, ich sprach vor deren Studenten über meine Probleme, und sie äußerten sich vor meinen über ihre. Man hätte mich eigentlich genausogut durchhängen lassen können in meinem Zimmerchen, aber davon war keine Rede.

Sie fragen mich, ob ich nach alledem, was ich in Kalifornien erlebt und hier aufgeschrieben habe, ob ich nach alledem Studenten oder jüngeren Kollegen einen Rat geben könnte? Nein, das möchte ich eigentlich nicht. Jeder muß sein Leben so einrichten, wie er es für richtig hält. Ich kann nur für mich sagen, daß es eines der aufregendsten Jahre meines Lebens war und mir, obwohl ich fast ein ganzes Berufsleben lang immer wieder im Ausland gearbeitet habe, unendlich viel gegeben hat. Ich werde bestimmt noch einmal ins Death Valley fahren und auf den Hanaupah-Fächer gehen.

If you're going to Hanapauh ...

There wasn't a table to be had in the Heathrow Airport restaurant. But I was hungry, and had a lot of time to kill in the break on my flight from Berlin to San Francisco. So I asked a sophisticated-looking couple if I could join them. I could. Listening to their conversation in German, I realized that they weren't lovers, or married, but colleagues travelling together to a history conference in San Francisco. The man, about my age, was very articulate, and had a smile I thought recognized from 30 years ago. I asked him straight out: »Are you Armin Wolf?« And he was. We'd been in the same class at school, and once went cycling round South Germany together, in the early fifties. We'd lost touch because he did his school leaving exam somewhere else. That's over half a century ago now. What a wonderful coincidence. I didn't really remember very much about our trip to South Germany. But strangely enough I do remember that we happened to hit Ansbach in its Bach week, and heard Wilhelm Kempff playing the Goldberg Variations. I didn't understand a single note of that at the time, even though I could already play the cello quite well. It was not until later, in 1985, that I found out that there is a marvellous transcription for string trio by Dmitri Sitkovetsky.

During the long flight I had a window seat on the right-hand, north side of the plane. The sun was high in the sky throughout the flight, but it wasn't dazzling on that side, and I was able to take photographs of the glaciers thrusting out into the sea from the eastern side of Greenland. I am, or rather I was, a geologist, and so I always tried, if at all possible, to choose a seat in the plane, from which I could see, photograph and film anything important we were passing over. There are still high, rugged mountains right on the coast of Greenland, but they get more and more thickly covered in ice towards the interior, until eventually they are completely covered over. Nothing to see but whiteness. Alfred Wegener's body must lie somewhere here. He was the father of the continental drift theory, and lost his life on an expedition into the Greenland inland ice in 1930. The next leg of the flight, over northern Canada, is a little boring, just the same glacial peneplain for hours on end.

I let my mind go back to where it had been in the weeks and months before my trip, remembering the delight and apprehension I had felt about the year I was about to spend as visiting professor in Hayward, a small California State University college, south of Berkeley and Oakland, opposite San Mateo on San Francisco Bay, in the Bay Area. I was on an exchange with Detlef Warnke, a colleague there who was taking over my post in Berlin for a year. He was a German who had emigrated very early, and he had become a lot more American than many Americans. When we first got in touch we went to Spandau in Berlin together to look for the site of the flak battery where he had had to defend Germany as a sixteen-year-old, in 1945.

After I had got through customs, pretty weary and excited, I found that my most important case was missing, with all my lecture notes and hundreds of slides in it. I was devastated for two whole days, then the case turned up, what a relief. That was in July 1980. The Fall Quarter did not start until late September, but I wanted to use the time to settle into the country and learn English, or rather, American. My parents had felt that the best thing was to send their boy to a grammar school that offered a great deal of Latin and Greek, but not very much English. I didn't have any trouble with reading English, especially in the geology field, but I was terrible at speaking and understanding. As a young student, and later as well, I had worked in Italy for years, and learned to speak Italian fairly fluently almost in the street, as it were, and I wanted to do the same thing here in California. It all went horribly wrong.

There was no room in the student hostel, so I lived in various motels at first, and then took an apartment in Hancock, at no. 10 Crest View, with a wonderful view of the San Mateo Bridge and the bay, but that didn't teach me any English. My salvation was the television, but above all the radio. I always had a little Dictaphone on the passenger seat of the car I'd had to buy as well, and listened to the radio all the time. If there was something I didn't understand I recorded it on the Dictaphone and looked it up in the dictionary at home in the evening. My favourite station was: »This is North California's Radio Concert Hall, KBFC, FM 102.1, San Francisco and KIB Palo Alto«, spoken by a sonorous, enormously reassuring man's voice; they always broadcast good music, and news. I remember a programme about the fugue in Mozart. I understood almost every word of that, but I couldn't understand the football reports at all, though the phrase »Billy is not the quickest« has stuck in my mind. Significantly enough, I've never forgotten that. The San Francisco Chronicle did my colloquial English a lot of good. I started to take it, and on Saturday or Sunday it always had a few extra pages of cartoons. I found Herman by Unger particularly funny, it's a shame there's nothing like that in Germany, at least not in the major dailies.

I didn't follow much of day-to-day American politics. Jimmy Carter was still president, and the Teheran hostages were constantly talked about in the media. I could relate to this problem particularly well because I had worked in Iran for a few months in late 1978, at the eastern end of the great salt desert, in the Chorassan; the end of the Shah's regime was in sight, but we had got out of the country unscathed. I could imagine the hostages' fate vividly. They were not released until Reagan took office in January 1981. I was struck at the time by how little the Americans understood about Iran as a Muslim country, and actually that's true of almost all the non-American world, which the average American knows scarcely anything about. So there was not very much at all about Europe in the San Francisco Chronicle, and scarcely anything about Germany.

Before I had a car of my own I hired one, and got my American Driver's Licence. It was called LeCar, and was the smallest and certainly the cheapest car I'd ever driven. When I went on a trip to Half Moon Bay a typical American car stopped next to me at the traffic lights, a gigantic vehicle, a car like an aircraft carrier. It had a black family in it, Dad, Mom and five little children, with frilly pink dresses and big bows in their hair. They crowded up to the windows, flattened their noses on them and pointed at my tiny car, they had never seen anything like it. I had to take a practical driving test, with every detail meticulously recorded. Then the examiner said: »Please turn round here.« It was a wide road with no traffic. So I looked ostentatiously in the mirror, pulled over to the left and turned LeCar in such a tight circle that I was in the middle of the road pointing in the opposite direction. »No sir«, he said, »not like that, I want a nice three-point turn.« So I drove as though I was commanding an aircraft carrier and drove forward and reversed three times to achieve exactly the same result.

I'd rather not say anything about my attempts to get the Faculty Administration to admit me as a full Faculty member. Administrations are administrations the world over. But people were always very friendly, and I quickly came to think if America as the land of »May I help you?« After some time I at last got my Social Security number, and I gave my first lecture on 25 September. I noted in my somewhat sparsely kept diary at the time: »Oh God«. And it turned out rather like that.

But it soon changed. At the end of the next quarter but one, the Spring Quarter – I had delivered a two-hour lecture on geological oceanography for students of all faculties, and I was chatting to some students there after the last lecture – a beautiful student came up to me, a Mexican woman, I think, in a kind of white tulle dress, not in jeans, in other words, dropped a hint of a curtsey, beamed at me and said: »I enjoyed your lecture.« And off she went. I was walking on air for the rest of the day.

The Americans were very friendly and forthcoming, at least compared with Germany as it then was. Perhaps especially so with strangers. It surprised me from the first day on. A girl student showed me San Francisco, especially the coast, Point Lobos and the Giant Camera at Cliff House. A revolving lens on the roof projects whatever is going on to the inside of the building, on to a large bowl lying flat on its side, accompanied by esoteric music. She spoke to the young man, a bearded hippie guy, who was selling the admission tickets. The two of them talked as though they were brother and sister who had not seen each other for a long time, really warmly, there weren't any other customers to disturb them. »How did you get to know him then?«, I asked her later. »Who do you mean?«, she asked. »The man selling tickets.« »I don't know him«, she said, »never seen him in my life.«

On a walk in the Lassen Volcanic National Park I'd gone on ahead a bit on the way down, so I was on my own when I met an elderly man resting by one of the few trees. He had taken one of his shoes off. I don't think he even said hello, but just went straight into: »Just look at that for a blister, I said to my wife I'd rather not wear my new shoes, they're bound to be too tight, and look here, that's what you end up with.« As though I'd been his best friend for years, but he didn't know me from Adam.

As my family had not come with me for various reasons, and only my eldest son joined me at Christmas, but quickly went off to his German host family, leaving me alone, I had to do something about a social life. I went to the Dean of the Music Department and asked him for a cello. He was a charming man, and I got one at once, and he asked me to play in the university orchestra; I kept that cello for a year. I also got a locker in the department to keep the instrument in, and I was allowed to practise in the sound-proof rooms whenever I liked. Fred, the institute technician and an oboist, recruited me for PATS, the Palo Alto Telemann Society, a loose association of music-lovers who sometimes made music at Anna's in Berkeley, Irma's in San Jose or Bill's in San Francisco; everyone brought their own drinks, just like Australia, BYO, bring your own. So I played in the university orchestra twice a week, at lunchtime, two hours, a full symphony orchestra, a full programme, a concert every quarter, I won't list the programmes here. The high point came when there was a sudden dearth of cellists in the Bay Area, and I was approached to see if I would like to play Oliver Messiaen's *Transfiguration* with the Berkeley Symphony Orchestra, sitting right at the back, of course, under Kent Nagano, who was very young at the time, assisted by the composer in person. Kent Nagano is now chief conductor of the DSO, the Deutsche Symphonie Orchester Berlin. The concert was held in the Davies Symphony Hall in San Francisco, which had just been completed at the time, in May 1981, and I was enormously impressed. I also greatly enjoyed John Gay's Beggar's Opera, which we performed with with each instrument a soloist in Hayward in April; I shall never forget the little whores up there on the edge of the stage trying to get off with the double-bass player down in the orchestra pit. During the performance, of course.

I became very friendly with Dieter Bergmann, a Jewish émigré who ran a gynaecological practice in Castro Valley. His home was very welcoming, with a lot of music. He didn't play the violin very well any more, but he knew all the repertoire and managed even the most difficult passages. He was an excellent cook. »That's why people still like coming to see me«, he used to say. Unfortunately he is no longer alive.

There was one misunderstanding I'd like to mention. The conductor, Denis DeCoteau, called a dress rehearsal before the concert. »Right«, I thought, »I know what dress means, I know what rehearsal means, so I'll dress for a concert.« I ironed my only white shirt as well as I could without an iron, I put on my suit, which I had never worn because lectures were delivered in jeans, and knotted my only tie. As I was driving up to the college I noticed some heavy black clouds, it hadn't rained for weeks, months even, and now there was a storm brewing. I had to rush right through the university campus because the faculty car park and the music building were at opposite ends, and the Campus Police were very hot on illegal parking. Inevitably I was caught by the downpour, and so was the cello, which I had with me, unusually, because I'd taken it home to practise a difficult passage. I arrived in the Music Building, an enormous round structure, soaked to the skin. There I met Dick, the double bass player, in tattered jeans as usual. »Well«, I thought, »dress rehearsal, he's going to have to get a move on.« Then I saw Anna, the trumpeter. She was in jeans too, and so were several others, not a dress or a suit to be seen. With great presence of mind I hurried to my locker, took my wet jacket off, and the tie, and rolled my sleeves up. Now I looked normal again. »We're only doing complete runs today«, said the conductor, »dress rehearsal.« And that was when the penny dropped, it was what we call a »Generalprobe« in Germany, the American musicians had borrowed the theatre term, I should have looked in the dictionary straight away. What would an American have done if he had been invited to a »Generalprobe«?

Geology still got its just deserts amidst all this. I'd really come just to do the teaching, but I was able to launch a little sedimentology project. Just north of the end of the San Mateo Bridge, on the Hayward side, there are former salterns or salt gardens that had probably been set up by the Spanish. Wide basins had been excavated there so that a public tidal park could be set up. The project had just got under way, and the whole area was fenced off and closed. There was already a sturdy wooden bridge over the main channel. Working with Phil, our departmental technician, I set up a tide-measuring station; I could take readings on current speeds as well. As I already knew the volume of the tidal area from excellent maps, I could investigate the water conditions in the area and use the suspended matter to establish whether new silt was being deposited in the basin or was being washed away from it. My colleagues in the biology department were interested in this, as they were running a programme at the same time to find out how the hitherto sterile area was to be populated by flora and fauna. As we had no self-recording equipment I spent many days and nights on the bridge measuring a particularly high tide, and that takes, because this is what the moon dictates, round about twelve hours a time.

The Tidal Marsh Project also had a side effect that was very welcome to me. Howard Cogswell, a colleague in the biology department, already close to retirement, was an enthusiastic pilot. He had learned to fly at an advanced age, and had bought a little four-seater Cessna, which he used to take aerial photographs of the Tidal Marsh for himself and his colleagues. I asked him if he would fly for me as well, and so we got together. He had had a hole drilled in the aircraft floor at the back of the cabin, so it was possible to take vertical shots as well. We flew a lot, and split the fuel costs. Whenever we took off he let out a joyous yell. A fantastic chap. We didn't just fly over the Hayward tidal area, but the whole south bay; the tidal gullies made bizarre patterns at low tide with their complex ramifications. We also flew over the San Andreas fault along the Upper and Lower Crystal Springs Reservoirs to Half Moon Bay, from where you can see San Francisco, the big city with its tall buildings and the Golden Gate Bridge. Or over Palo Alto and the Stanford Ranch with its high library tower, over the coastal mountains to the Pacific, to Año Nuevo Bay. I could take photographs through the hole in the floor with both cameras, the Leica and the large-format camera, which I will come back to in a moment. We never flew back to the Hayward Air Terminal without a great deal of photographic loot.

I had taken a lot of photographs in the first six months, especially of geological subjects, with my Leica; there were no digital cameras in those days, no computers either, incidentally, or if there were they were very rudimentary, no internet, and also hardly any credit cards you could use to get at your money anywhere, at least I didn't have one. Transferring money from Berlin to Hayward was a laborious process anyway. I had set up an account with the First Interstate Bank on the naïve assumption that it was in international bank. But it served only a few states in the west of the country. So, I had taken a lot of pictures with the Leica, but I also had a big Linhof camera in Berlin. I brought it back from a Christmas visit to Berlin, and was now in a position to photograph California and the adjacent states properly, not much in colour, but a lot of black and white. It was inevitable that I should come across the work of Ansel Adams, who was still alive at the time. I was particularly fascinated by his zoning system, which showed me the way to theoretical photography, which I pursued for a number of years. It was only the sophisticated filtering offered by Multigrade papers that made a simple solution possible here. Adams had more influence on landscape photography than anyone else. But he also had the good fortune to live in spectacular surroundings, which of course does not diminish the achievement of his positively theatrical shots. I always had to take things as they were in my photographs, I had neither the time nor the money to wait for dramatic clouds.

The whole of the American West is a geological wonderland. I would have been a fool not to have looked at as much as possible. My travels took me to the Yellowstone National Park and to Mesa Verde, including everything in between, for example Mount St. Helens, which had just erupted. I was particularly fond of Point Reyes, the sweeping countryside north of San Francisco, which could be reached from Hayward in simple day trips. I showed Point Reyes to everyone who came to see me. I often visited Yosemite National Park, but I probably went to Death Valley even more often, and I have been back to it on a number of occasions subsequently. My love of Death Valley was rewarded in 1989, when we worked for a month on the Hanaupah Fan opposite Dante's View, and I found some hitherto unknown sediments from the former Lake Manly, which used to ripple here many years ago. This is the »Hanaupah Fan Shoreline Deposit at Tule Spring«, deposited 145,000 to 128,000 years ago, according to the latest cosmogenic dating. We were living in Shoshone at the time, as Furnace Creek was too expensive, and had to drive the 130 km to and from the Fan every day, though this was not a problem, as there was so little traffic.

The landscapes of the American West are strangely attractive for historically-minded Europeans. A niece of mine who grew up in Australia was asked about her impression of a trip to England. Her reply: »Too much history.« She hit the nail on the head. There is no history, at least not in the European sense, in the American West. There is the occasional »historical landmark«, marking some little event or other, but nothing to compare with Europe's years of bloodstained soil. When I think of the way Europeans have suffered I am happy to accept this lack of history in Death Valley and don't smirk at the »historical landmarks«.

Perhaps the fascination of the American landscape, particularly the desert landscape, lies in this lack of history. In Germany, in Brandenburg, for example, the essentially plain landscape lives on its history. Here the Great Elector triumphed, Napoleon's army won a battle there. Actual nature, nature without people, is hidden under fields, under woodland and heath. In the American West, in the desert landscapes where admittedly Indians were killed or driven out, grandiose nature, without any people in it, reigns supreme, without any human history or human interventions to speak of, in comparison with Europe. Here the history of the earth is dominant, a particularly fascinating phenomenon. Anyone who can read it is doubly blessed.

I had come to California full of apprehension because I had a very high opinion of American research and teaching and I was worried about holding my own. But I soon realized that it was no different there from anywhere else. A little story about that: We had been on a student outing somewhere or other with John Cummings, a geologist who unfortunately died all too early, probably the most unusual colleague I ever had.

We were standing at an exposed outcrop of rock by the side of the road, and had all knocked off a specimen of the sandstone from it and were looking at it with our magnifying glasses. I had licked my piece to moisten it. I always do that because I am used to it from my Italian calcareous sandstone, as that's the only way you can see micro-fossils like globotruncanae, for example. »Good heavens«, said Cummings, »You're a real professional.« »What do you mean«, I said. He replied: »Because you licked the specimens.« It turned out that American petroleum geologists lick their samples so that they can see on site whether the spittle is absorbed by the rock, which would show it has a certain porosity, possibly indicating oil- or gas-bearing rock deeper down. Of course that's a primitive on-site experiment, not a laboratory test. I explained my method, which was just as new to him as his had been to me, and we patted each other on the back. So that was 1:1, a draw in other words. University teaching was and is a different matter. Even as students in the 1950s, it had struck us how very much better Anglo-Saxon textbooks were than German-language ones. Things are rather better today, but only because we have largely adopted Anglo-Saxon teaching methods. I am only talking about geology here, I can't really assess the situation in other subjects. Nevertheless, the two most important German textbooks on the history of geology and general geology published by the Spektrum Verlag are by American authors, translations of the American first editions and published in 1994 and 1995. It would be a good idea to analyse the teaching methods thoroughly to work out why that is. It would certainly also touch on the different mentalities, indeed the languages, of the Germans and the Anglo-Saxons. I am not the person to do this.

Whether teaching is better in America than it is in Germany has long been a topic of discussion, not just now in 2006. As far as geology is concerned, I can say that both systems produce geologist who are just as good or just as bad. But the Americans study more quickly and effectively, and they have a lower drop-out rate. This is because of the universities are more school-like in their structure, especially in the early stages, and teaching and learning are constantly monitored. Every course was examined in Hayward, even in the middle of the quarter, in other words teachers could set an intermediate examination after a very few weeks to show whether he had gone through the material too quickly, to slowly, or whether he had got it just right. This meant that the students knew where they were as well. That is one side of the coin. The other side is that every teacher was assessed by the students after every class, through faculty questionnaires. It took quarter of an hour at the most, even then the answer sheets were read electronically. So each teacher could see where his or her weaknesses lay. I was not assessed, incidentally, because I was a visiting lecturer. My attempt to introduce this system in Berlin fell flat on its face. Now individual university departments are assessed on the internet. But its not within the scope of this California reminiscence to go into that.

So how can I sum up that wonderful year? I had lived abroad before. I had worked in Italy for twenty years, not continuously, but always for months at a time. But I had never been so profoundly involved professionally and personally. I would identify three themes, the landscape, the people and the job. Perhaps in that order.

Compared with the essentially small-scale Central European landscapes, with their abundant vegetation, the desert landscapes of the American West are wide and empty, they are petrified. I think, it is this almost horizontless breadth that shapes our experience of the landscape. It is like a stone world before plants and animals, and then people, took possession of it. A kind of primeval landscape. Beyond any aesthetic considerations it is a particularly attractive world for the geologists, because apart from desert varnish and other weathering crusts they have direct access to the object of their desire.

In the twenty-five years that have passed since my time in California a lot has changed for the better in Germany on the simple level of the way people live together. People have become more friendly and more sociable, including officials, so that things are not as different from California as they used to be. You might even get a friendly word or a smile from a check-out girl in a supermarket here now. That was something that particularly struck me in California at the time. A policeman had stopped the traffic on a country road because a tree had fallen over, and it was just being taken away. I was the first in the queue of cars. The policeman waved me on and said: »Thank you for your cooperation.« I was staggered. I still think something like that would be impossible in Germany.

It is very difficult to assess my professional work in California correctly and to relate it to Berlin. I was a guest, almost an exotic creature, there was no sense of competition, of being superior or inferior to anyone else. I delivered the prescribed lectures and exercises, ran trips and in fact only had very committed students to deal with. If I wanted anything in the department or the lab I got it straight away. Working with colleagues from the biology department on the tidal project was perfect, I talked about my problems in front of their students and they talked about theirs in front of mine. They could easily have let me hang around in my little room, but that was out of the question.

You ask me if after everything I experienced in California and have written down here I could give students or younger colleagues any advice? No, I wouldn't like to do that. Everyone must live his or her life as they think fit. I can only say for myself that it was one of the most exciting years of my life, and it gave me a very great deal, even though I have regularly worked abroad for long periods throughout my professional life. I shall certainly go back to Death Valley and revisit the Hanaupah Fan.

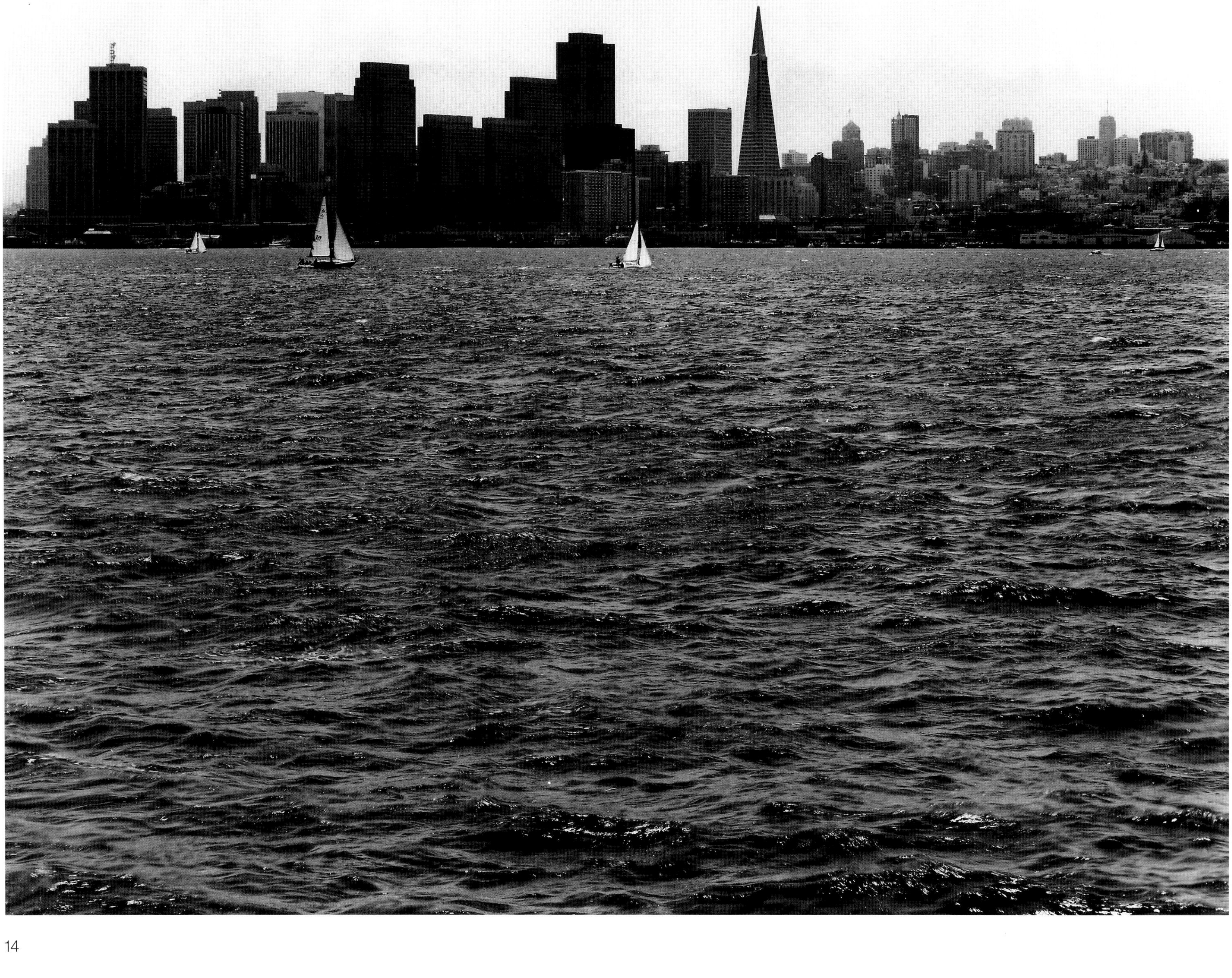

1. San Francisco. Blick von Treasure Island auf die Stadt.
2. San Francisco. Blick von den Twin Peaks auf die Stadt.

1. San Francisco. View of the city from Treasure Island.
2. San Francisco. View of the city from Twin Peaks.

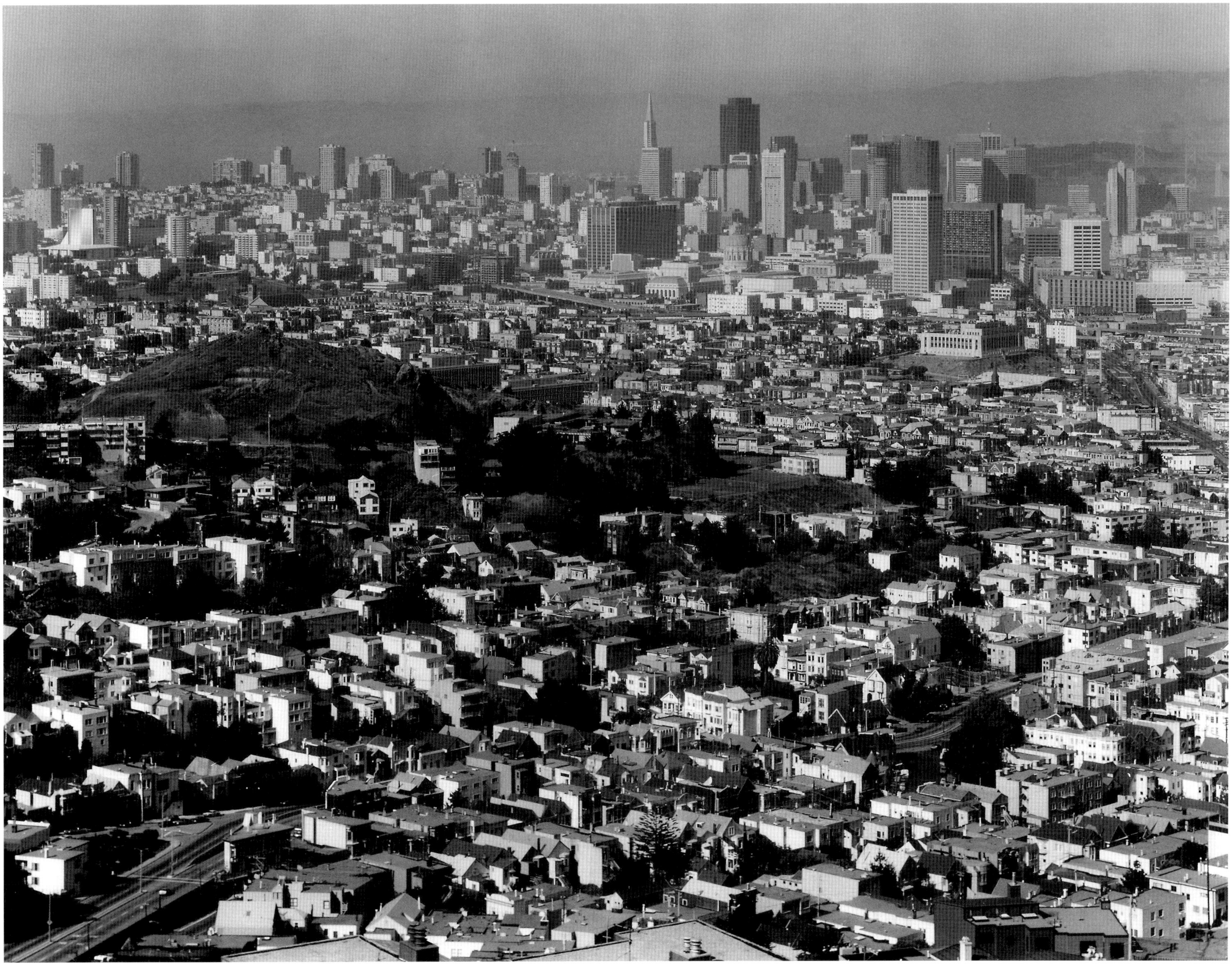

3. San Francisco. Columbus Street, Ecke Kearney Street.
4. San Francisco. Market Street, Ecke Sutter Street.

3. San Francisco. Columbus Street on the corner of Kearney Street.
4. San Francisco. Market Street on the corner of Sutter Street.

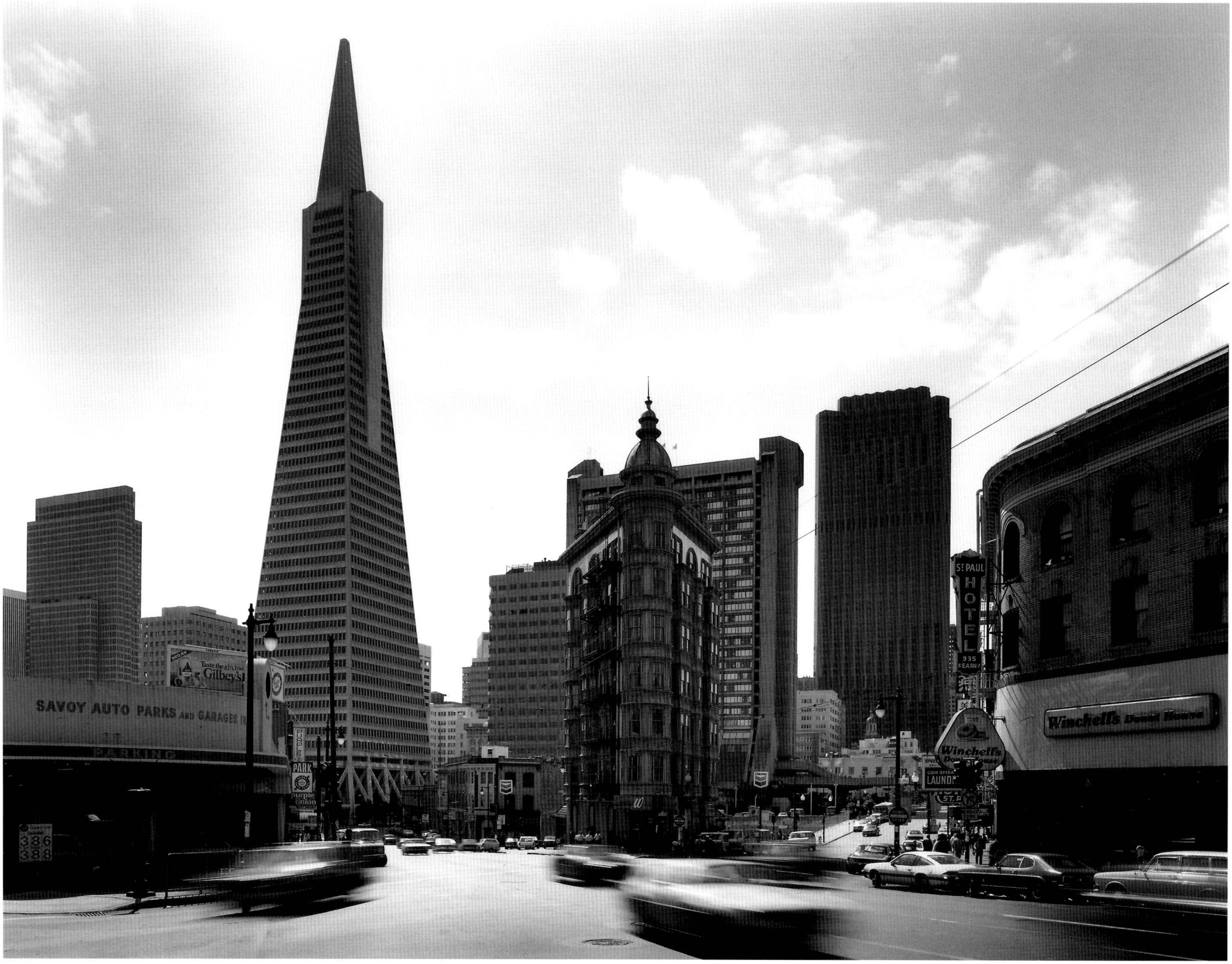

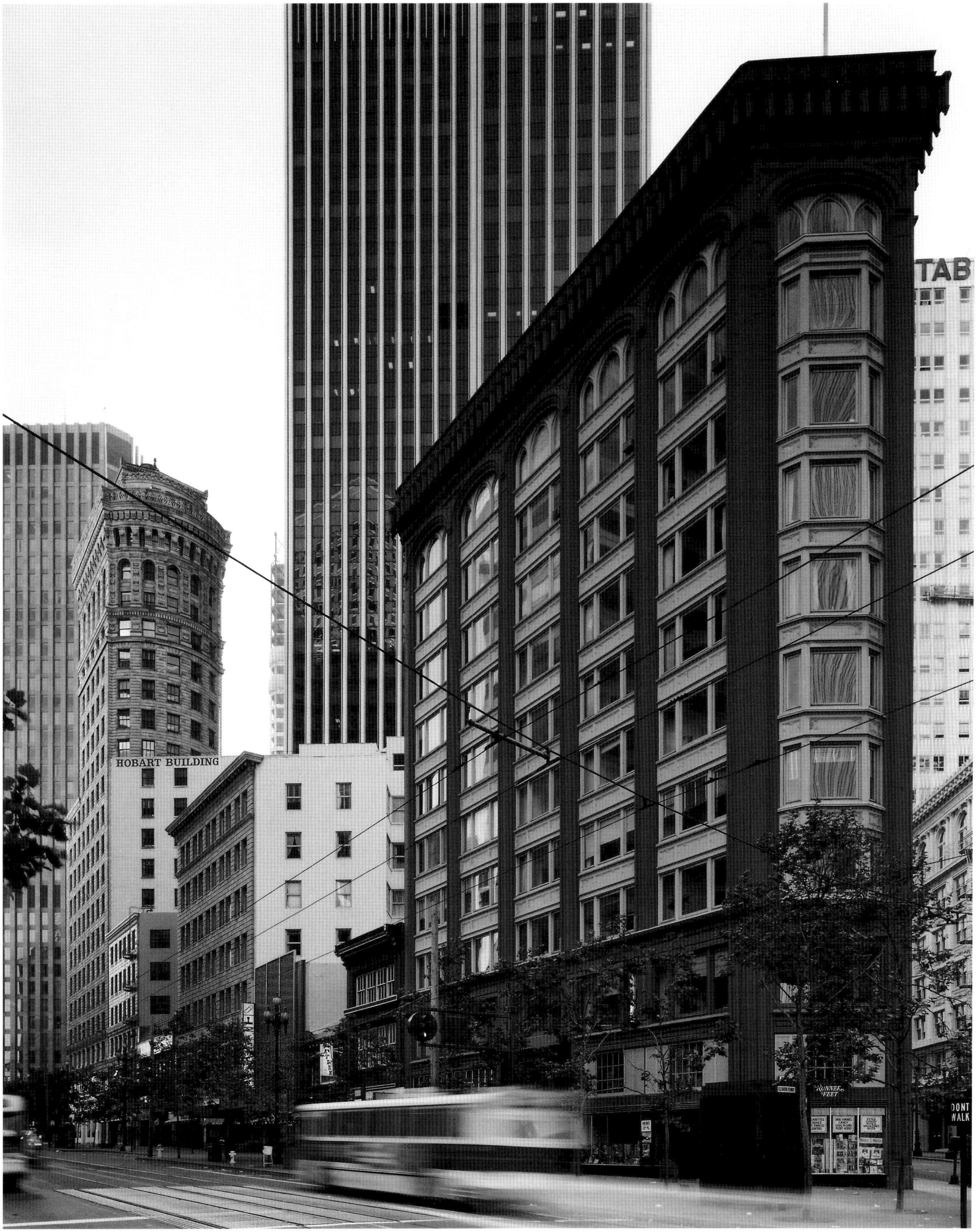
HOBART BUILDING
TAB

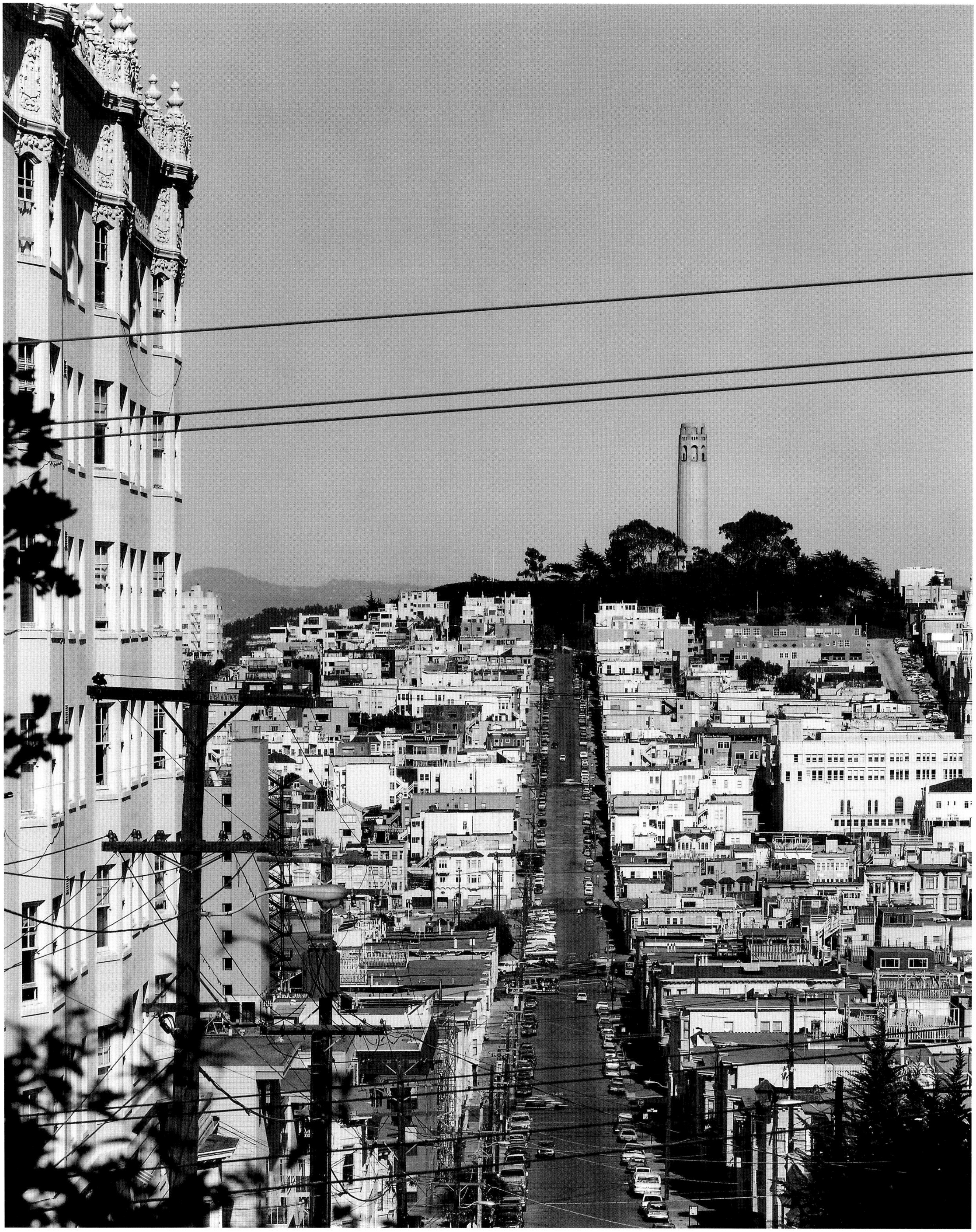

5. San Francisco. Greenwich Street und Telegraph Hill.
6. San Francisco. Sacramento Street.

5. San Francisco. Greenwich Street and Telegraph Hill.
6. San Francisco. Sacramento Street.

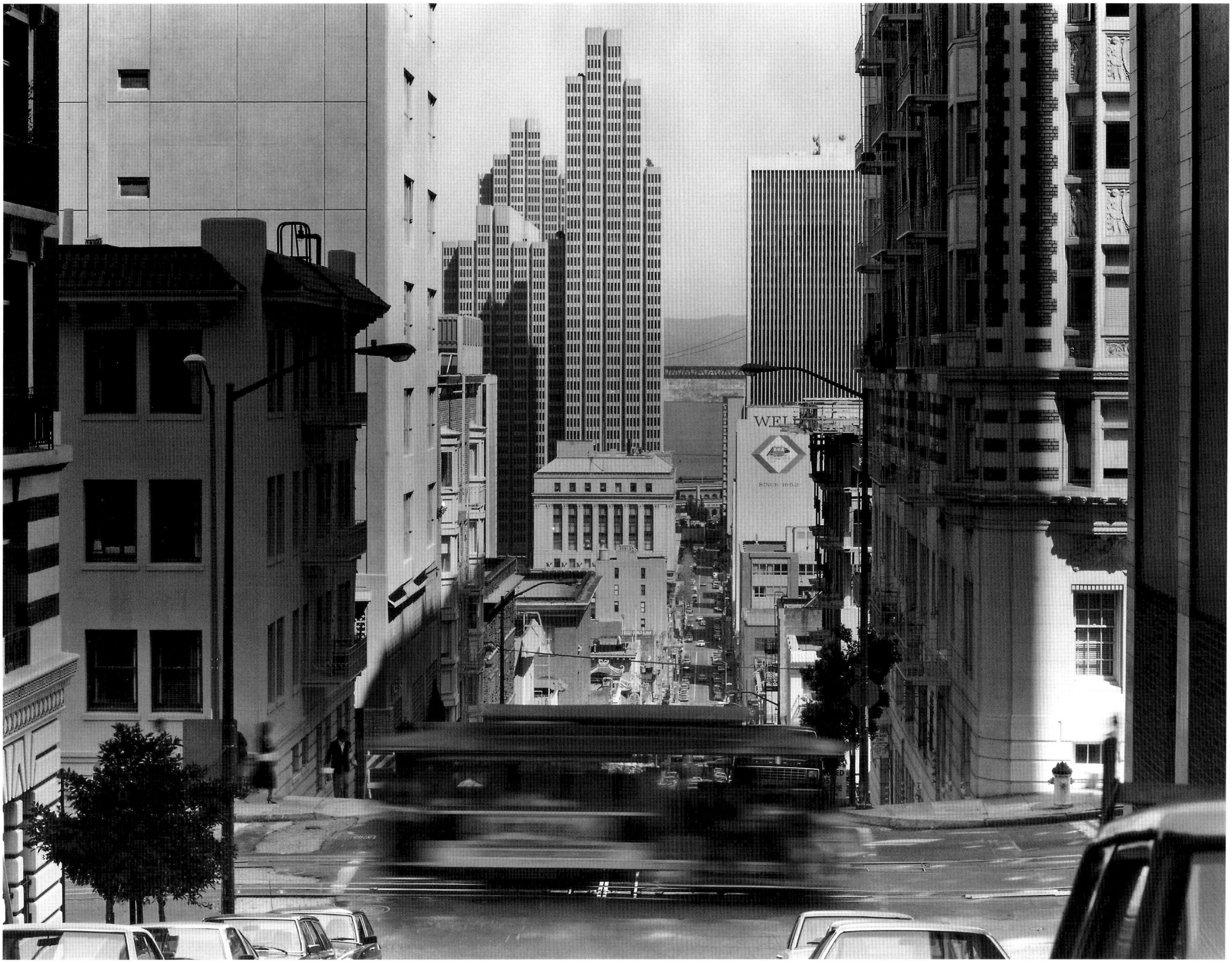

7. San Francisco. Jackson Street mit der Bay Bridge im Hintergrund.
8. San Francisco. Die Bay Bridge von Pier 24 aus gesehen.

7. San Francisco. Jackson Street with Bay Bridge in the background.
8. San Francisco. Bay Bridge seen from Pier 24.

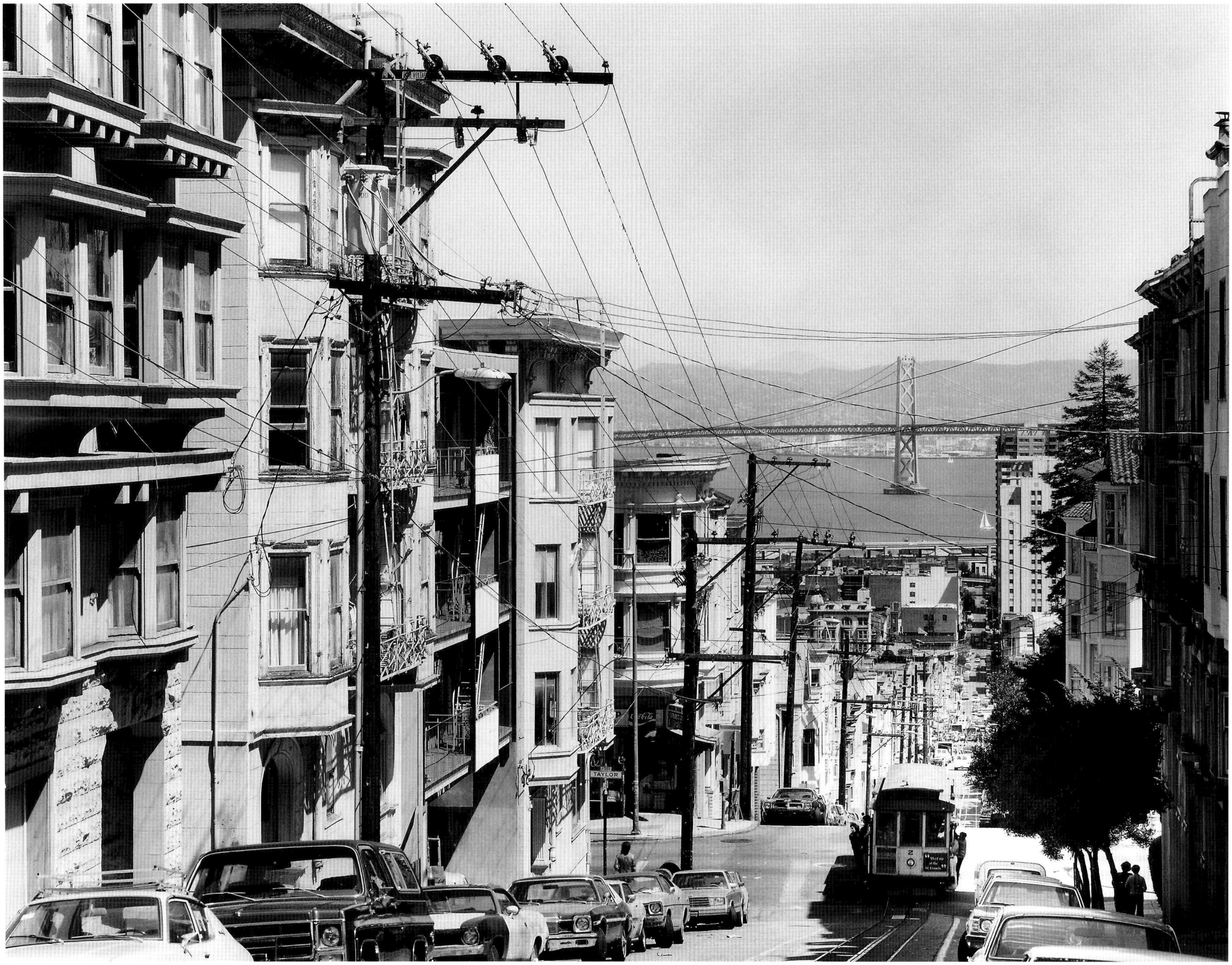

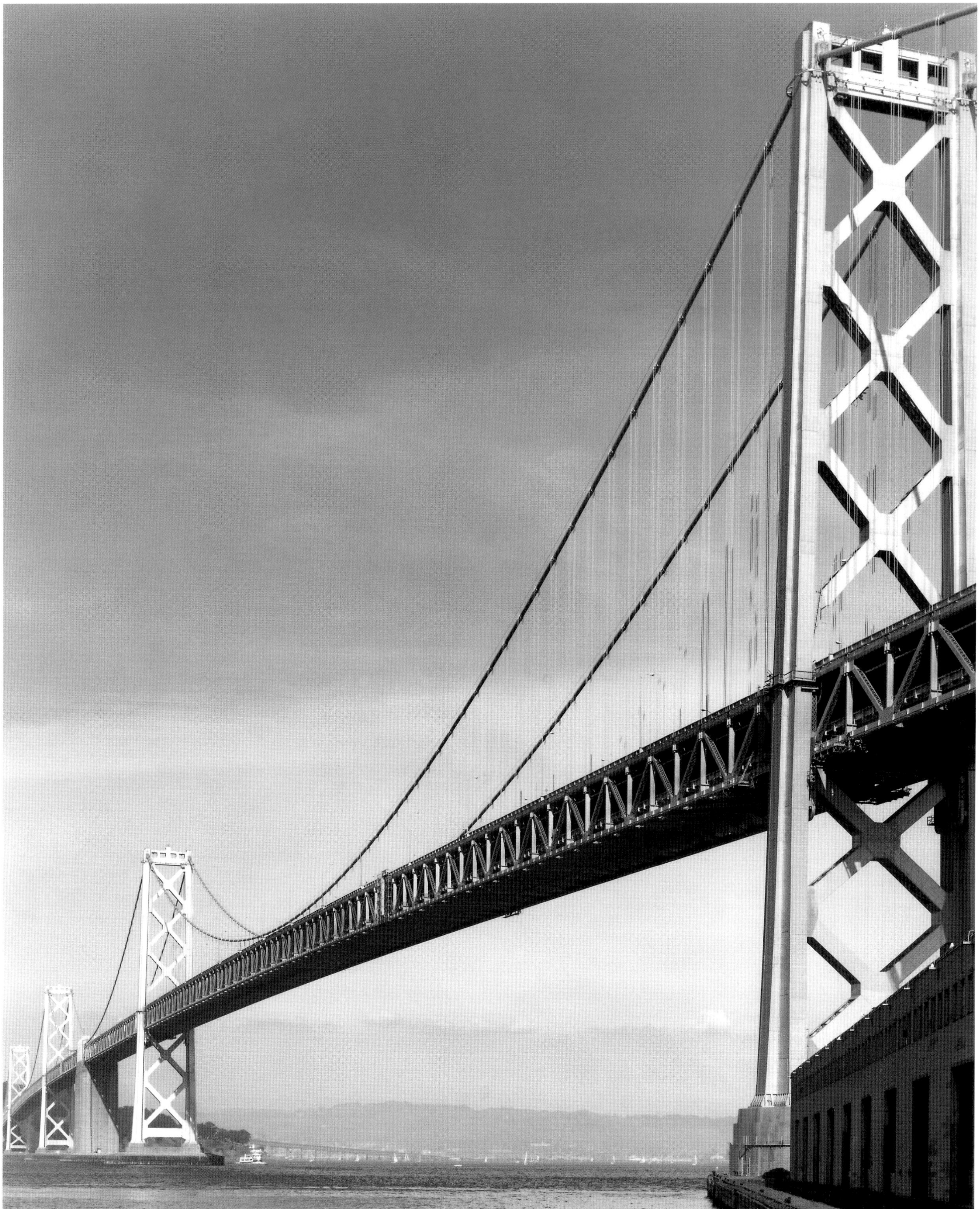

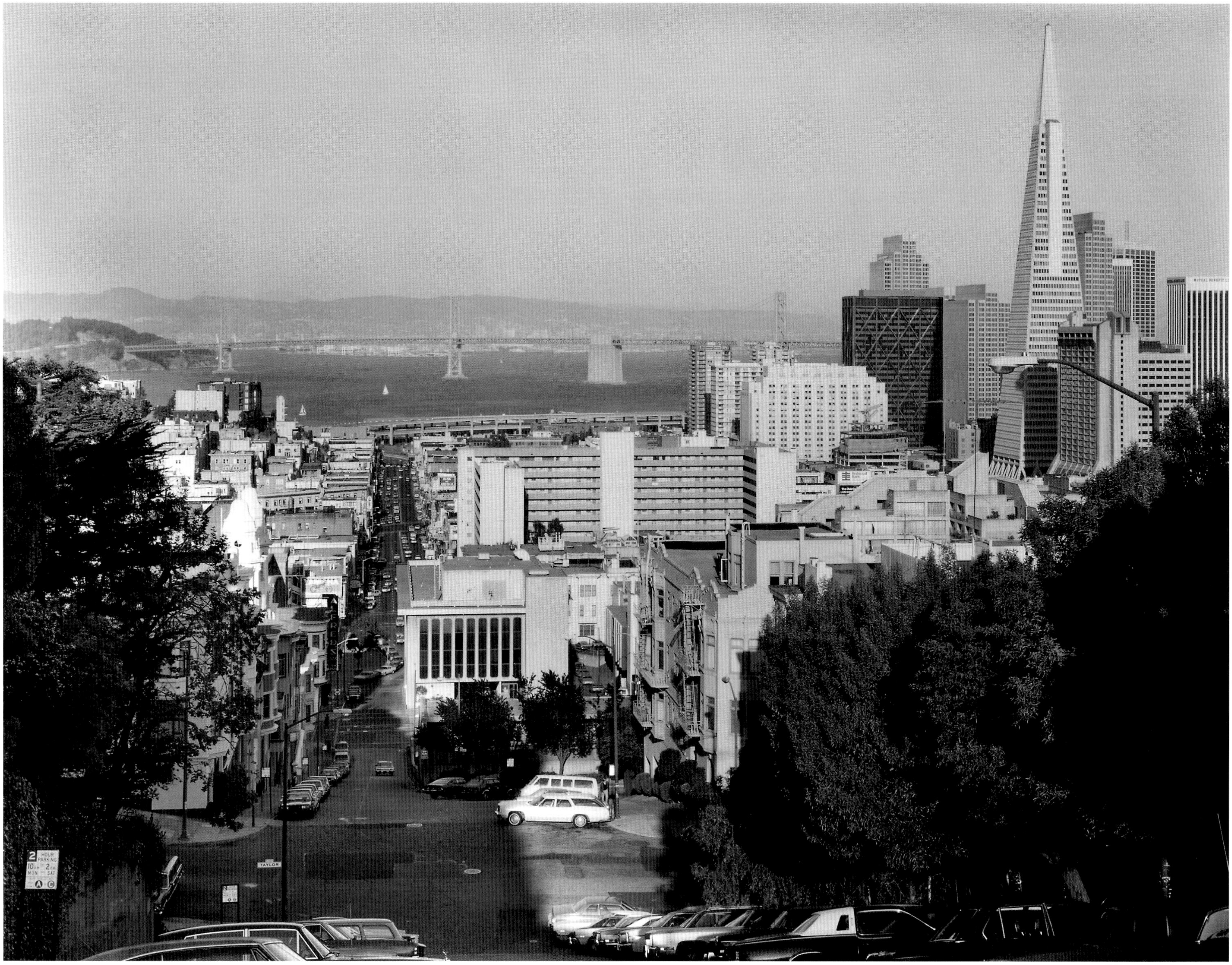

9. San Francisco. Broadway mit der Bay Bridge im Hintergrund.
10. San Francisco. Taylor Street.
11. San Francisco. Alamo Square mit viktorianischen Häusern.

9. San Francisco. Broadway with Bay Bridge in the background.
10. San Francisco. Taylor Street.
11. San Francisco. Alamo Square with Victorian houses.

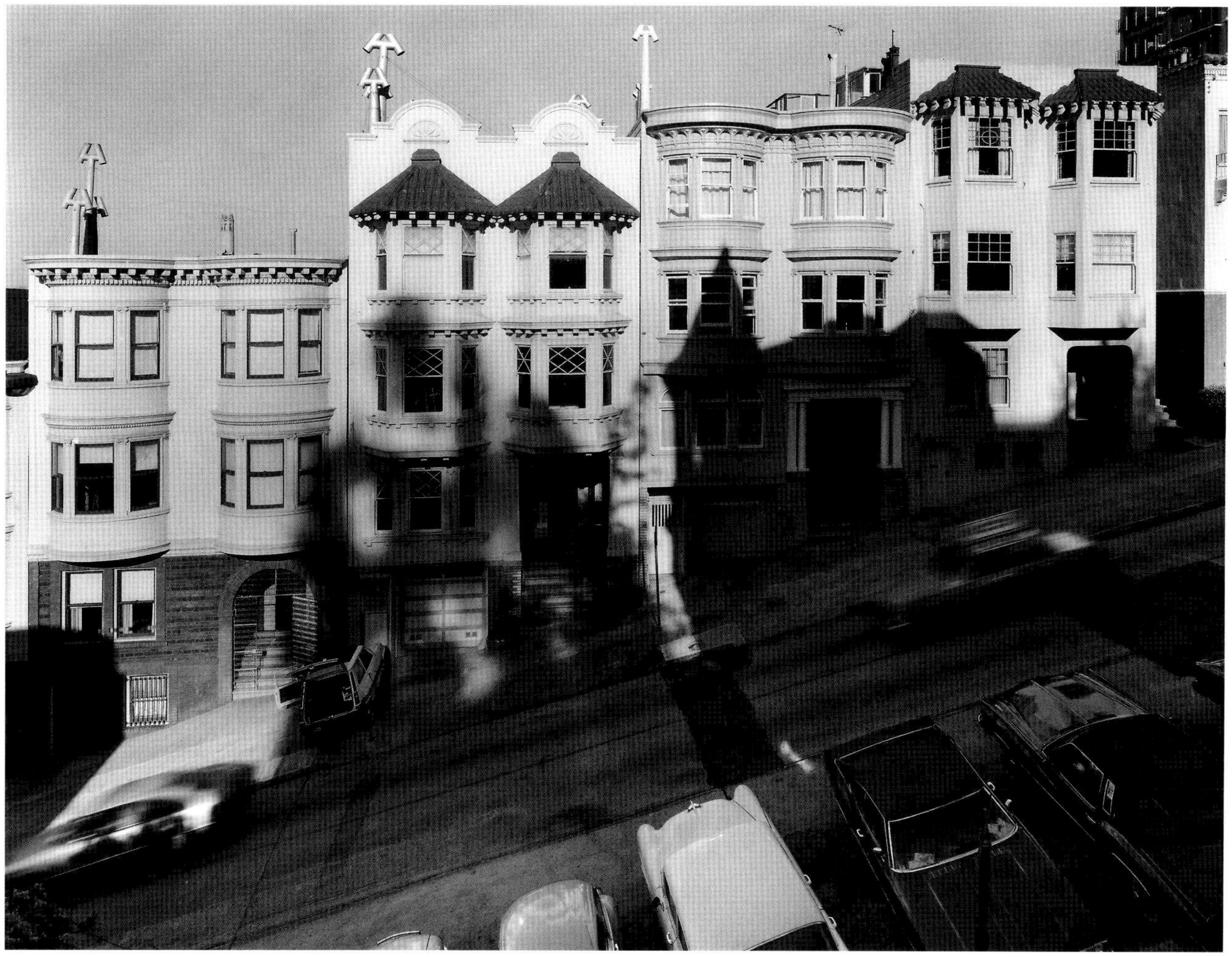

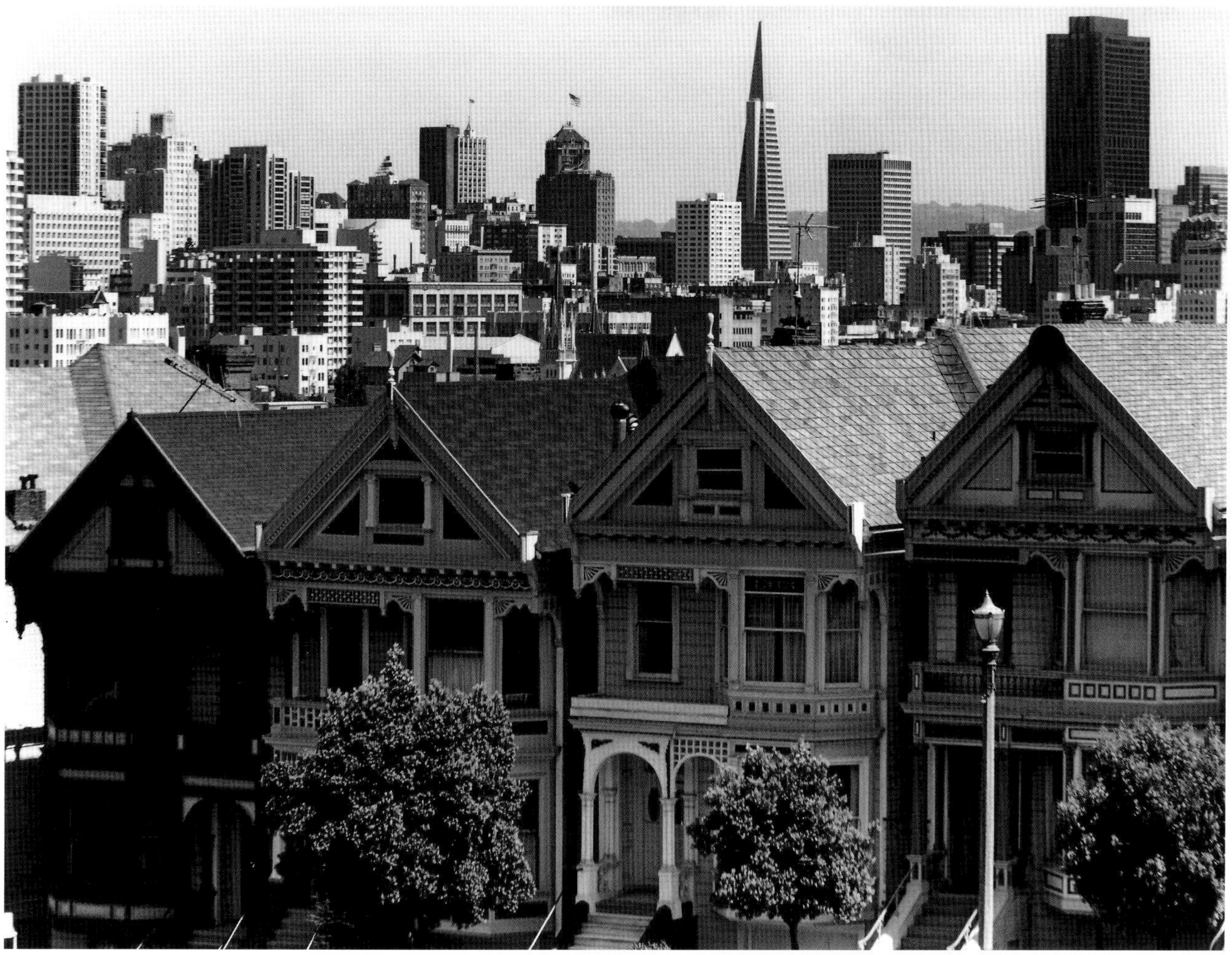

12. Golden Gate Bridge mit San Francisco im Hintergrund von Point Diablo aus gesehen.
13. San Francisco. Die Golden Gate Bridge von Fort Point aus gesehen.

12. Golden Gate Bridge with San Francisco in the background seen from Point Diablo.
13. San Francisco. Golden Gate Bridge seen from Fort Point.

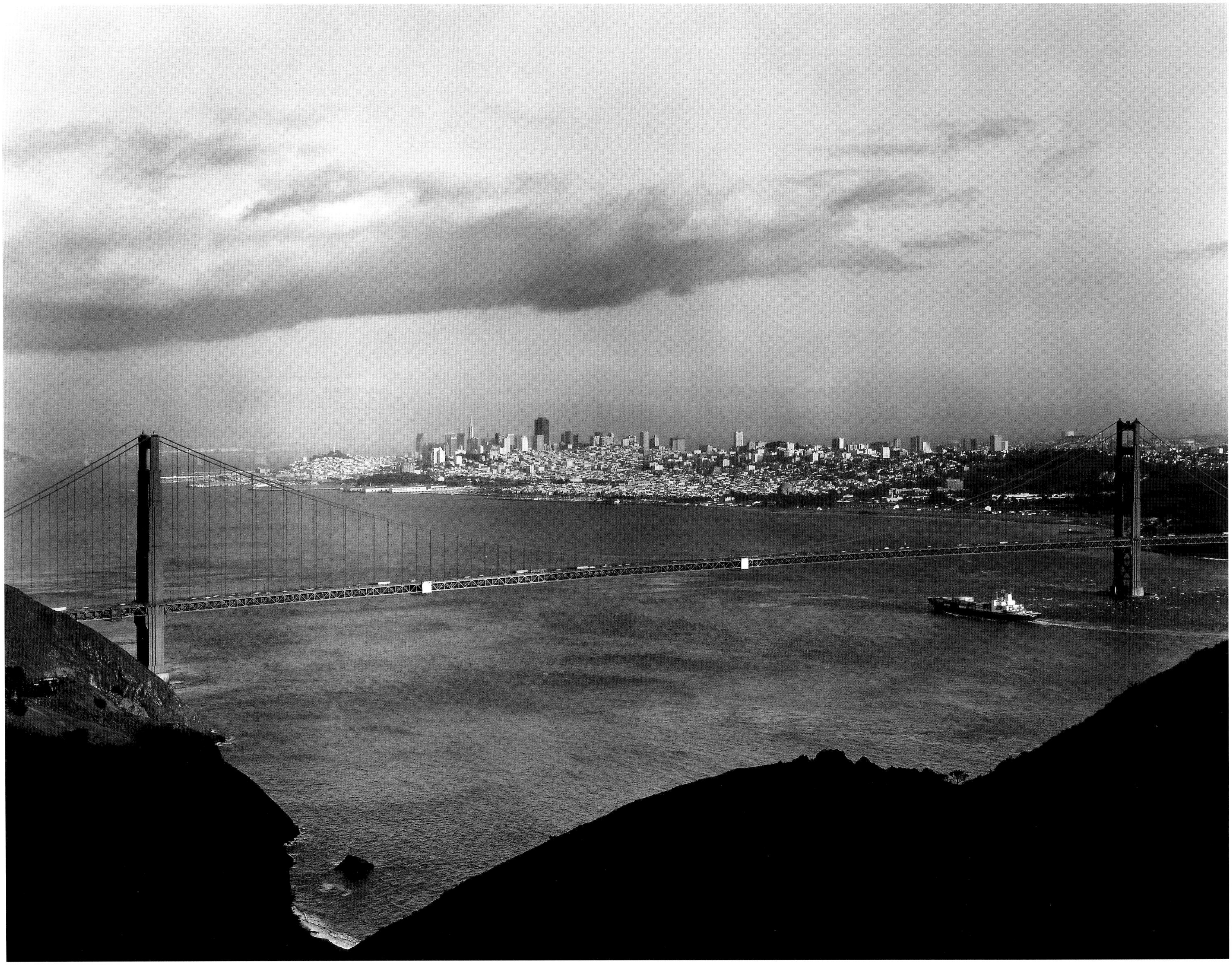

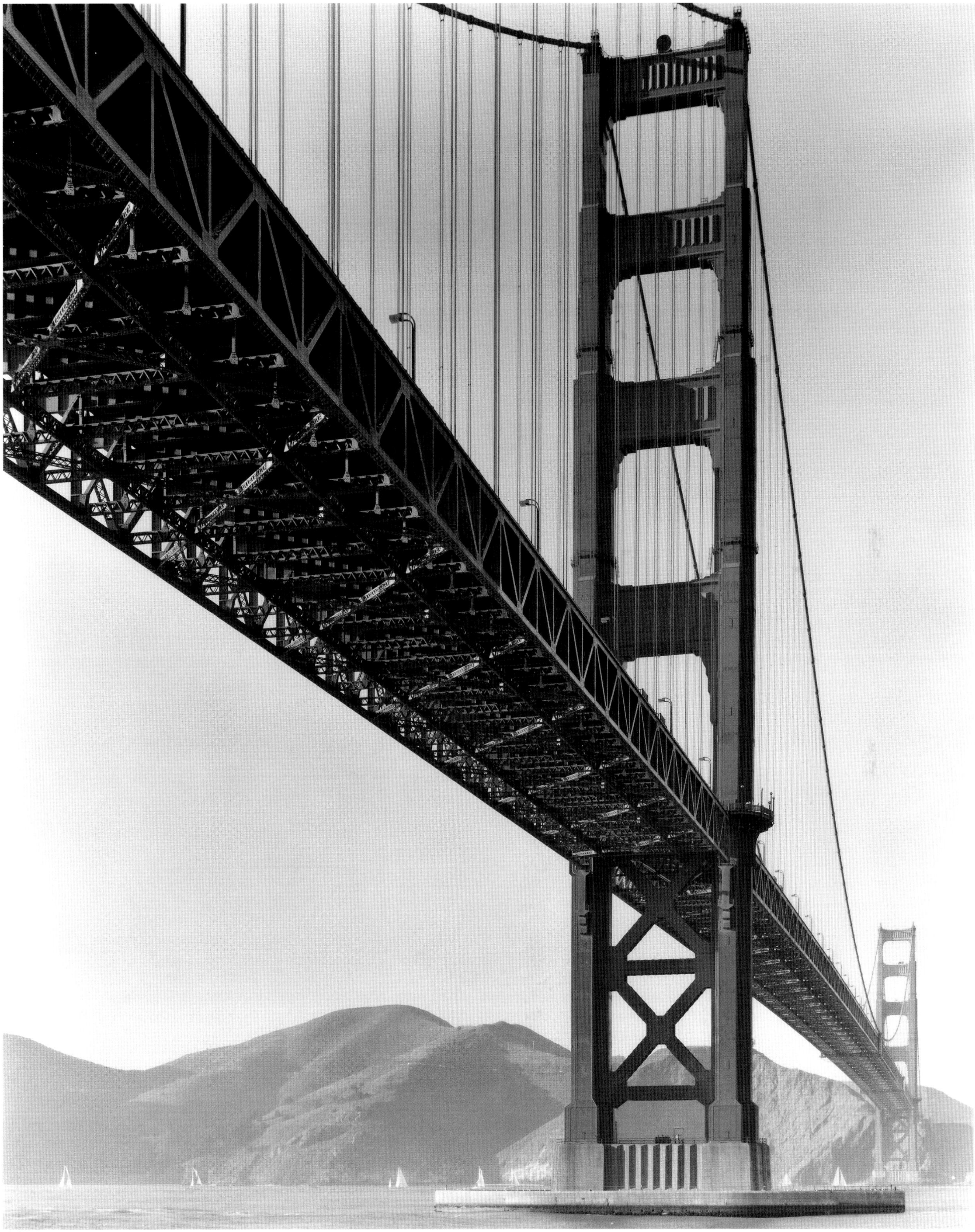

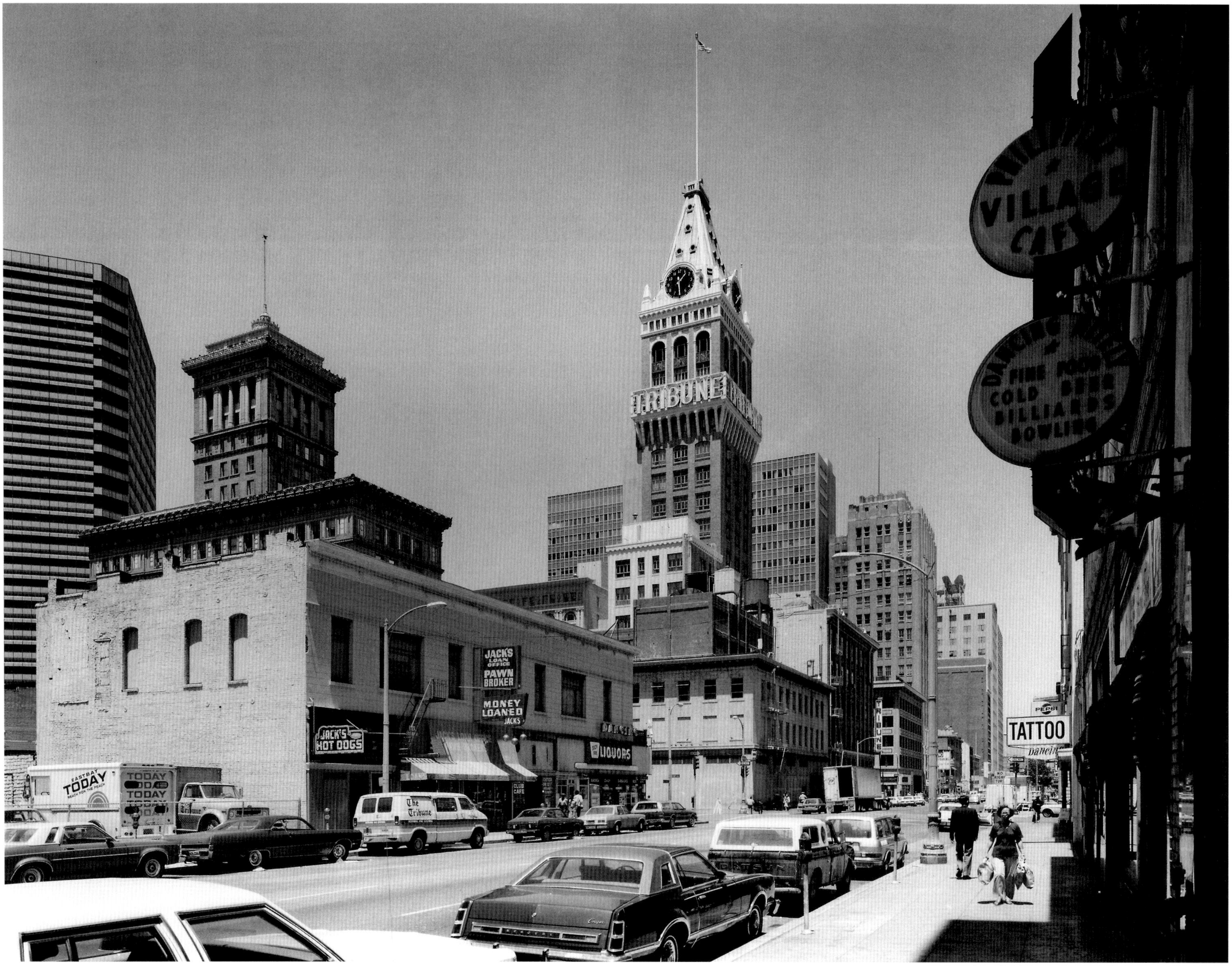
TRIBUNE
JACK'S
LOAN OFFICE
PAWN BROKER
MONEY LOANED
JACKS
JACK'S HOT DOGS
LIQUORS
EASTBAY TODAY
TODAY
The Tribune
TATTOO
CLUB CAFE

14. Oakland. Franklin Street, Ecke 11. Street.
15. Hayward. Blick vom Calstate Tower auf die Bucht von San Francisco, die San Mateo Bridge und die Küstenberge.

14. Oakland. Franklin Street on the corner of 11. Street.
15. Hayward. View of San Francisco Bay, San Mateo Bridge and the coastal mountains from Calstate Tower.

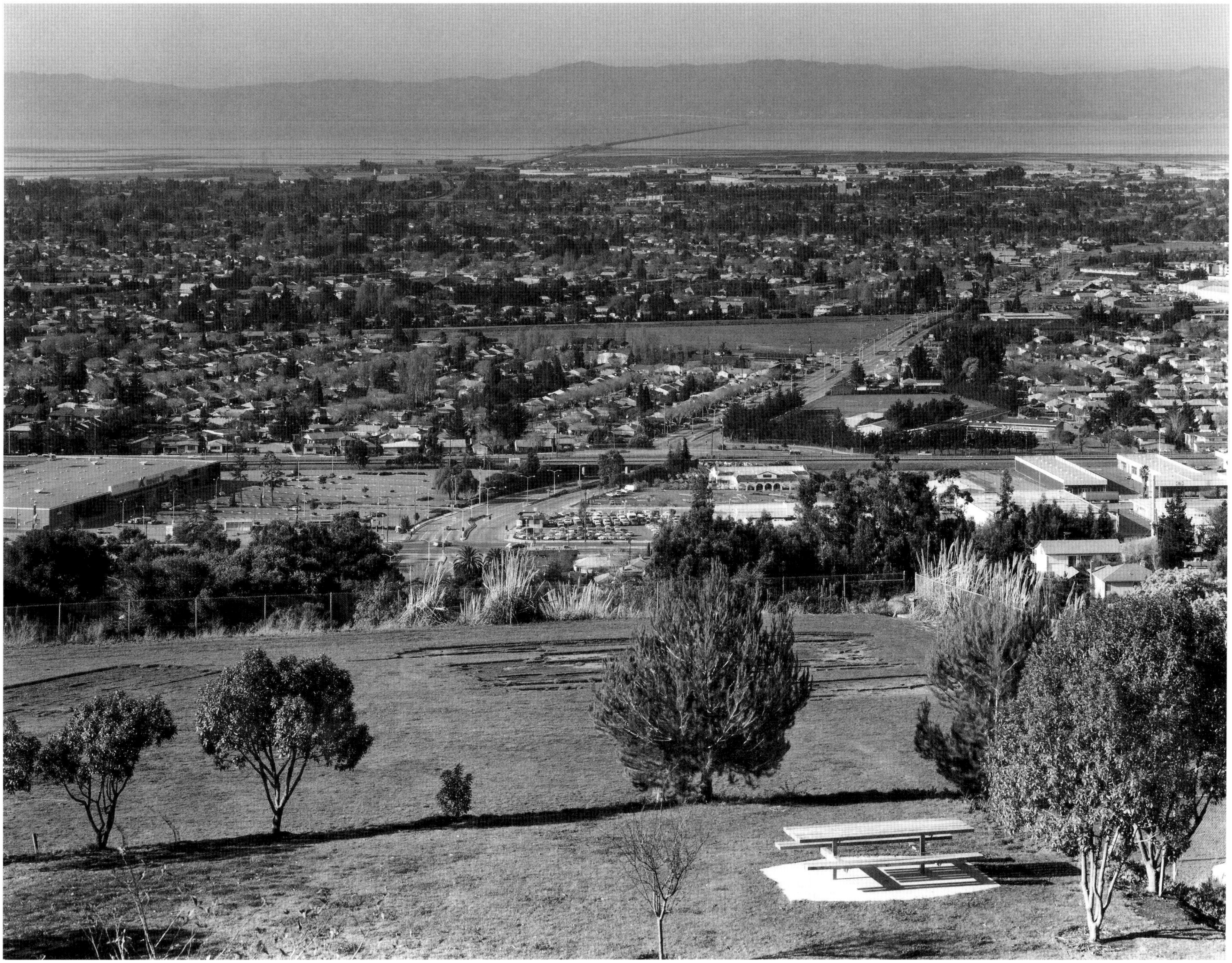

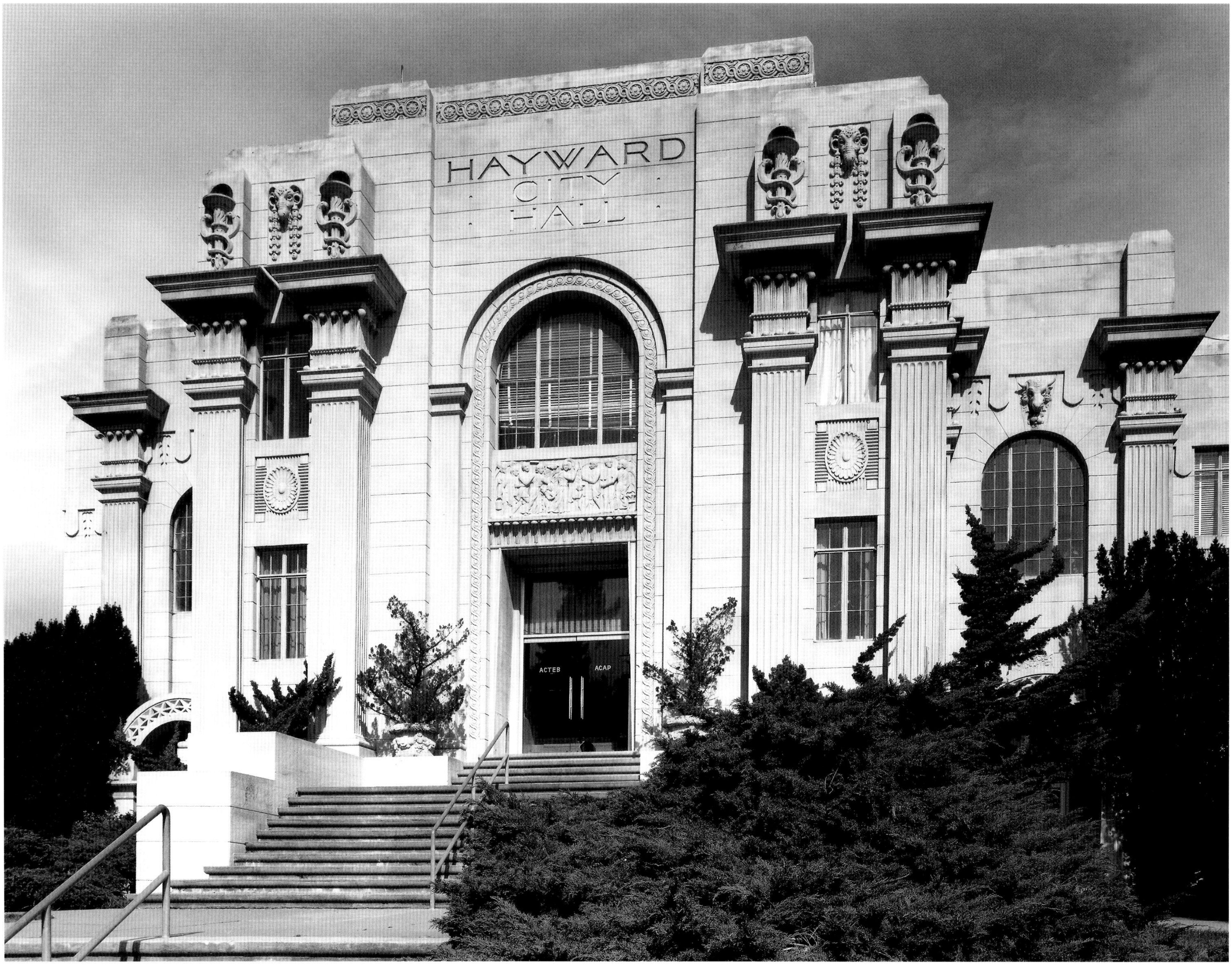
HAYWARD
CITY
HALL

16. Hayward. City Hall. Das verlassene Gebäude wird von der Hayward-Störung, die genau unter ihm verläuft, in zwei Teile gerissen.
17. Hayward. Die Hayward-Störung zerreißt Straße und Rinnstein. Die Kriechbewegung beträgt weiter nördlich 3 bis 9 mm im Jahr.
18. Hayward. City Hall. Aufgerissener Fußboden im Foyer.

16. Hayward. City Hall. The abandoned building is broken in two by the Hayward Fault, which runs exactly below it.
17. Hayward. The Hayward Fault is rupturing the street and the gutter. Farther north the creep is 3 to 9 mm per year.
18. Hayward. City Hall. Torn floor in the foyer.

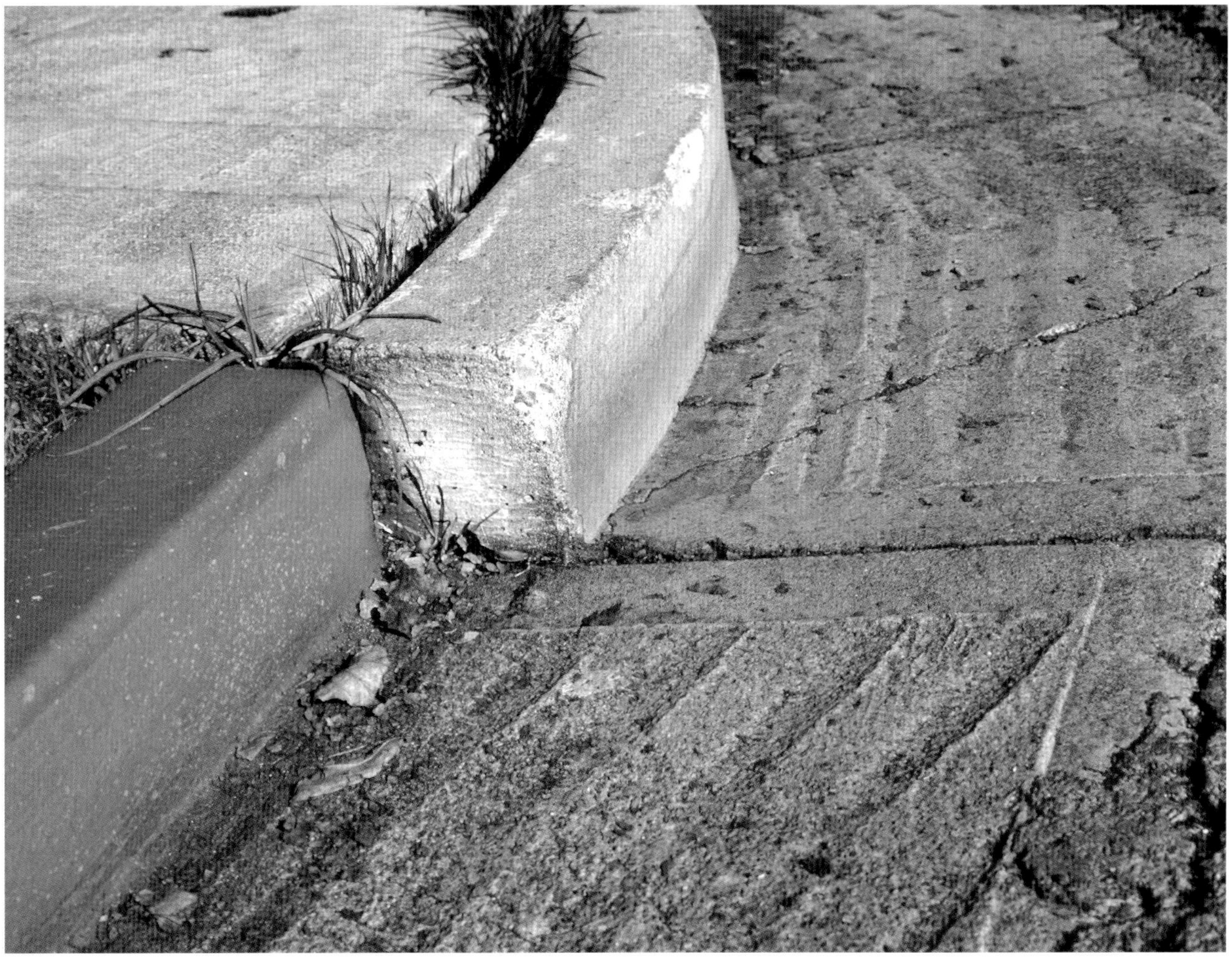

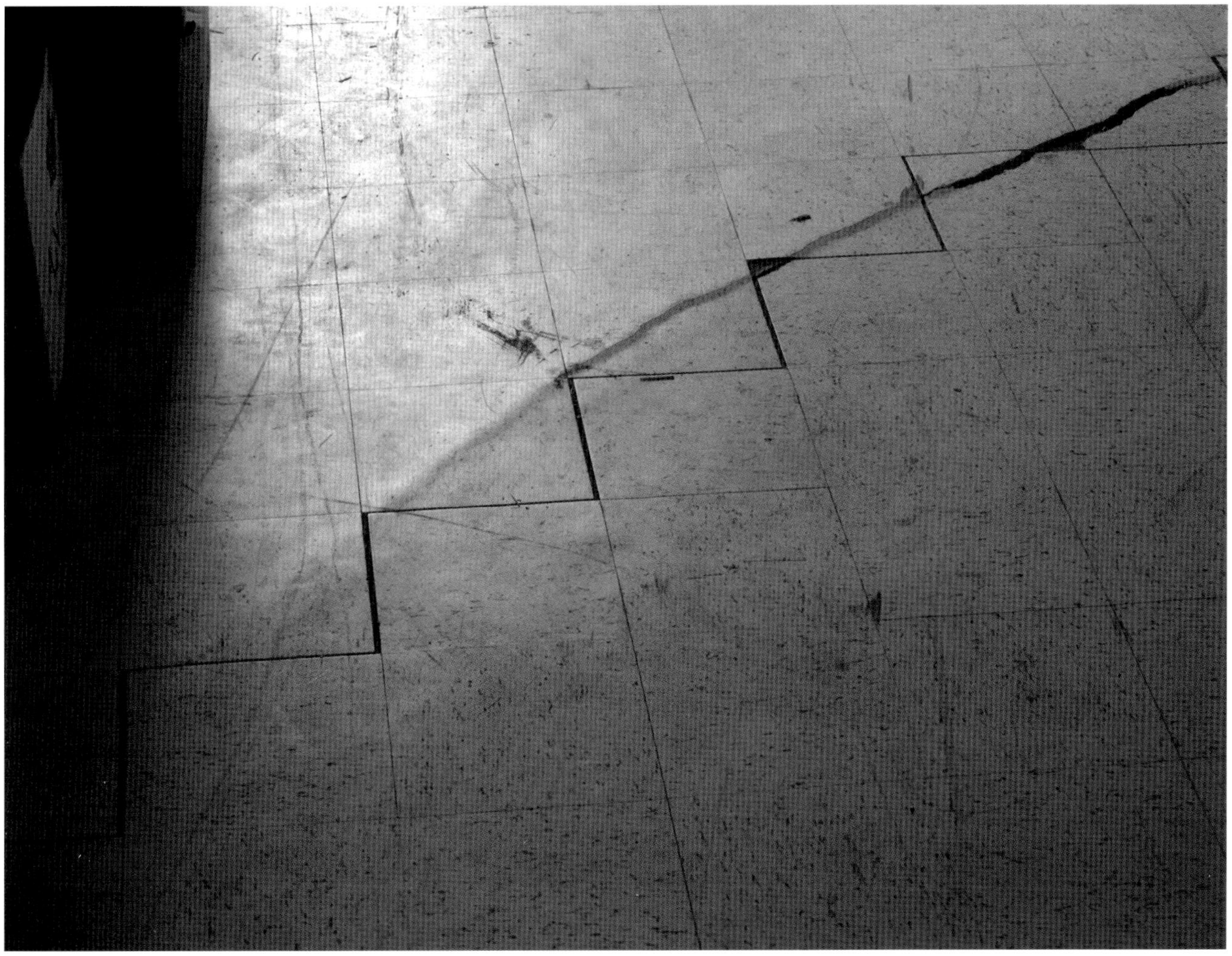

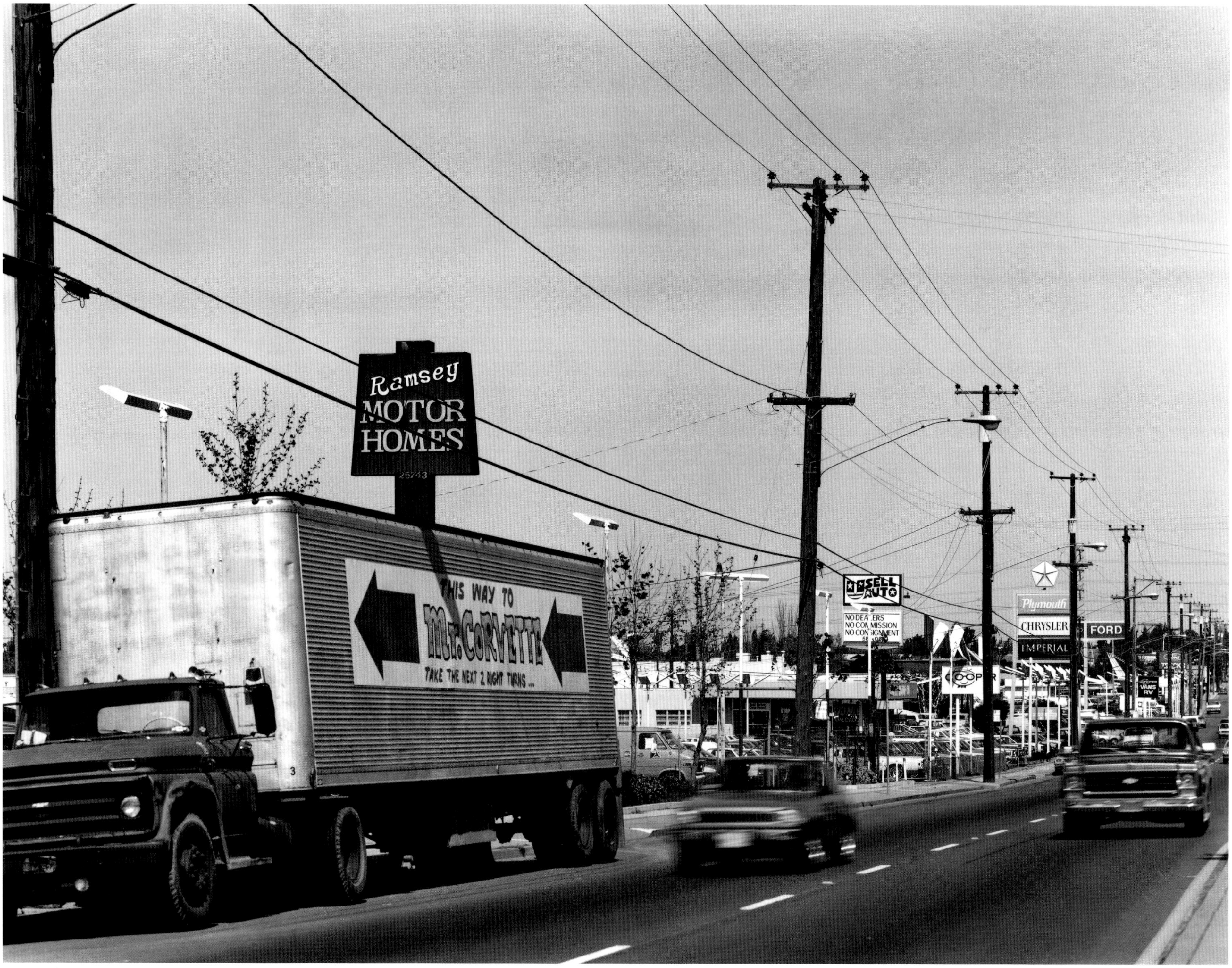
Ramsey
MOTOR
HOMES
THIS WAY TO
Mr. CORVETTE
TAKE THE NEXT 2 RIGHT TURNS ...
Plymouth
CHRYSLER
IMPERIAL
FORD

19. Hayward. Mission Boulevard am Devon Drive.
20. Hayward. Harder Street, Ecke West View. In dem erdbebengefährdeten Gebiet bietet sich die leichte Holzbauweise besonders an.

19. Hayward. Mission Boulevard near Devon Drive.
20. Hayward. Harder Street on the corner of West View. Wooden structures are especially appropriate when there is risk of earthquakes.

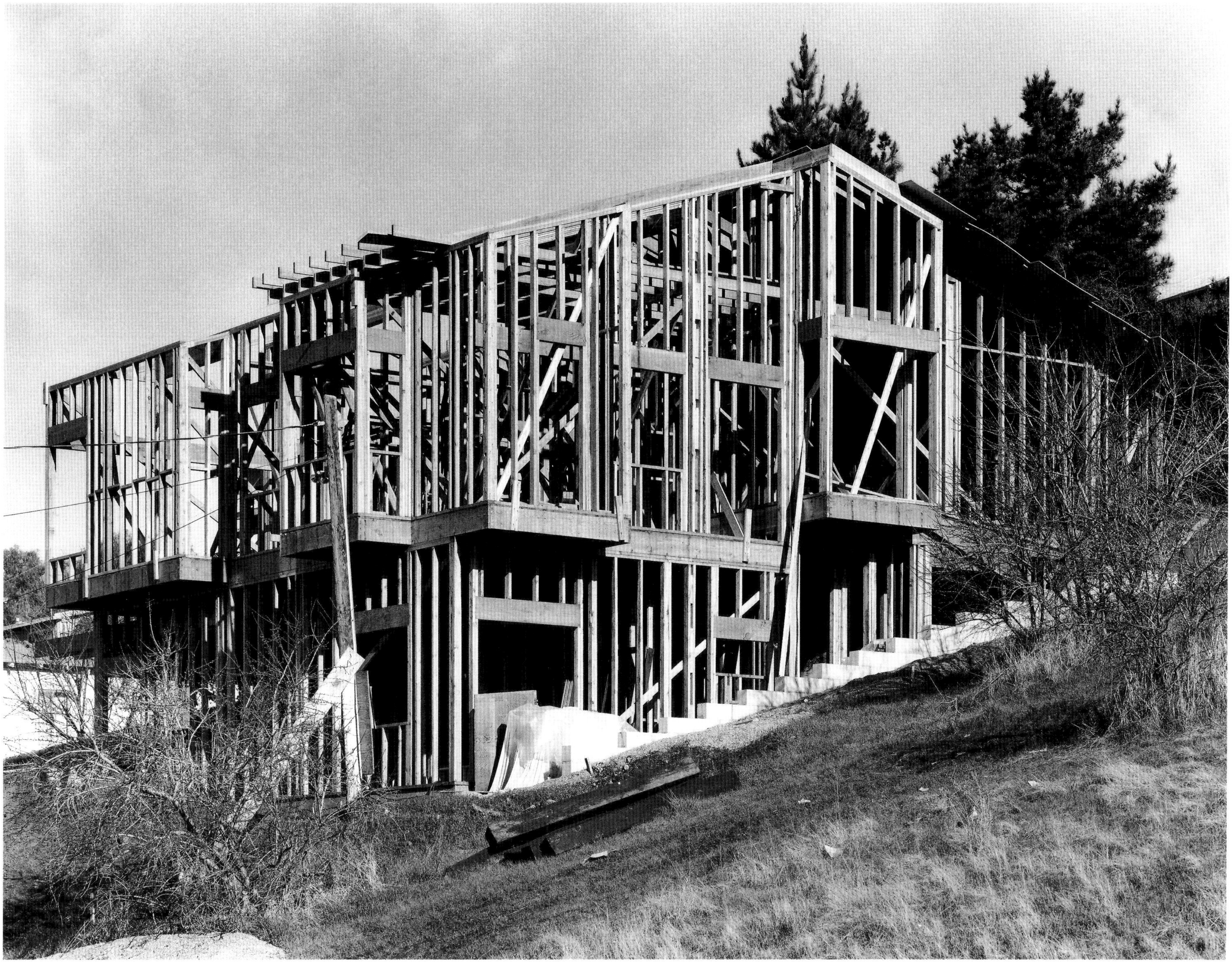

21. Hayward. Eden Landing. Alte Windräder und Wasserheber in den ehemaligen Salzgärten der San Francisco Bay.
22. Hayward. Eden Landing. Hölzerne Archimedes-Schraube zum Wasserheben.

21. Hayward. Eden Landing. Old wind wheels and water lifters in the former salt garden of San Francisco Bay.
22. Hayward. Eden Landing. Wooden Archimedean screw for water lifting.

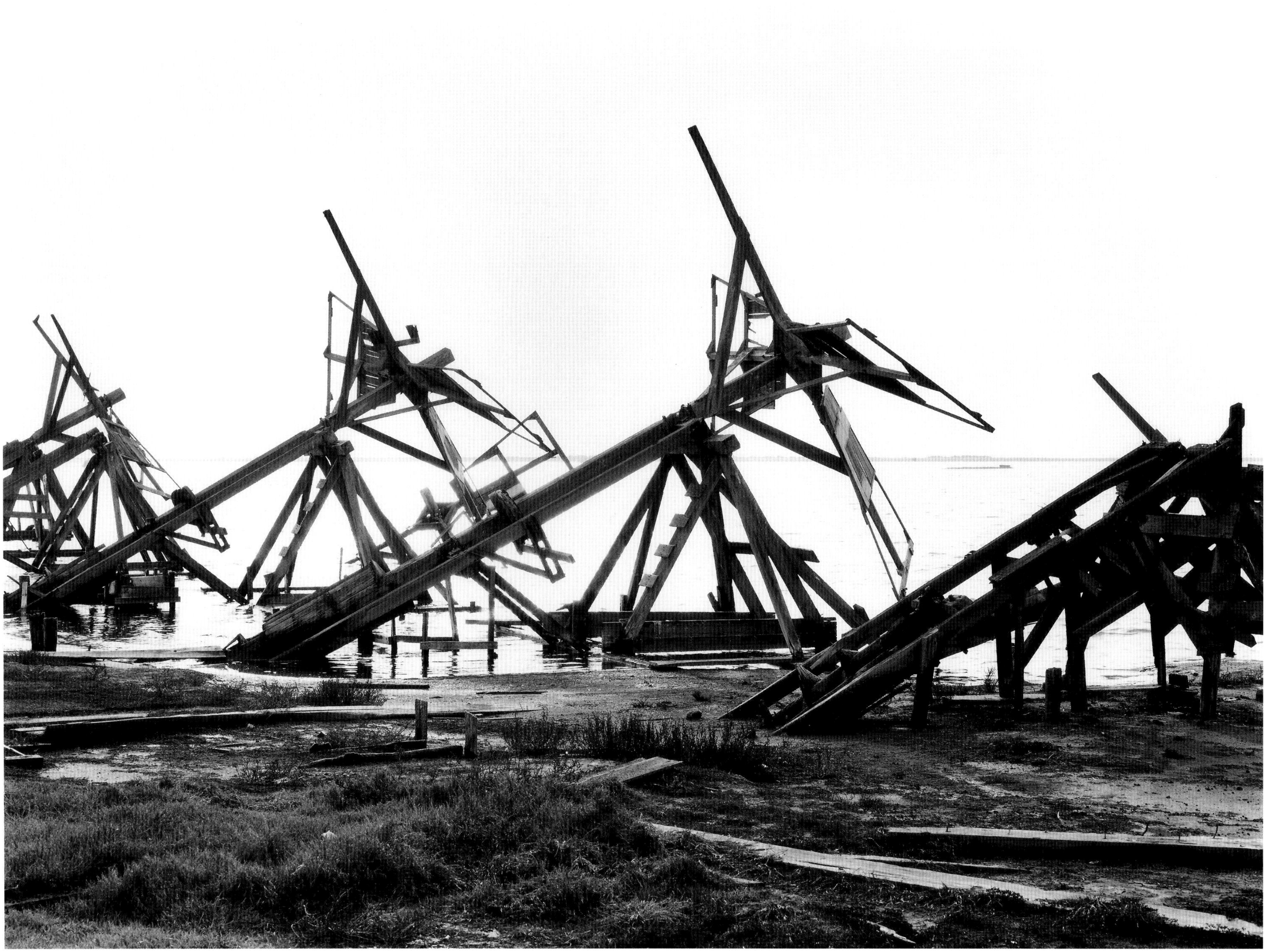

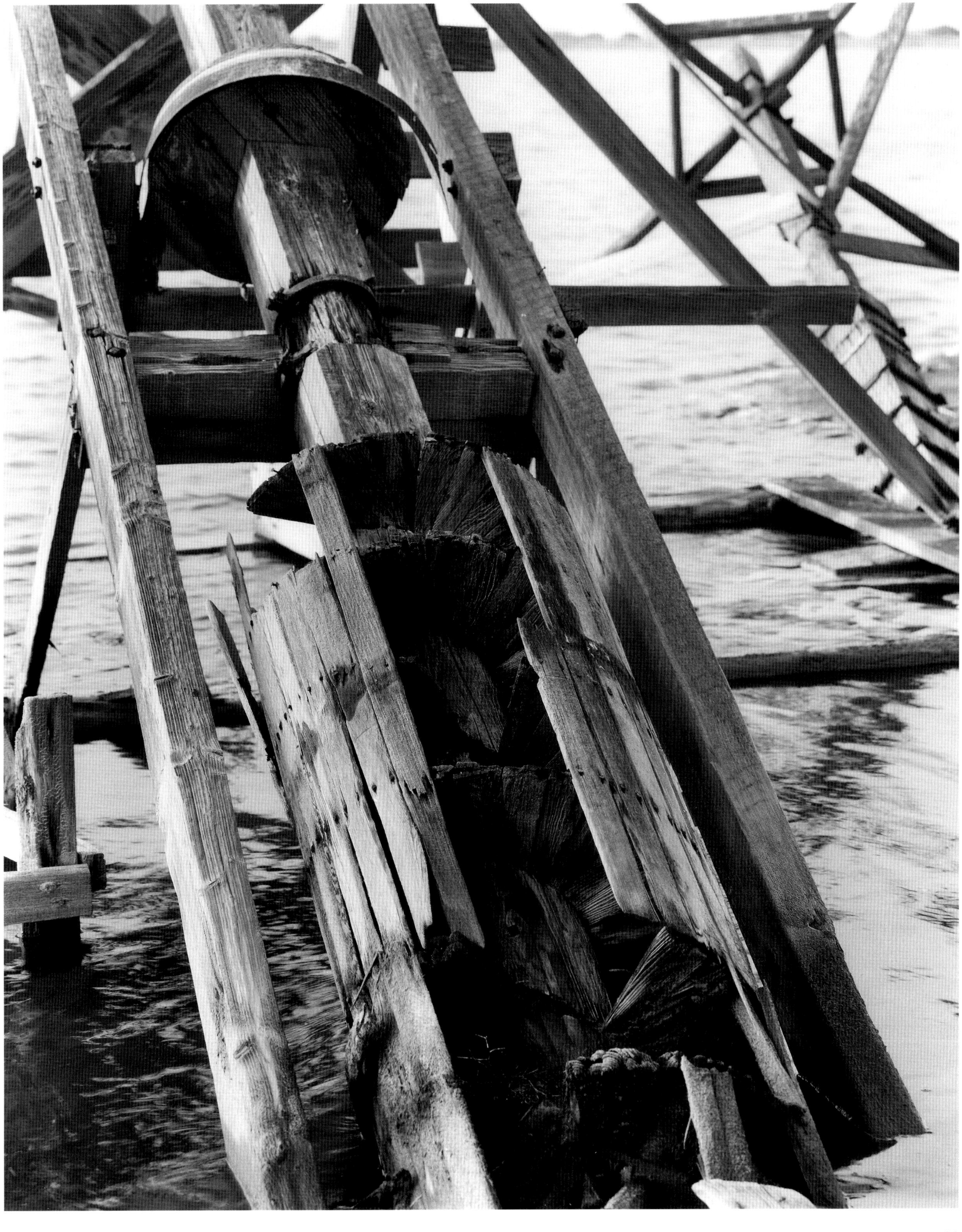

23. Moss Beach. Ausbiß einer Synklinale der pliozänen Purisima-Formation.
24. Pidgeon Point.

23. Moss Beach. Outcrop of a syncline of the pleistocene Purisima formation.
24. Pidgeon Point.

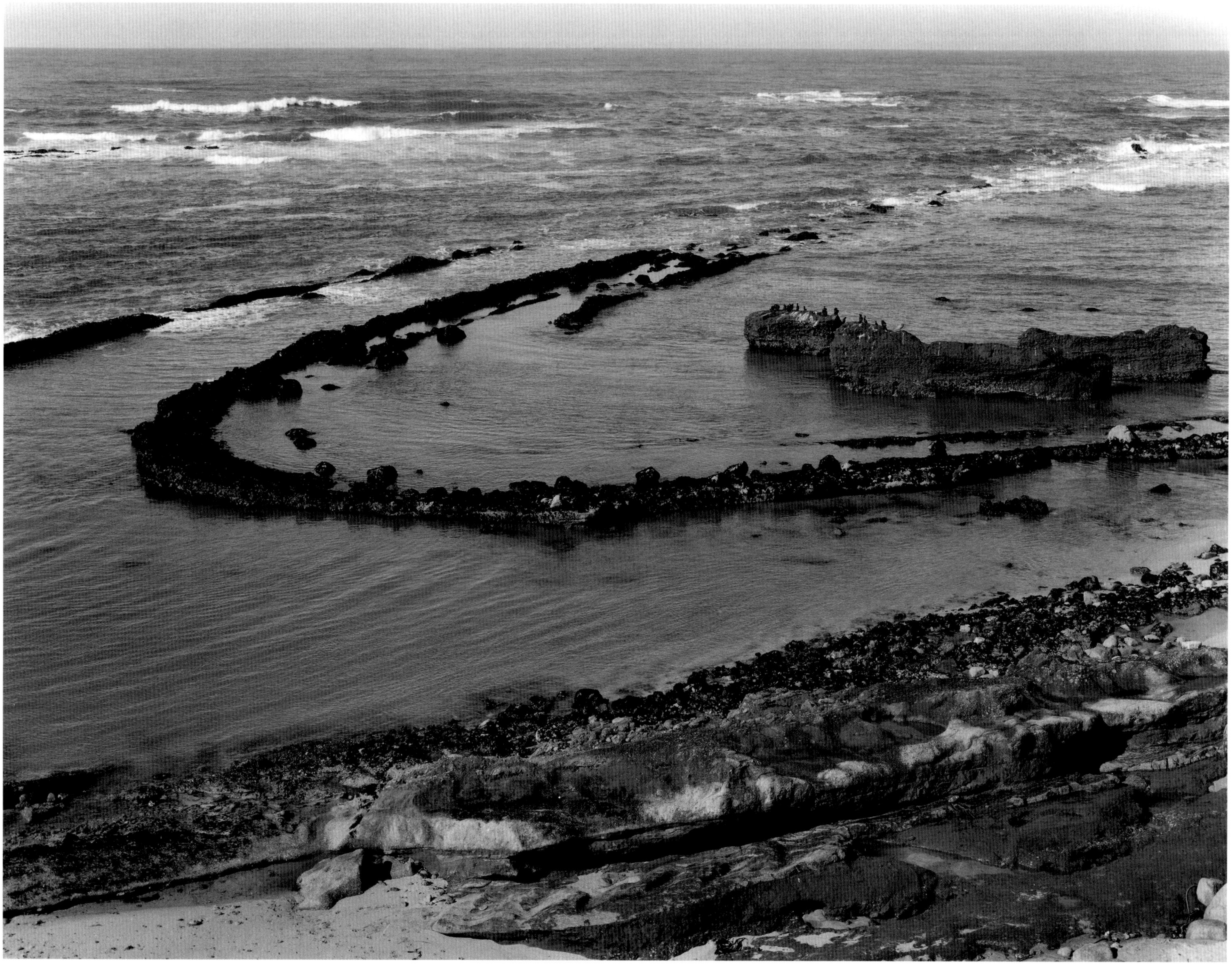

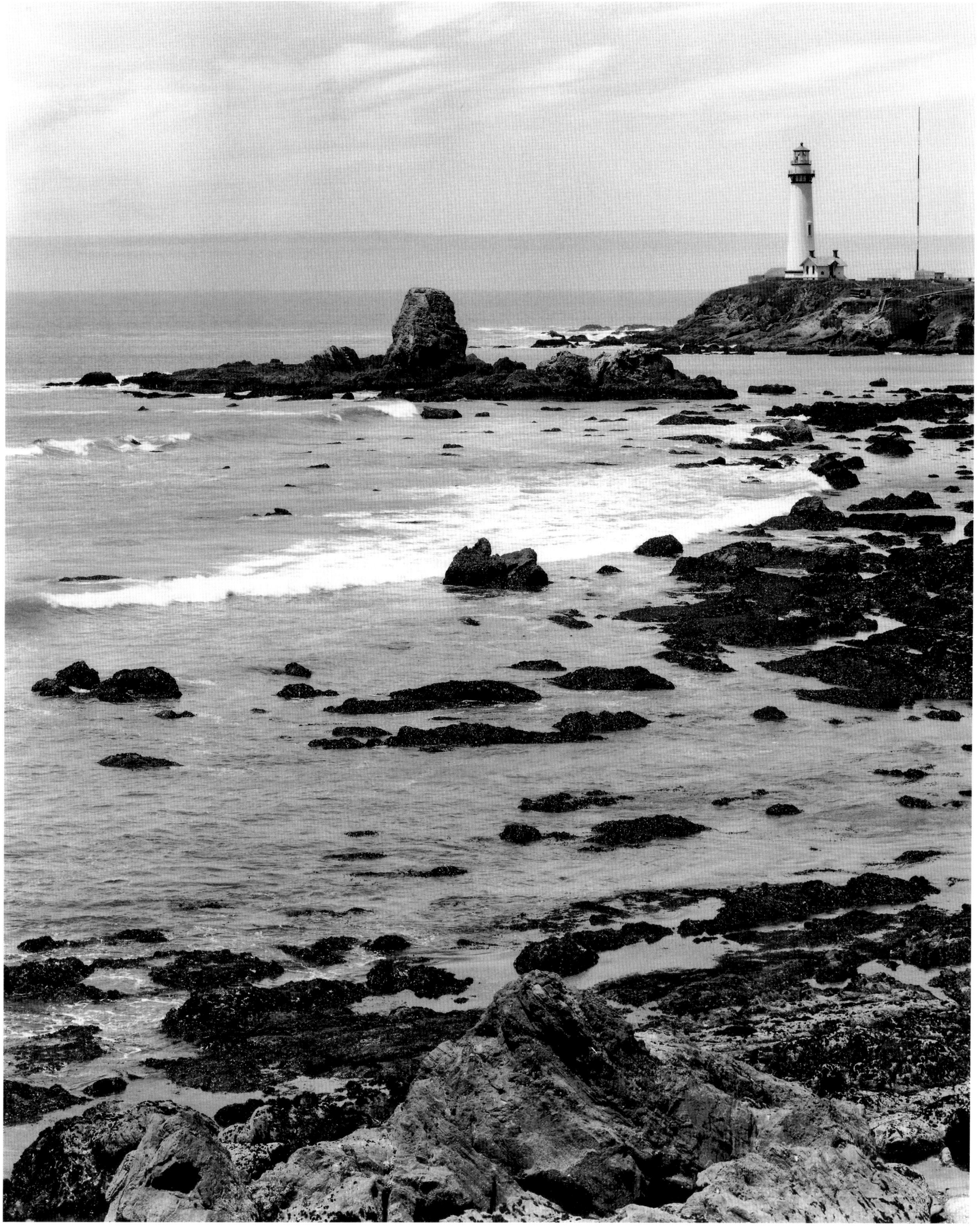

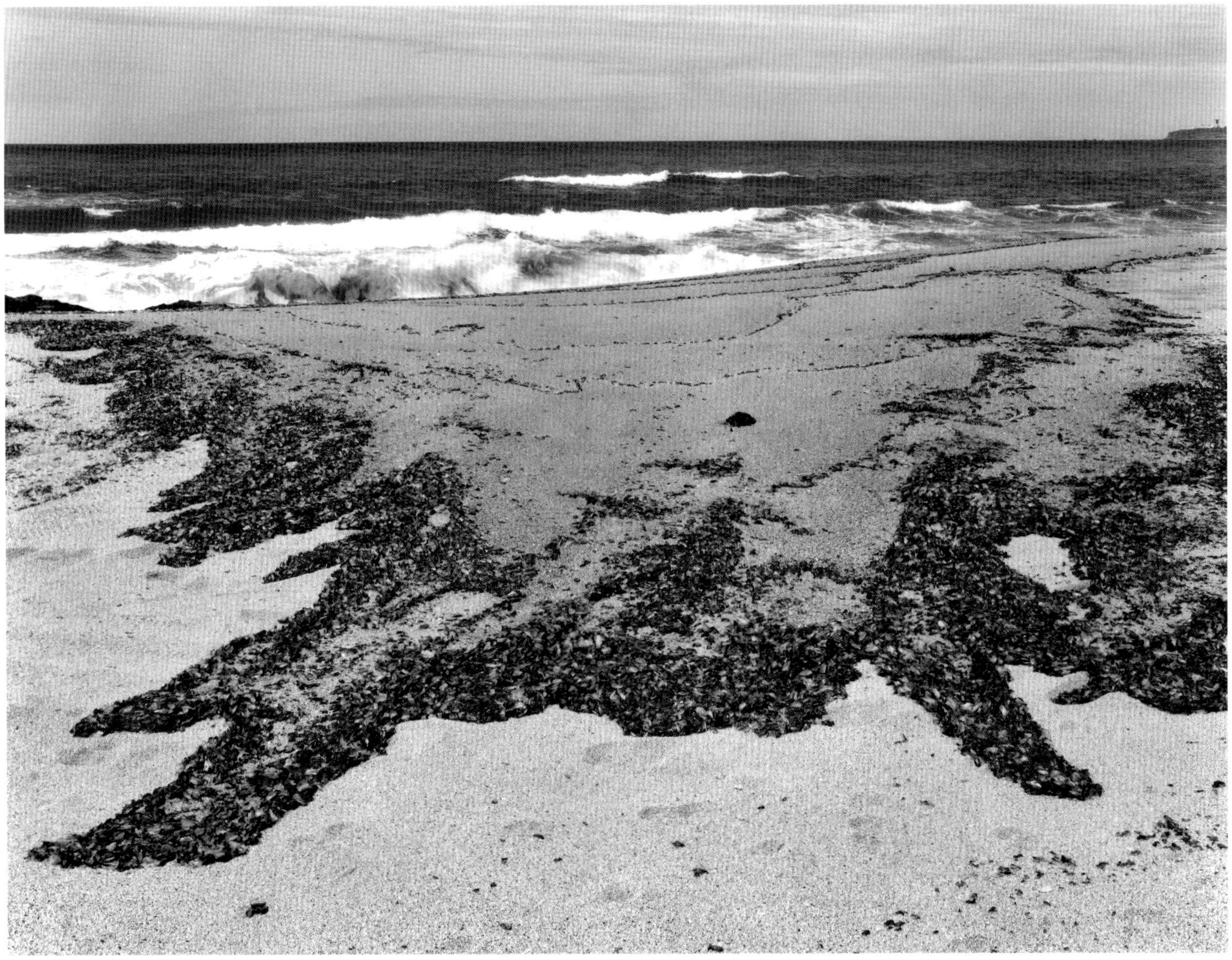

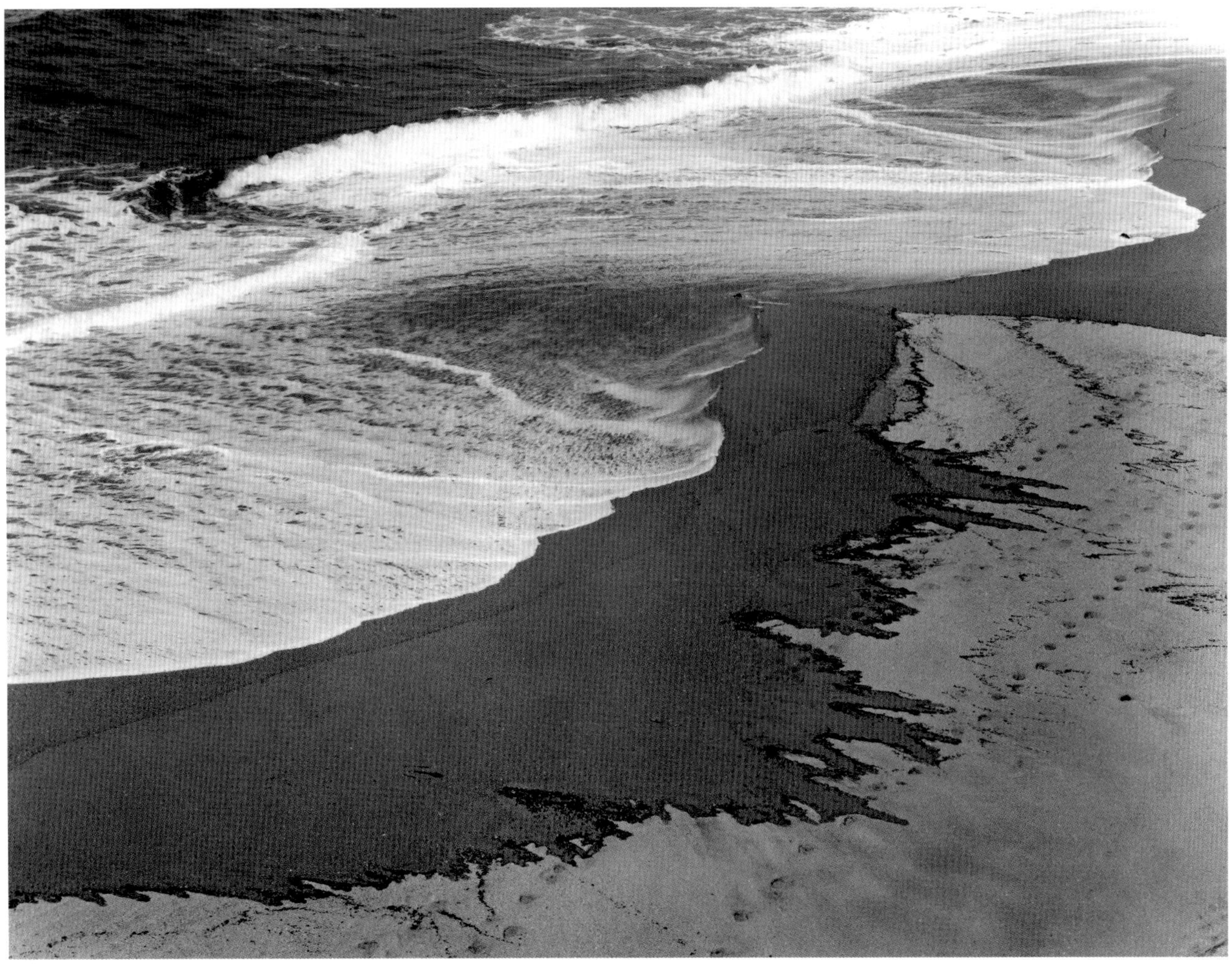

25–27. Half Moon Bay. Spülsaum von Velella Velella, mobilen Hydrozoen, die im Frühjahr massenhaft auftreten können.

25–27. Half Moon Bay. Drift line of Velella Velella, mobile Hydrozoans, which may appear in bulk during spring.

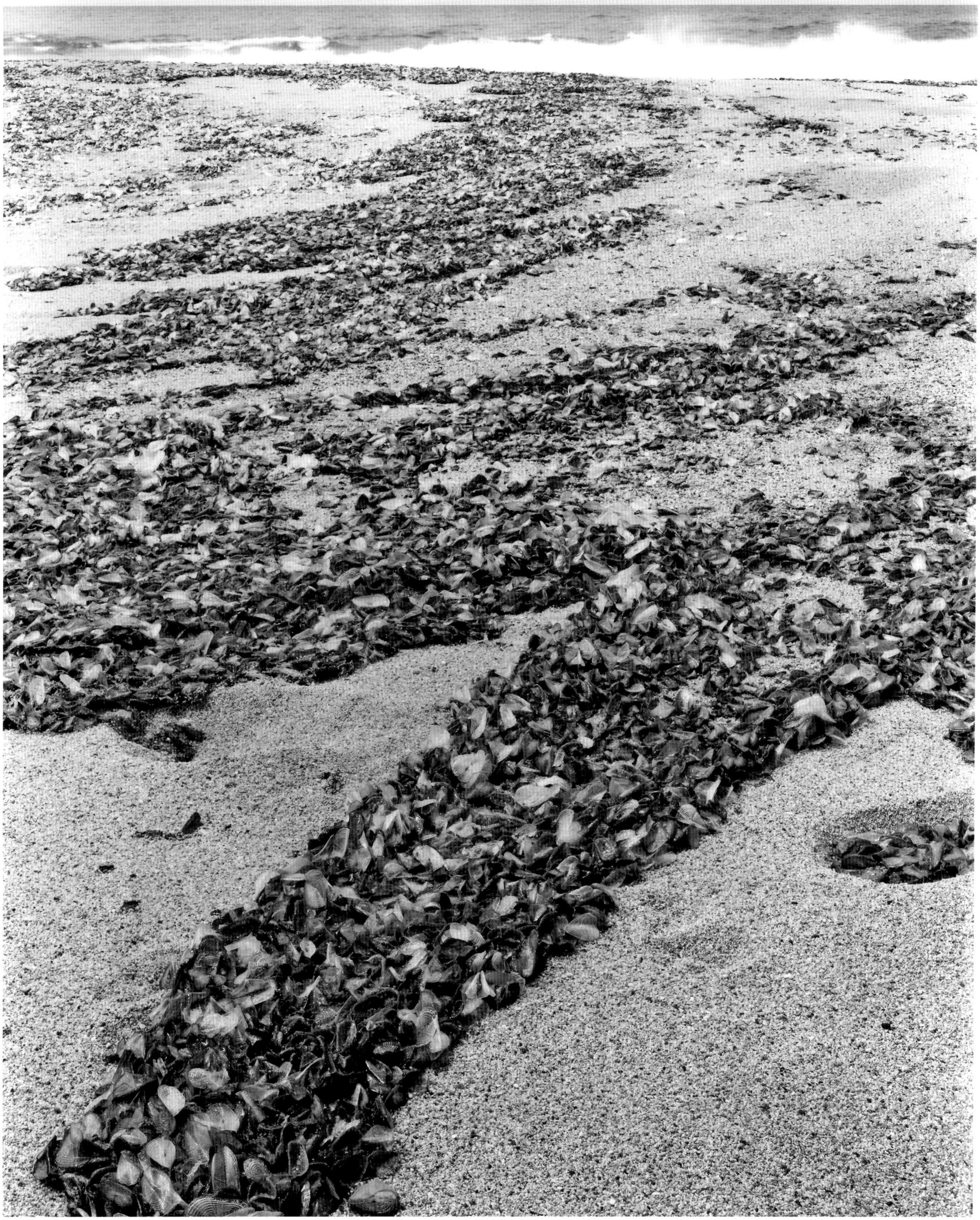

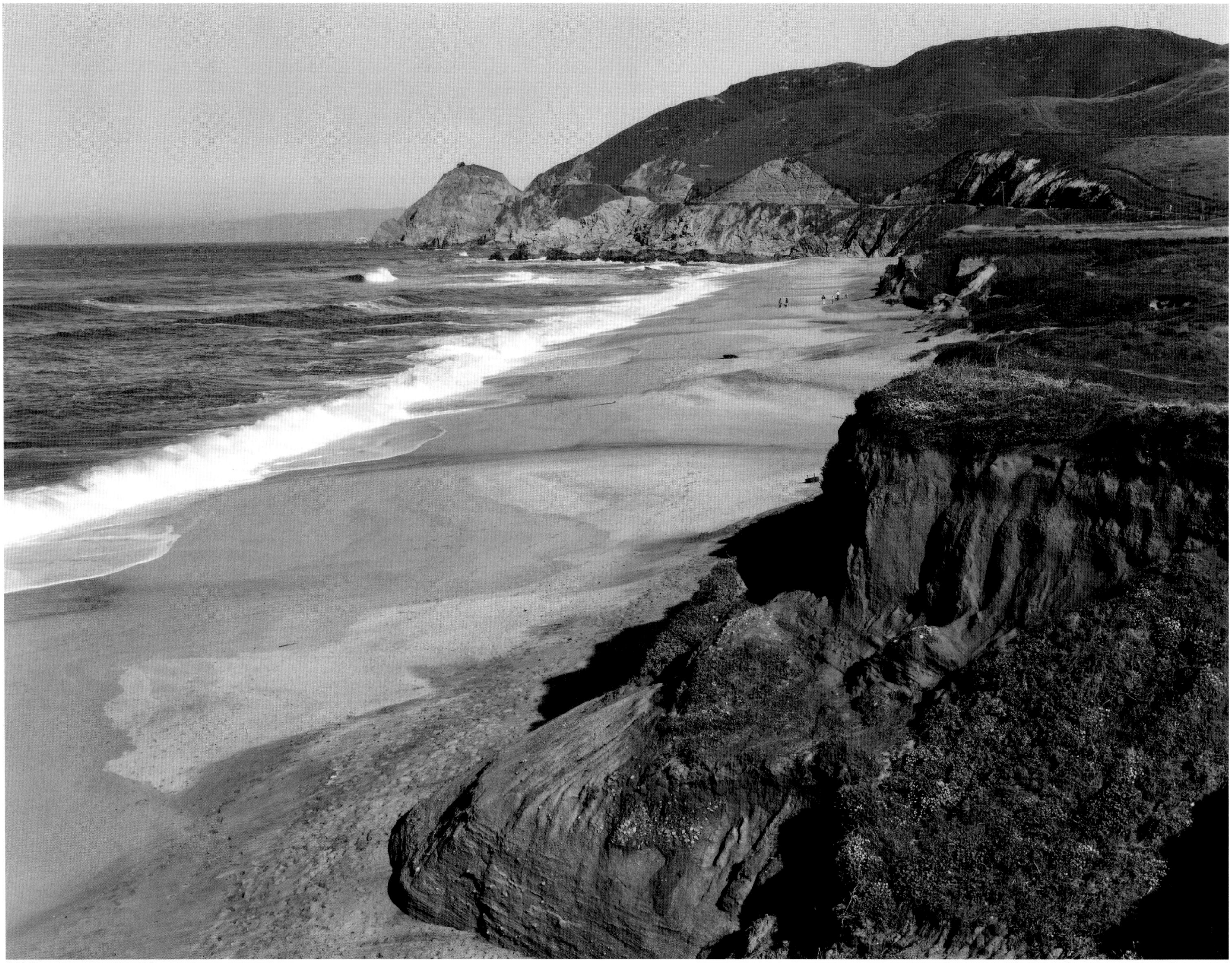

28. Montara Beach. Der California Stream ist hier so kalt, daß das Wasser auch im Sommer nicht zum Bade einlädt.
29, 30. Davenport. Kliff und Brandungsterrassen in den Monterey Shales.

28. Montara Beach. The California Stream is so cold here that it doesn't entice you into the water even in summer.
29, 30. Davenport. Cliff and wave-cut terraces on the Monterey Shales.

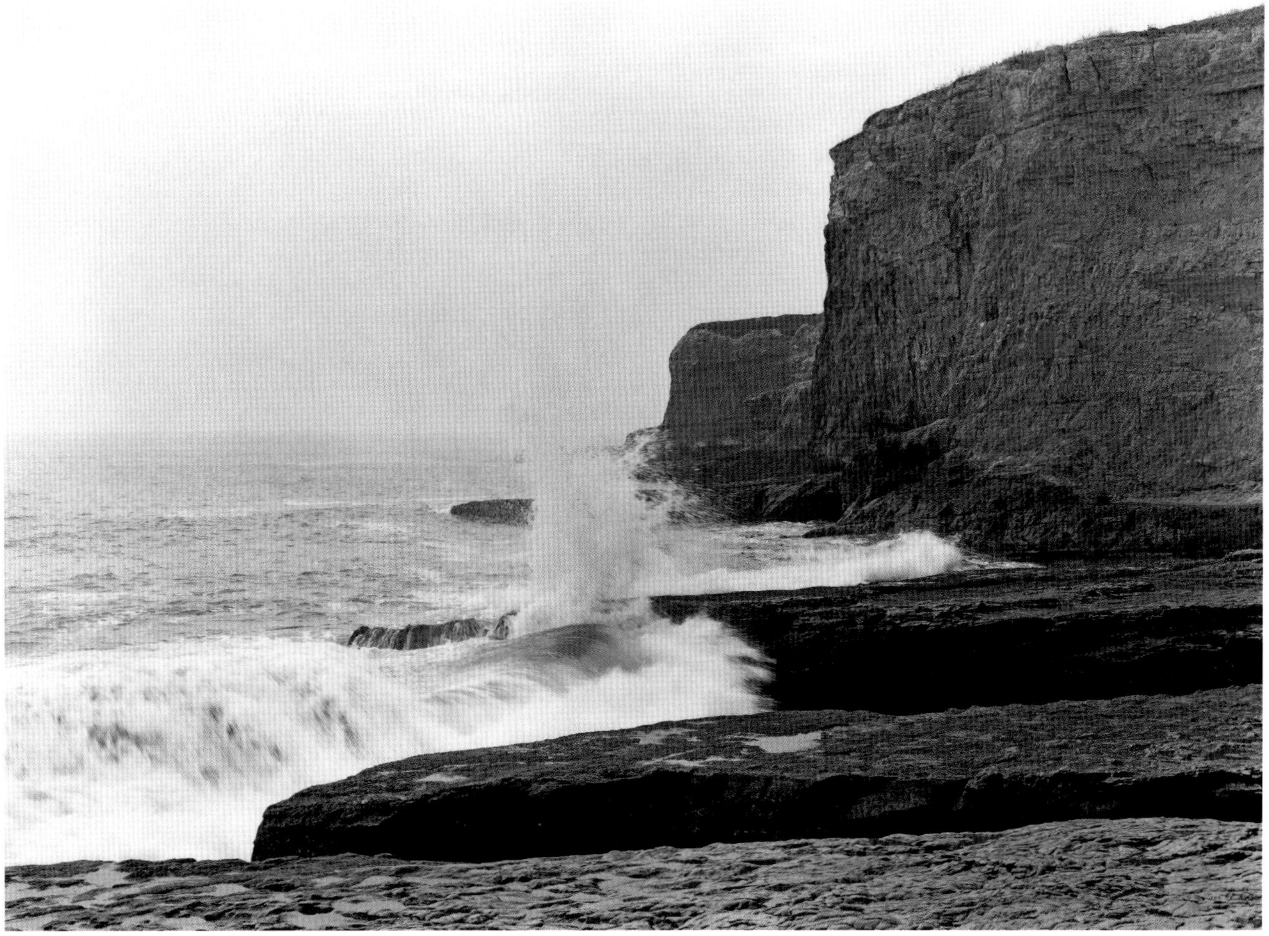

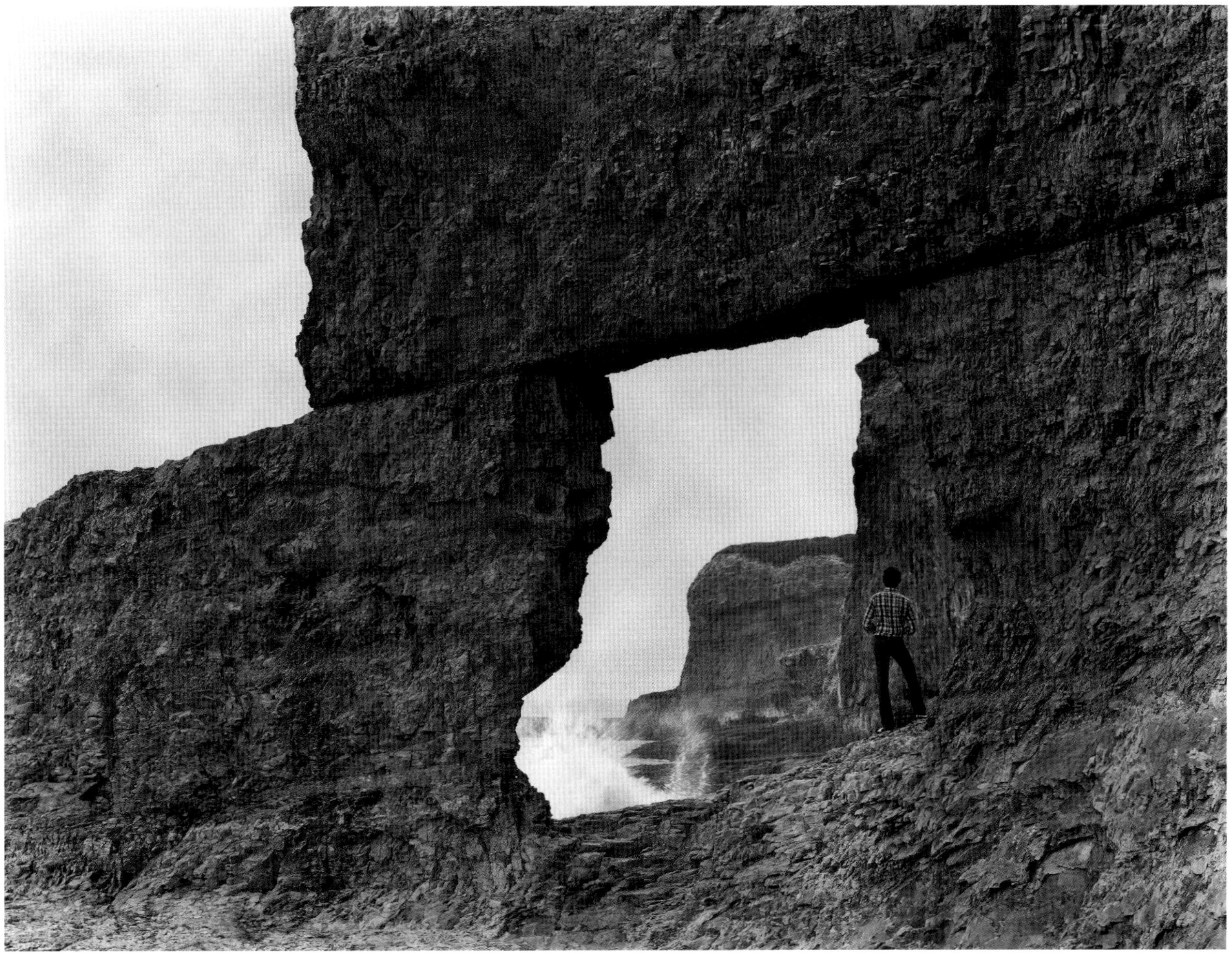

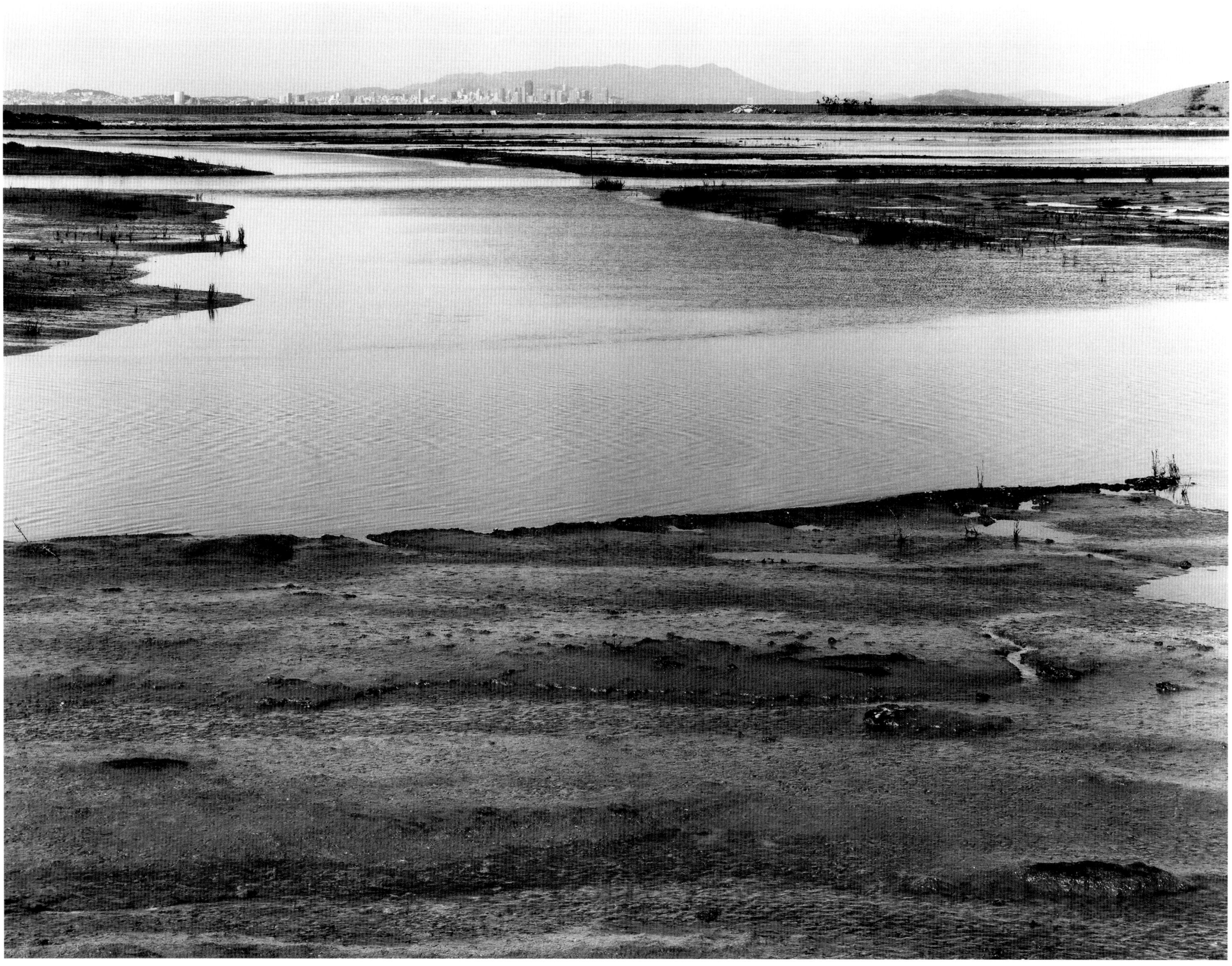

31. Hayward Tidal Marsh. Blick über die Bay hinweg auf San Francisco.
32. Blick vom Mount Diablo auf Alamo mit San Francisco am Horizont.

31. Hayward Tidal Marsh. View of San Francisco across the Bay.
32. View of Alamo from Mount Diablo with San Francisco on the horizon.

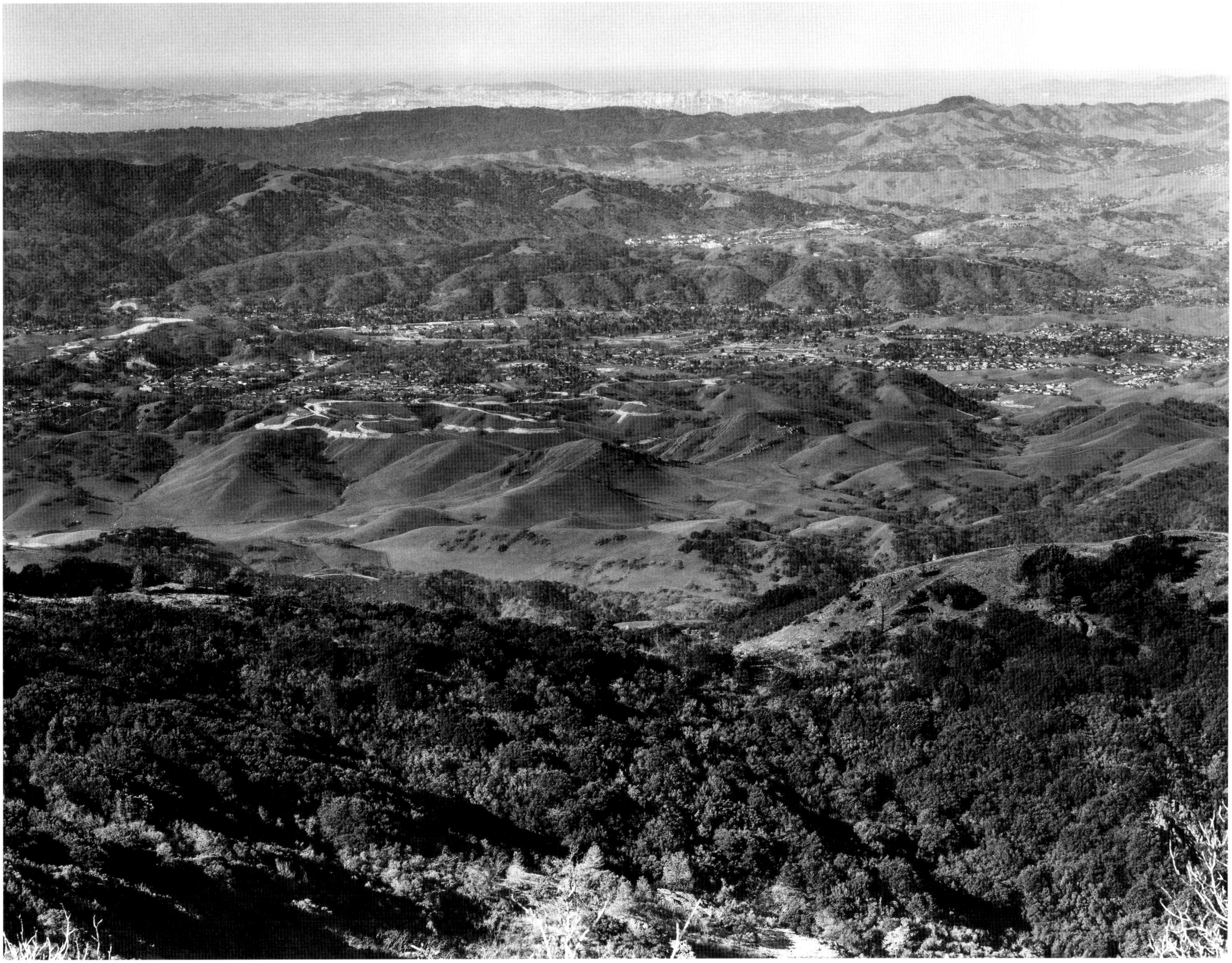

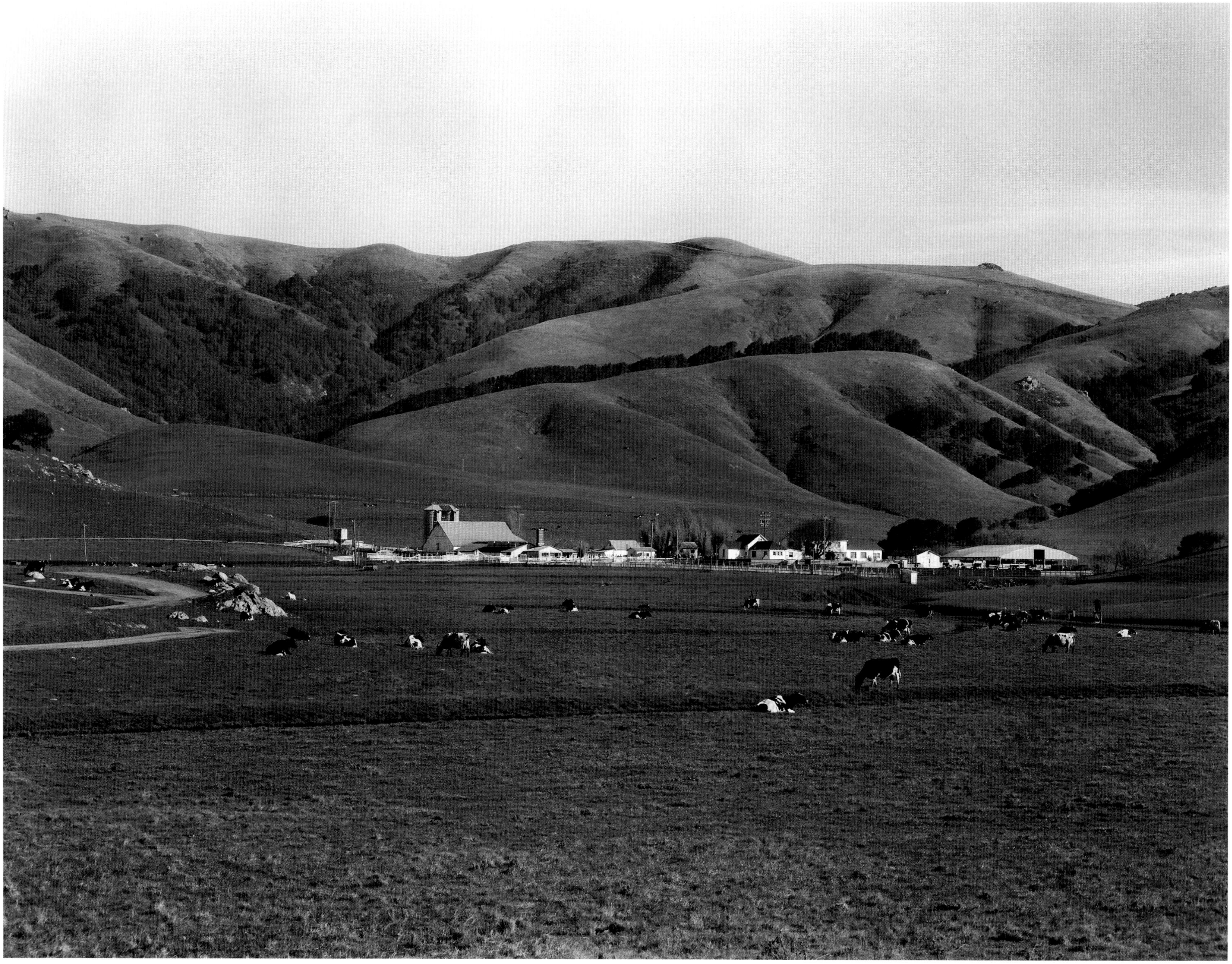

33. Halleck Nicasio Ranch nördlich von San Francisco.
34. Lobitos südlich von Half Moon Bay.

33. Halleck Nicasio Ranch north of San Francisco.
34. Lobitos south of Half Moon Bay.

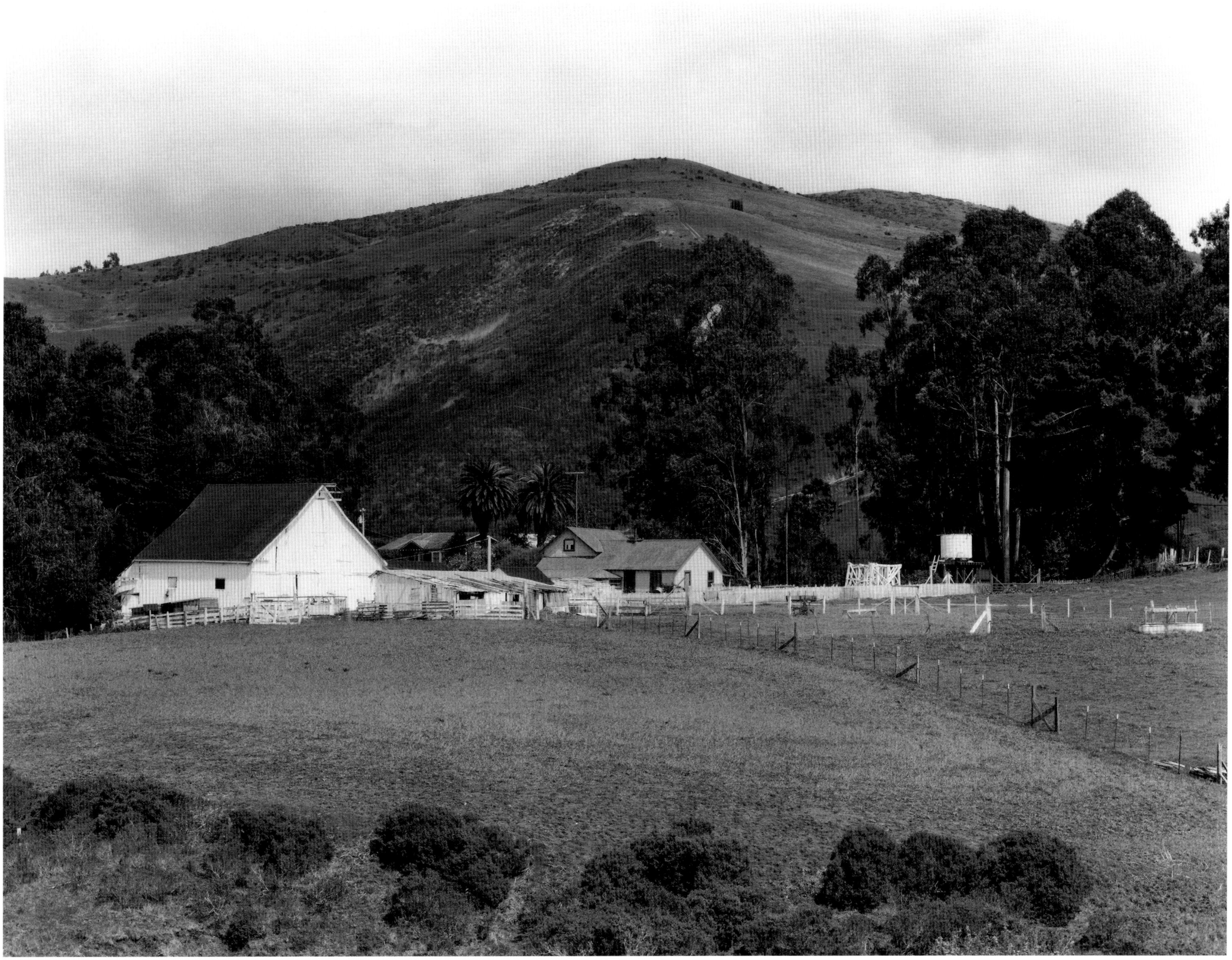

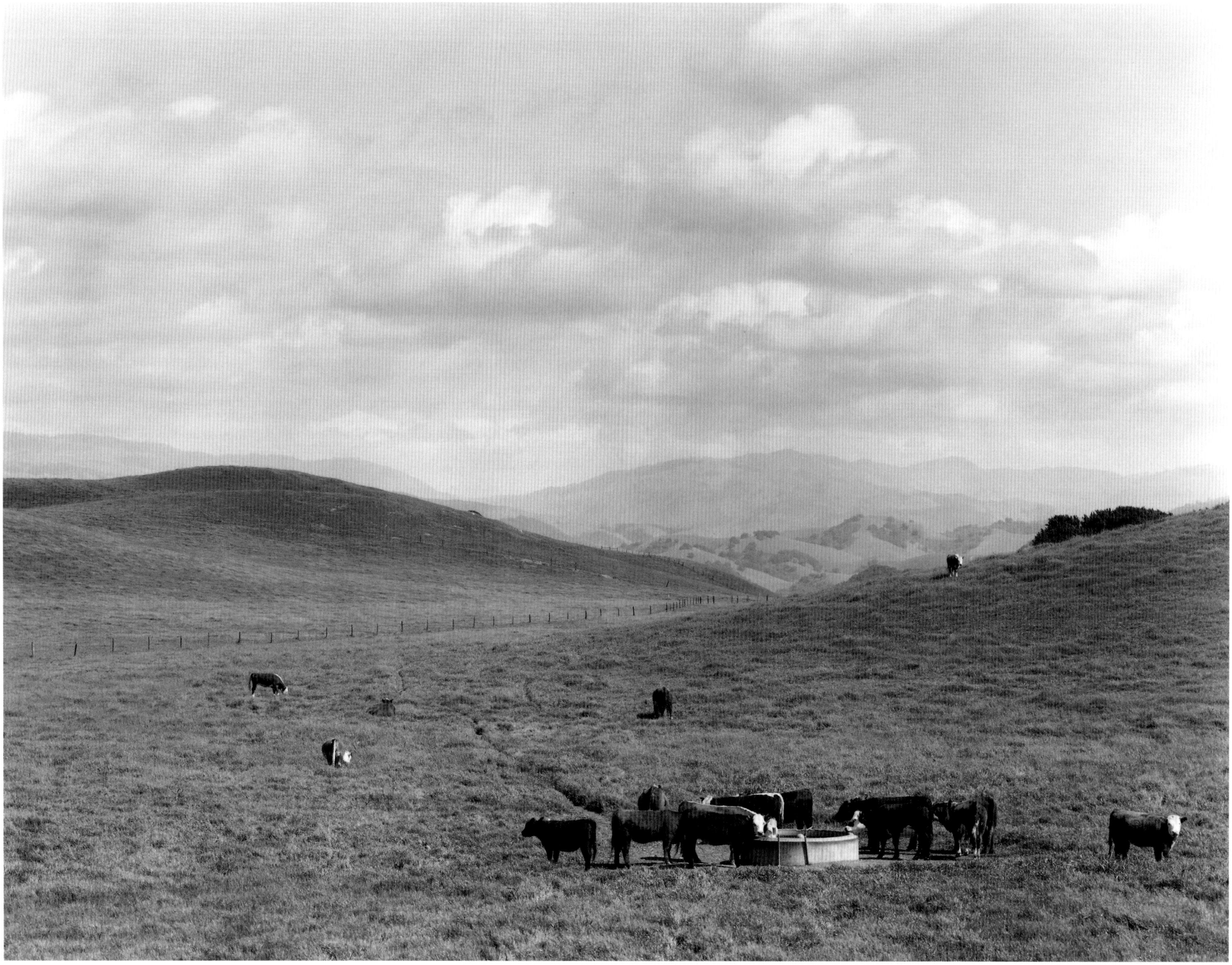

35. Mount Hamilton Group von der Morrison Canyon Road, Fremont.
36. Landschaft am Tunitas Creek zwischen Tunitas und dem Skyline Boulevard, der die Küstenberge südlich von San Francisco begleitet.

35. Mount Hamilton Group from Morrison Canyon Road, Fremont.
36. Landscape along the Tunitas Creek between Tunitas and the Skyline Boulevard, which follows the coastal mountains south of San Francisco.

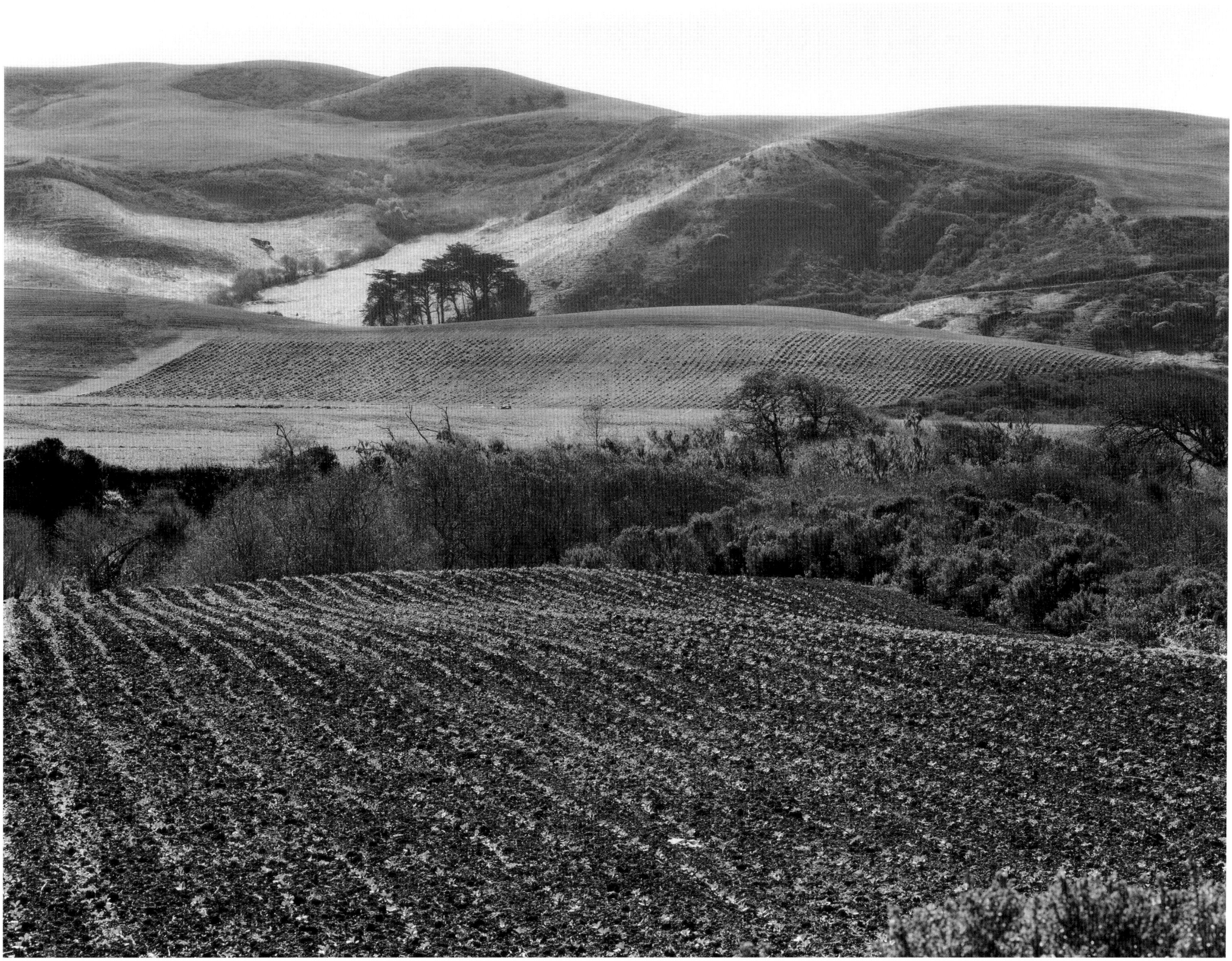

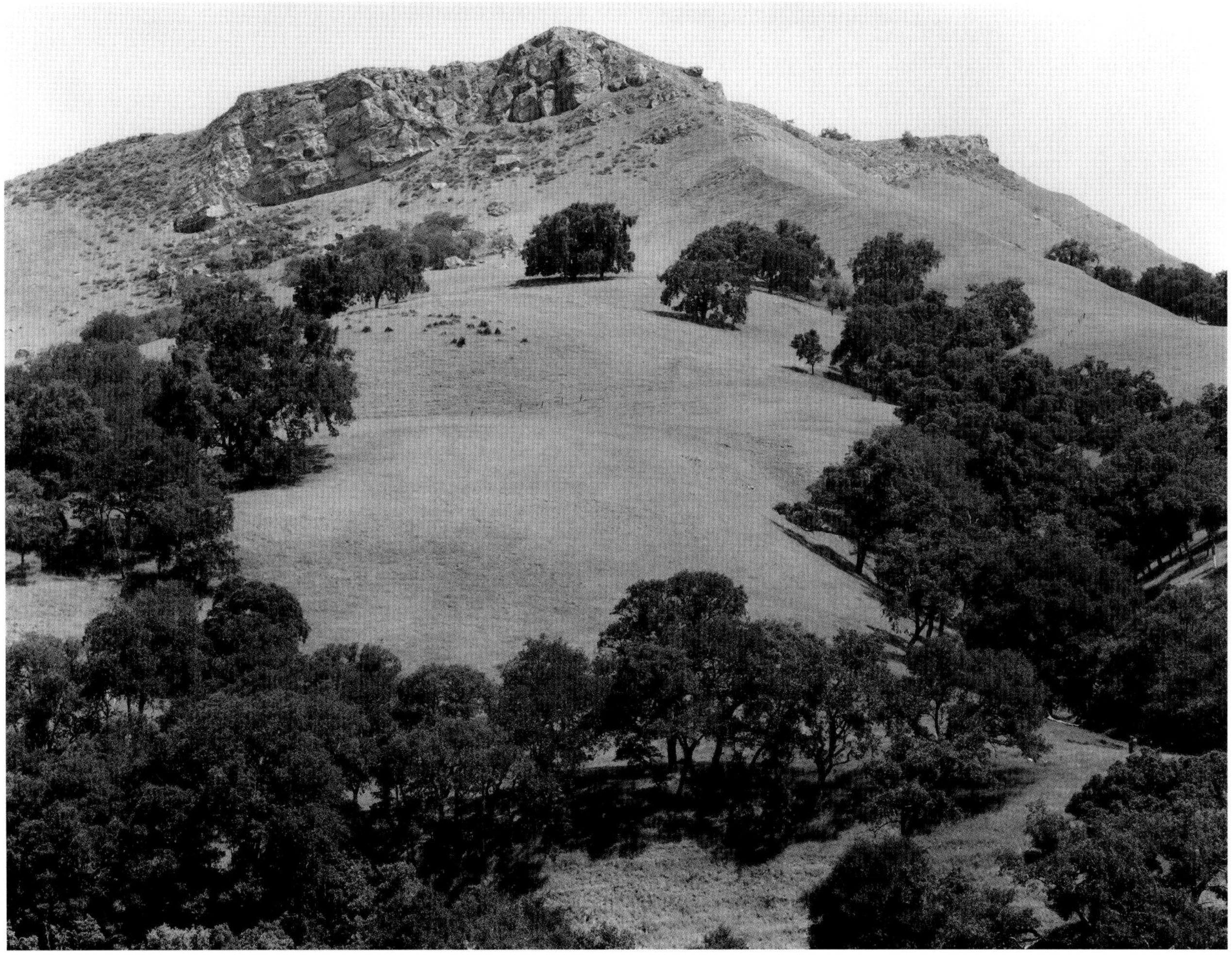

37. Sunol Regional Wilderness.
38. Del Valle State Recreation Area südlich von Sunol von der Del Valle Road / Mendenhall Road.
39. Landschaft südlich von Sunol von der Sherdan Road / Andrade Road.

37. Sunol Regional Wilderness.
38. Del Valle State Recreation Area south of Sunol from Del Valle Road / Mendenhall Road.
39. Landscape south of Sunol from Sherdan Road / Andrade Road.

S. 48/49
40. Butano State Park. Redwoods in Lot 16, südlich der Pescadero Beach.

p. 48/49
40. Butano State Park. Redwoods in lot 16, south of Pescadero Beach.

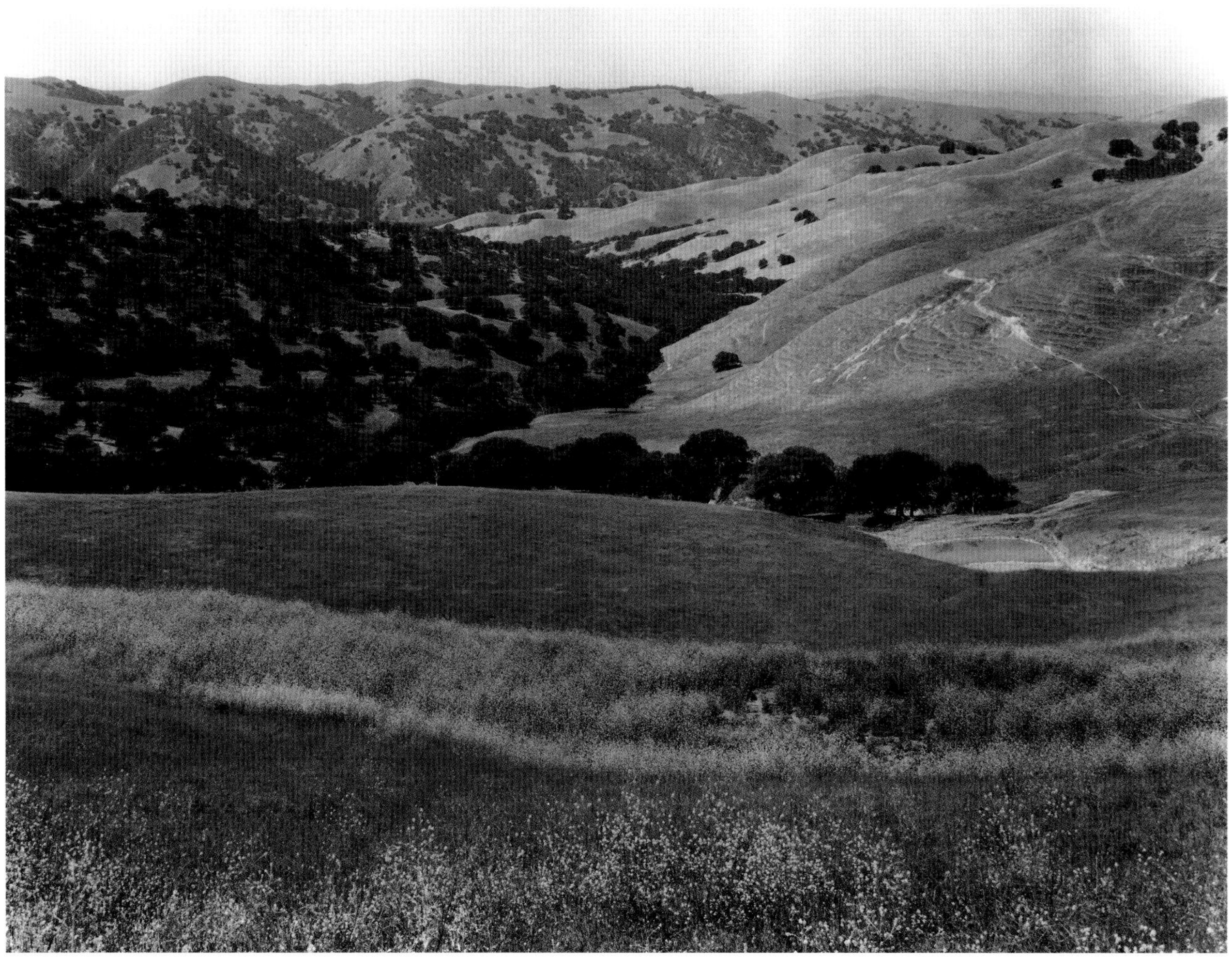

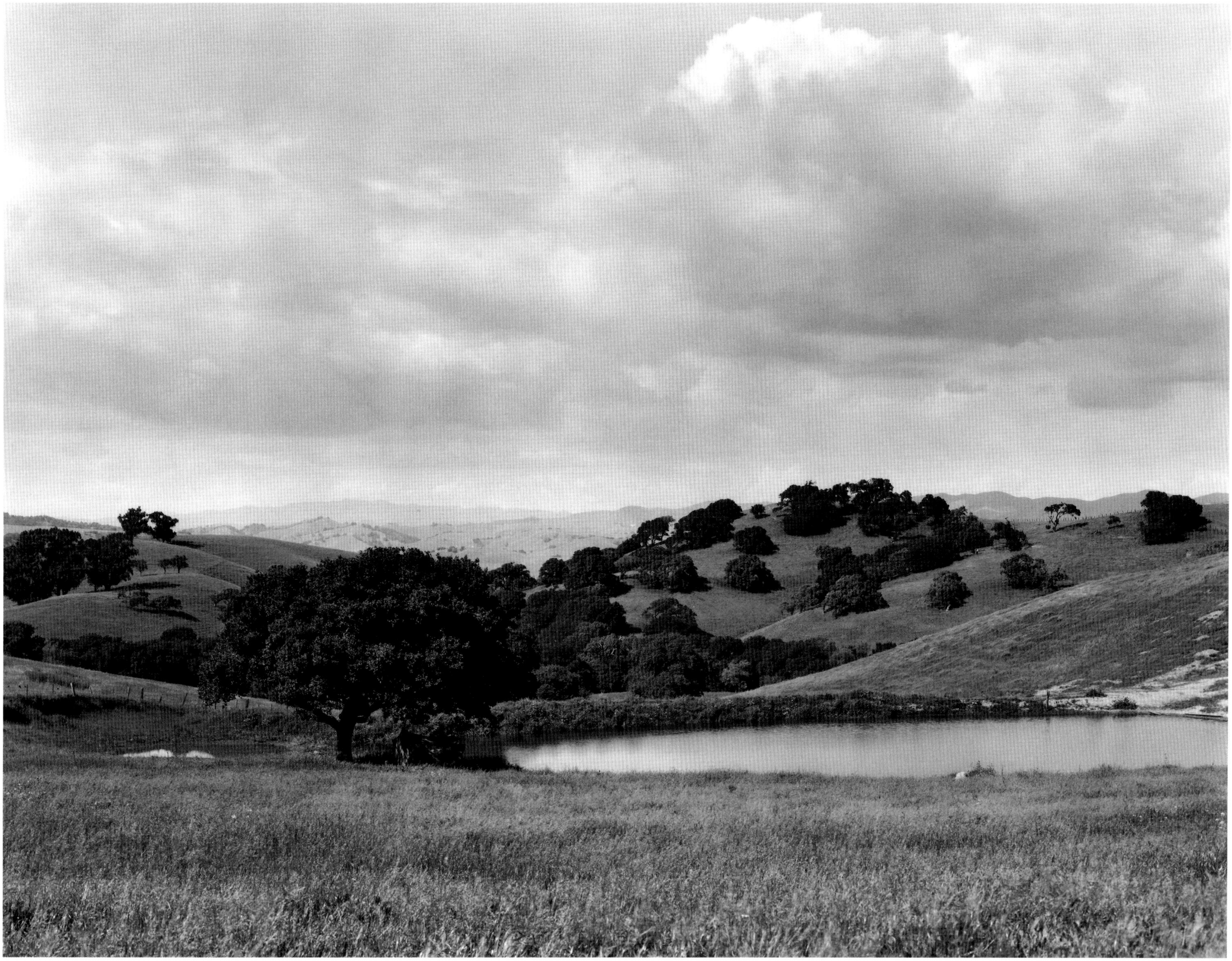

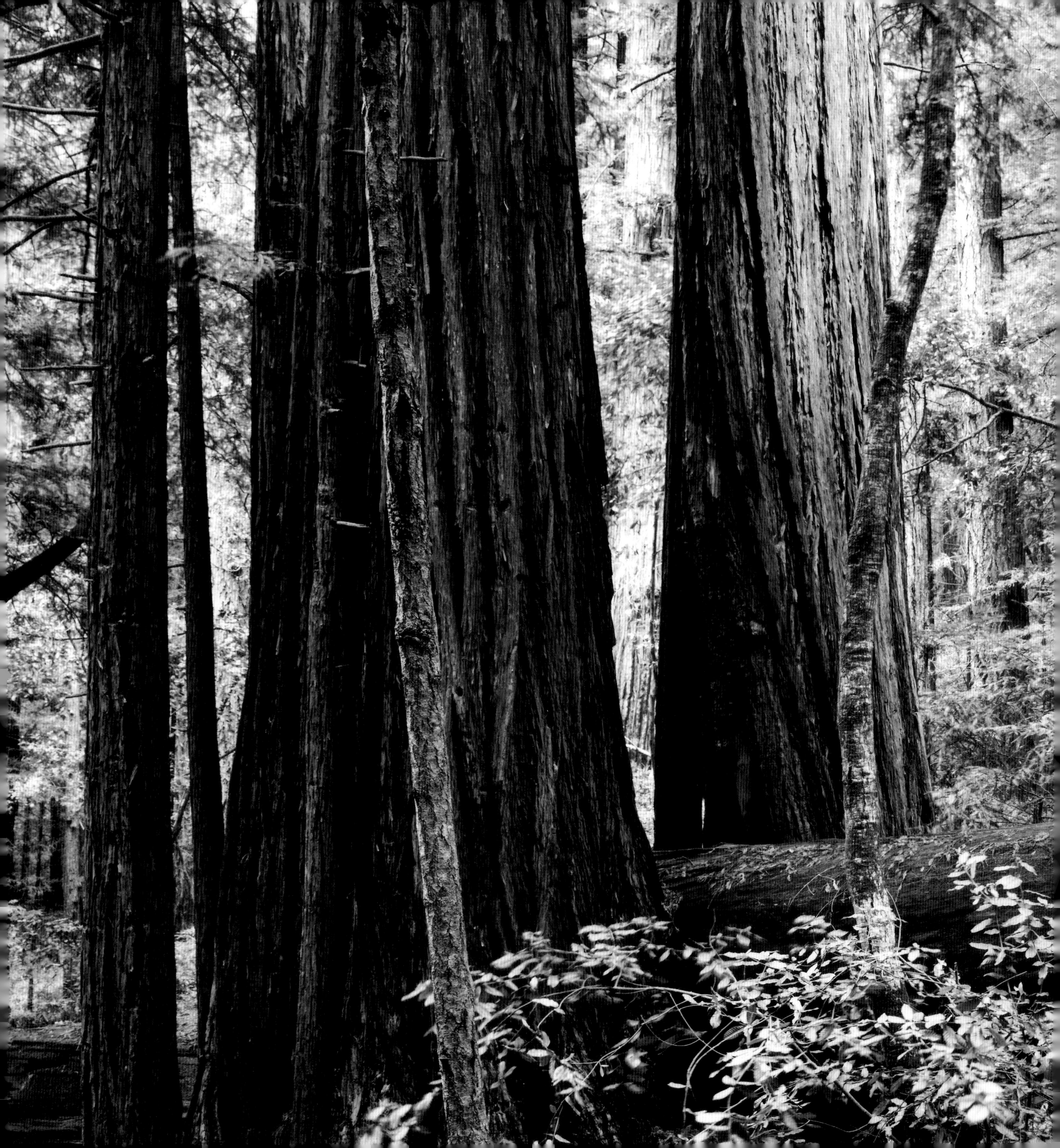

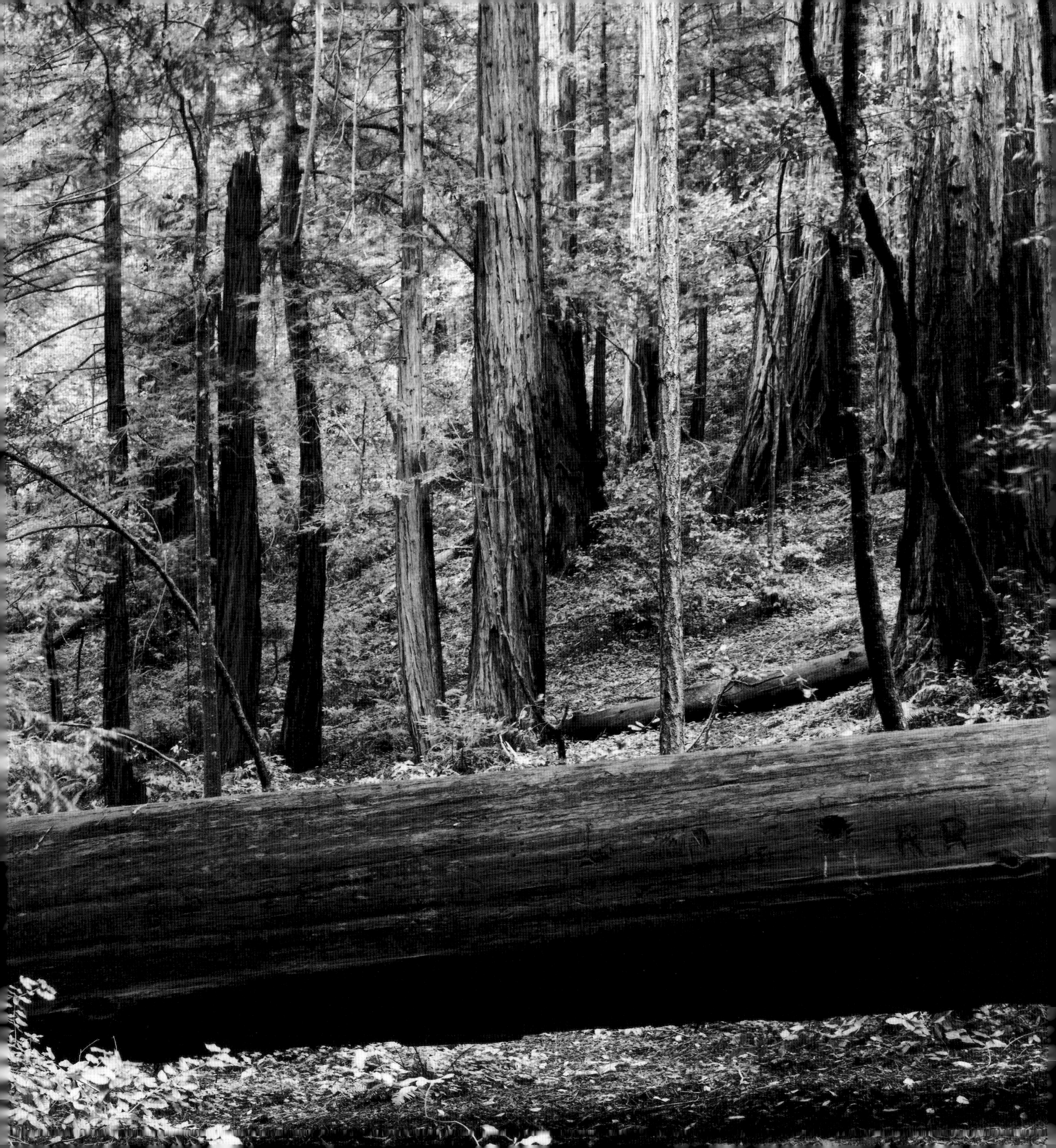

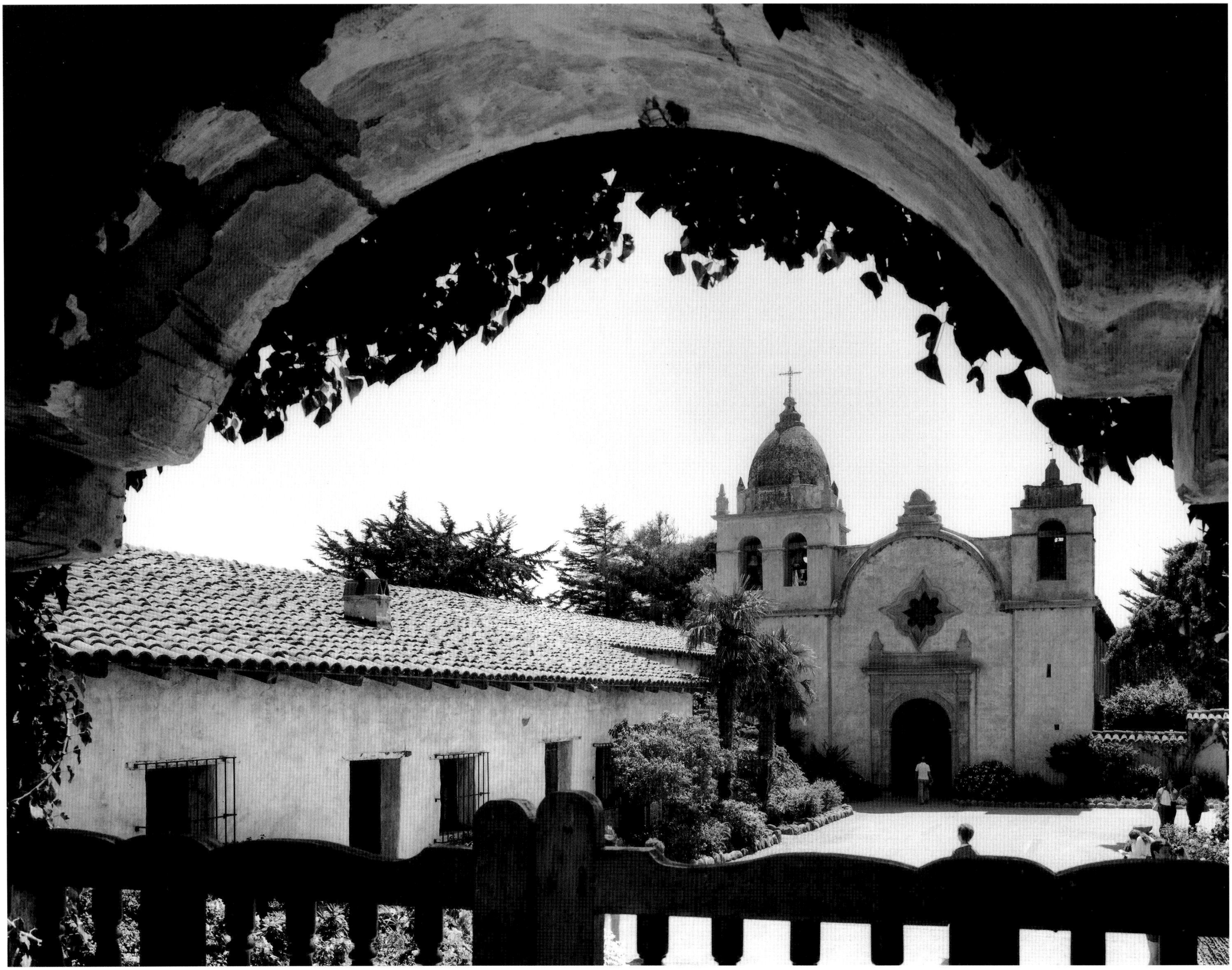

41. Carmel Mission südlich von Monterey (1771).
42. San Juan Bautista Mission östlich von Monterey (1797–1812).

S. 52/53
43. Point Reyes National Seashore. Blick von der Mount Vision Road auf die Drakes Bay.

41. Carmel Mission south of Monterey (1771).
42. San Juan Bautista Mission east of Monterey (1797 to 1812).

p. 52/53
43. Point Reyes National Seashore. View of Drakes Bay from Mount Vision Road.

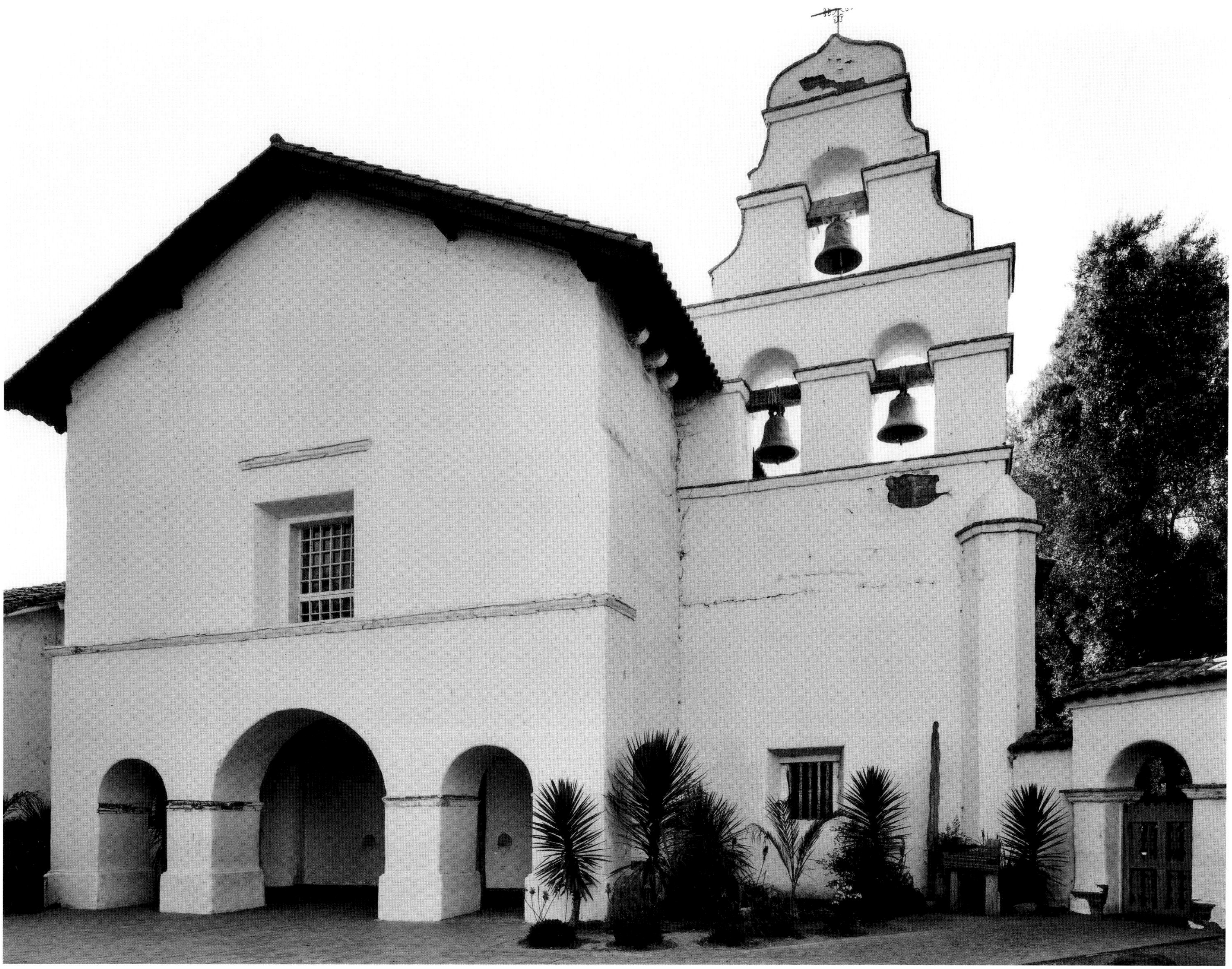

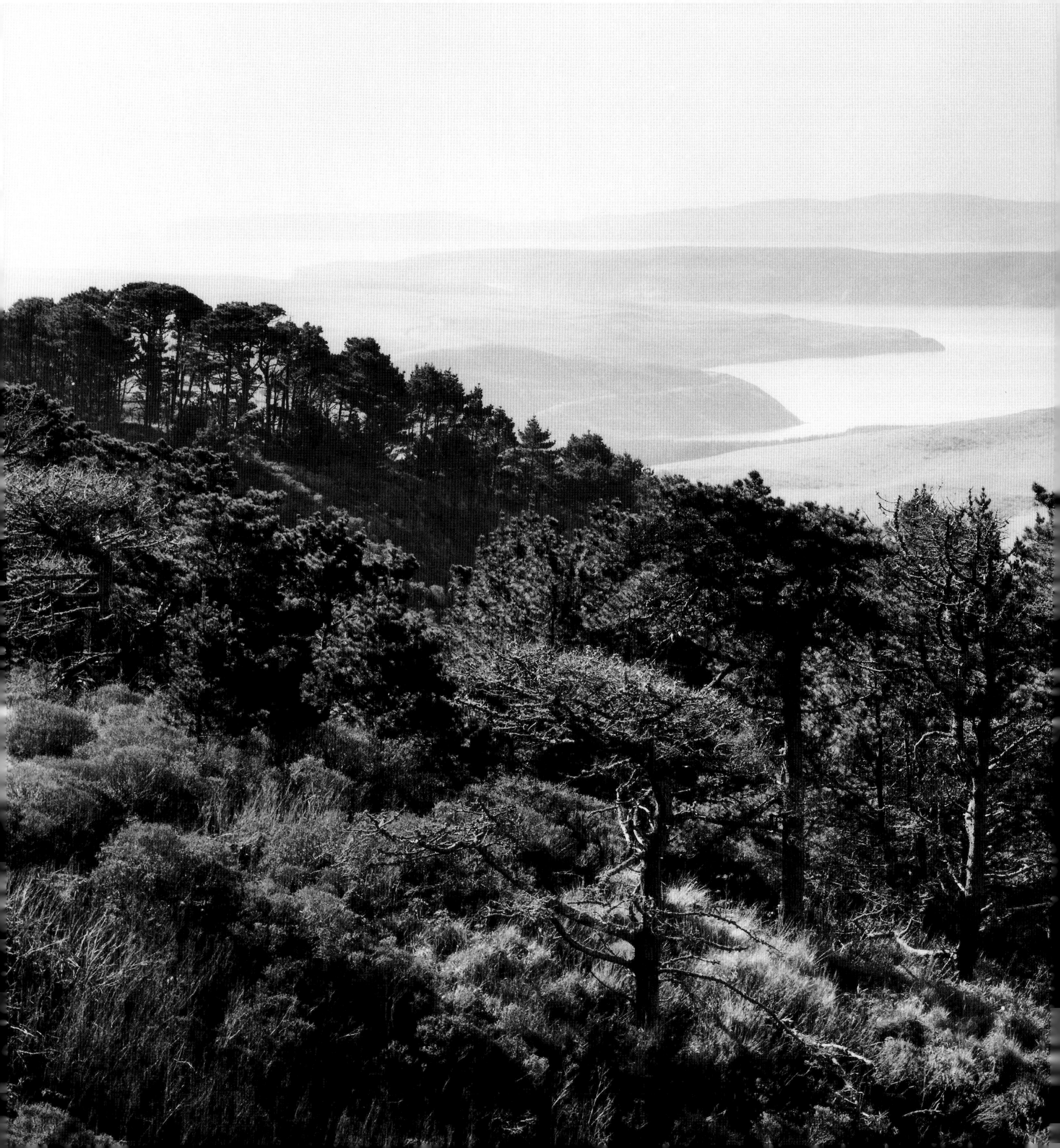

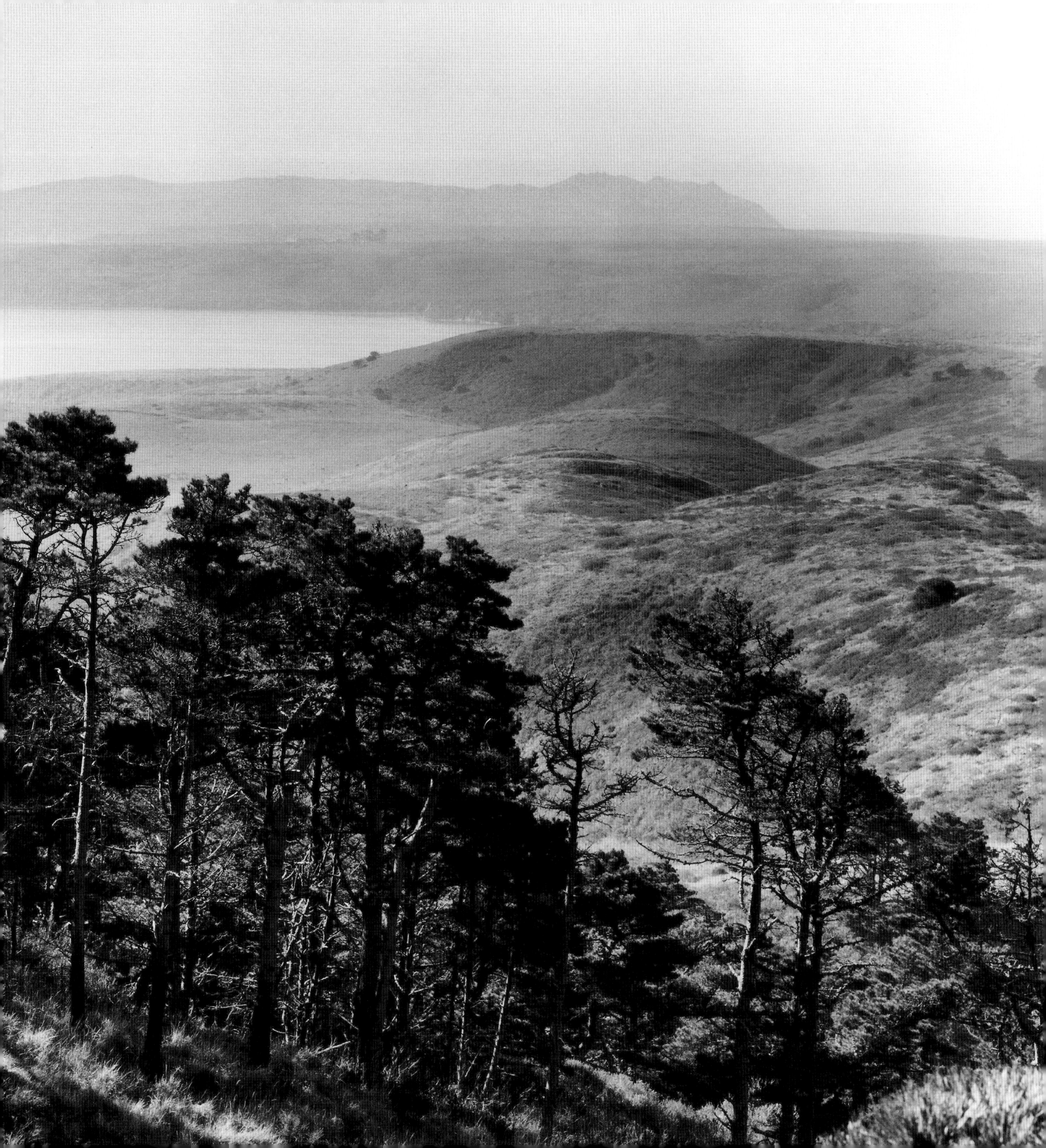

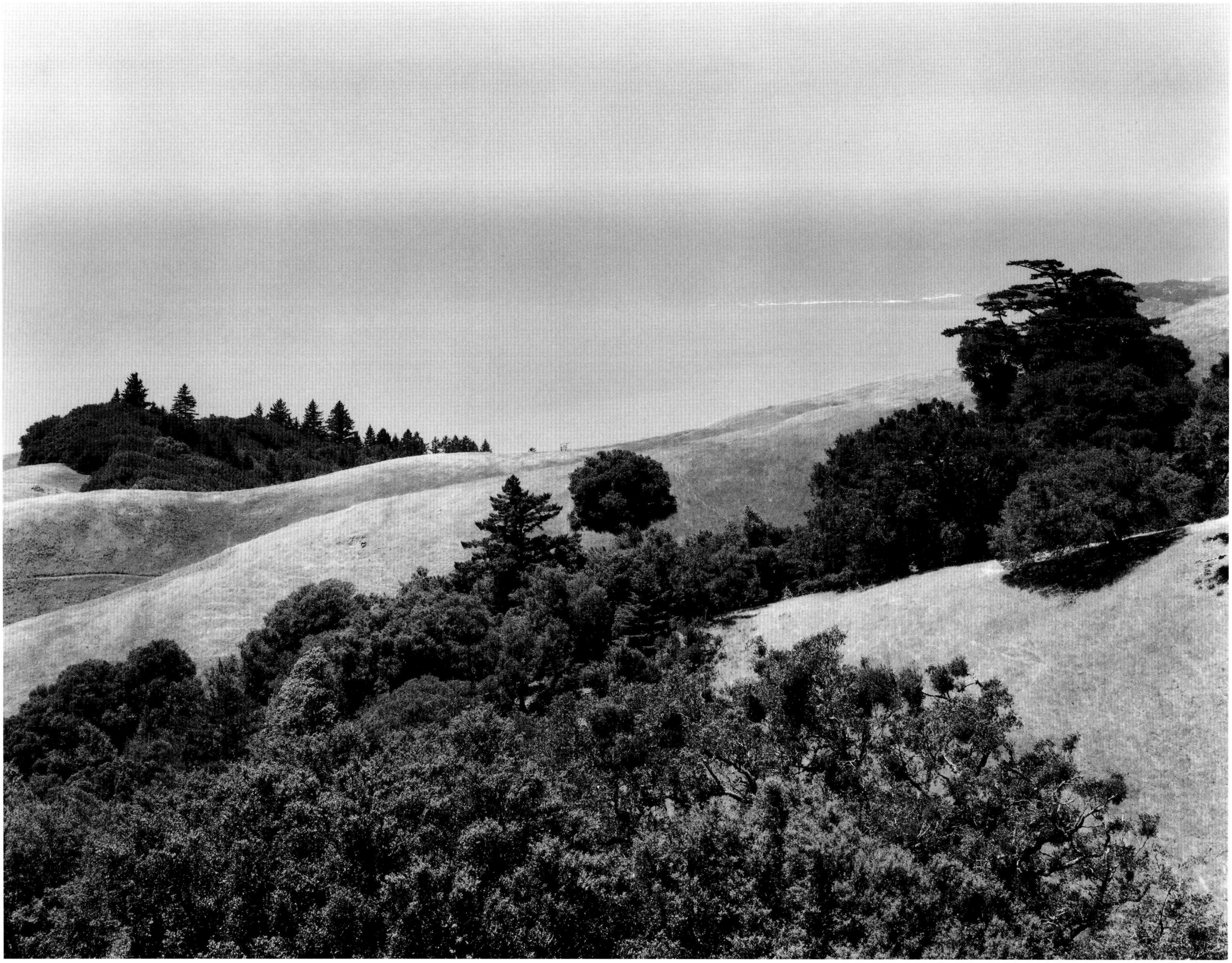

44. Mount Tamalpais State Park. Blick auf den Pazifik, rechts die Stinson Beach.
45. Point Reyes District. Tule Elk Range.
46. Point Reyes National Seashore. Blick vom Chimney Rock auf die Drakes Bay.

44. Mount Tamalpais State Park. View of the Pacific Ocean, on the right Stinson Beach.
45. Point Reyes District. Tule Elk Range.
46. Point Reyes National Seashore. View of Drakes Bay from Chimney Rock.

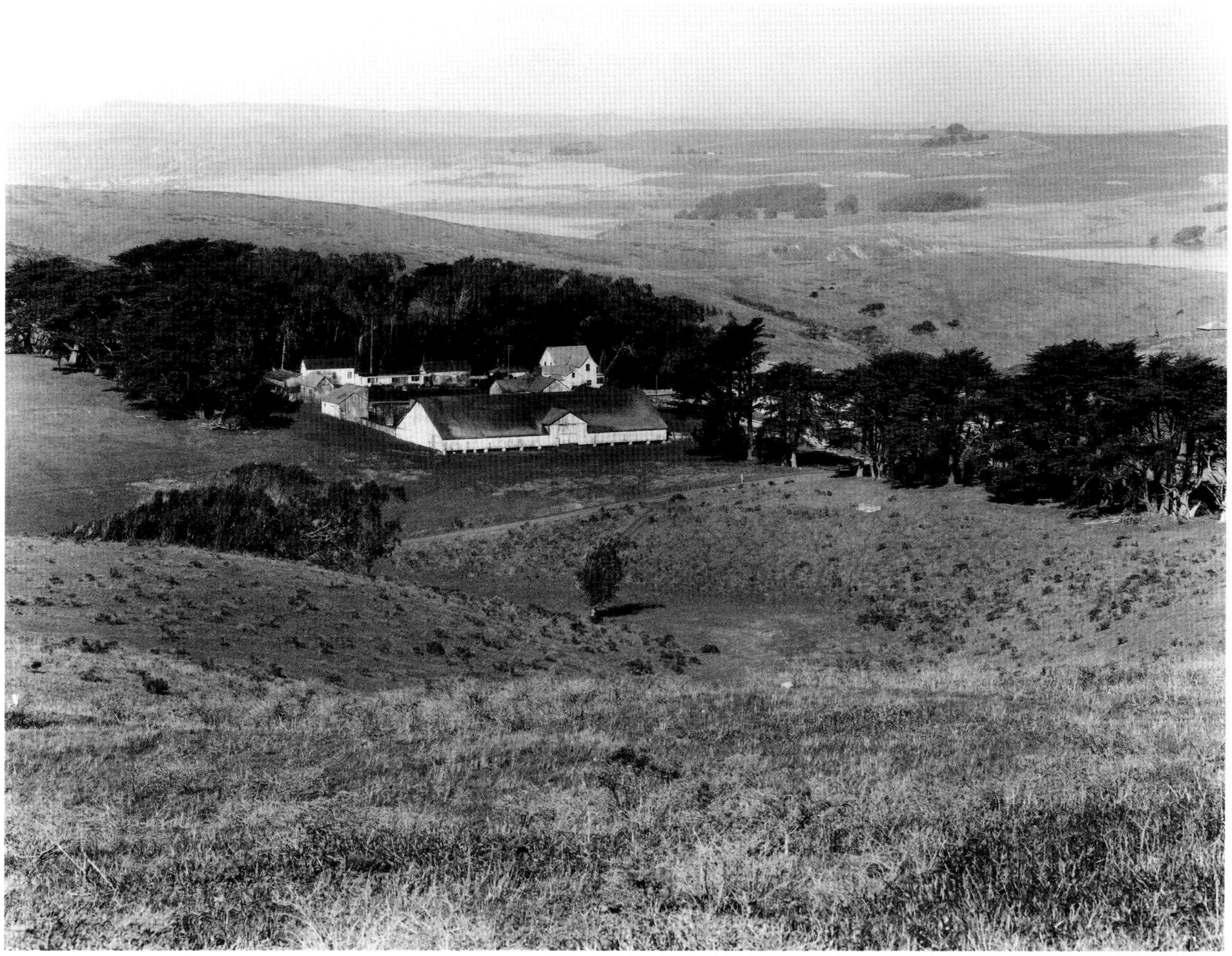

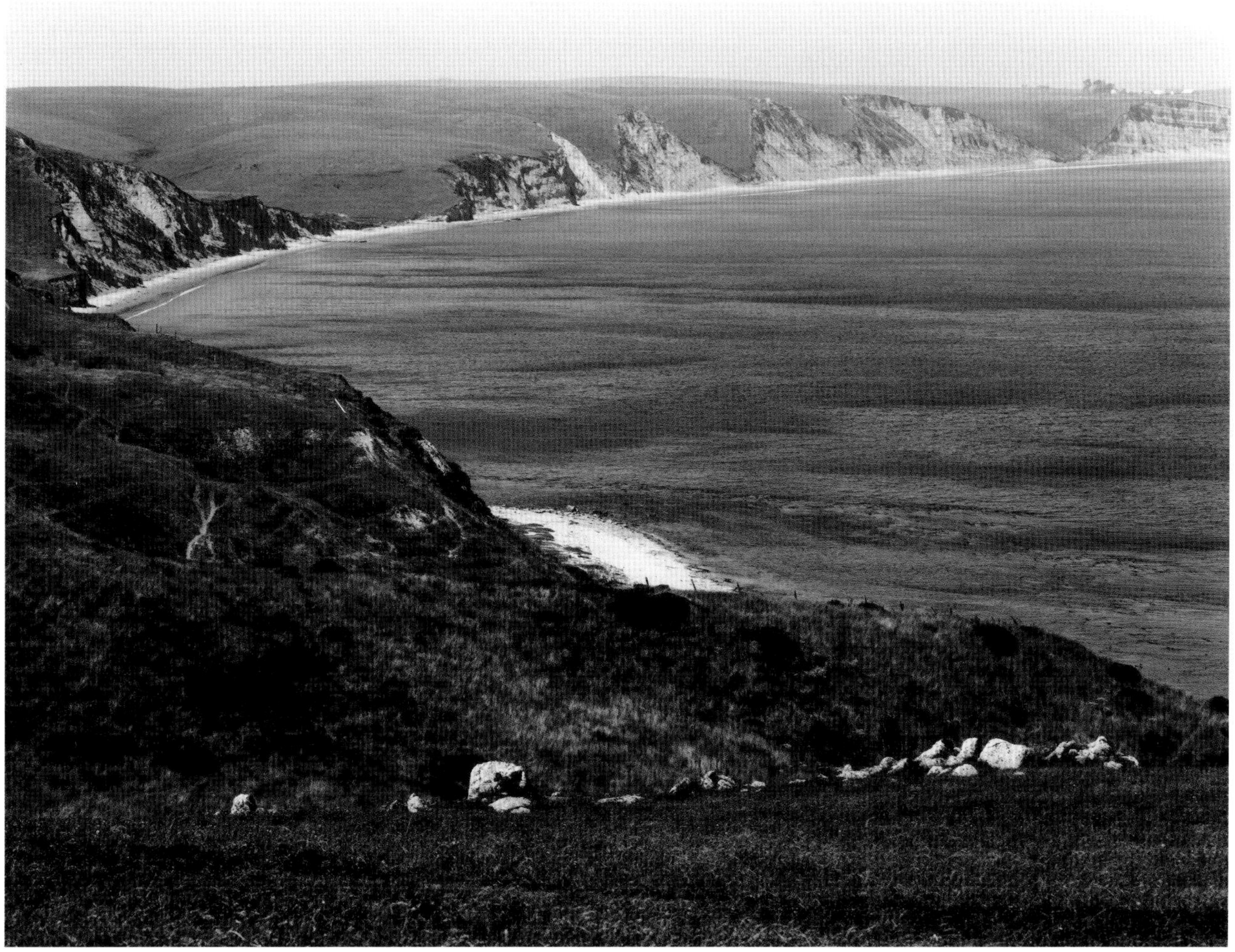

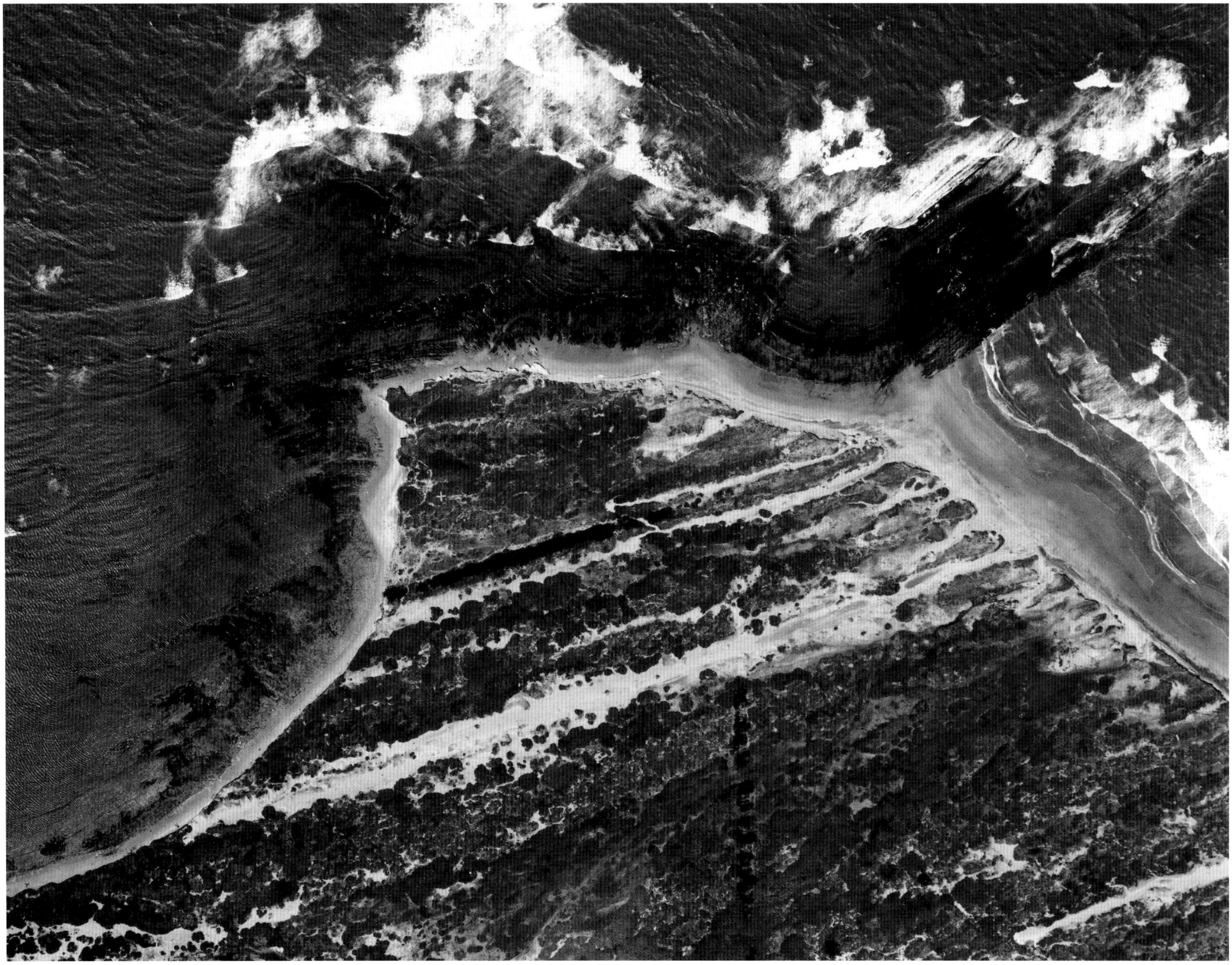

47. Küstenstreifen des Año Nuevo State Park südlich von Half Moon Bay.
48. Miramontes Point südlich von Half Moon Bay mit Golfplatz und Hotel.

47. Coastal strip of Año Nuevo State Park south of Half Moon Bay.
48. Miramontes Point south of Half Moon Bay with golf course and hotel.

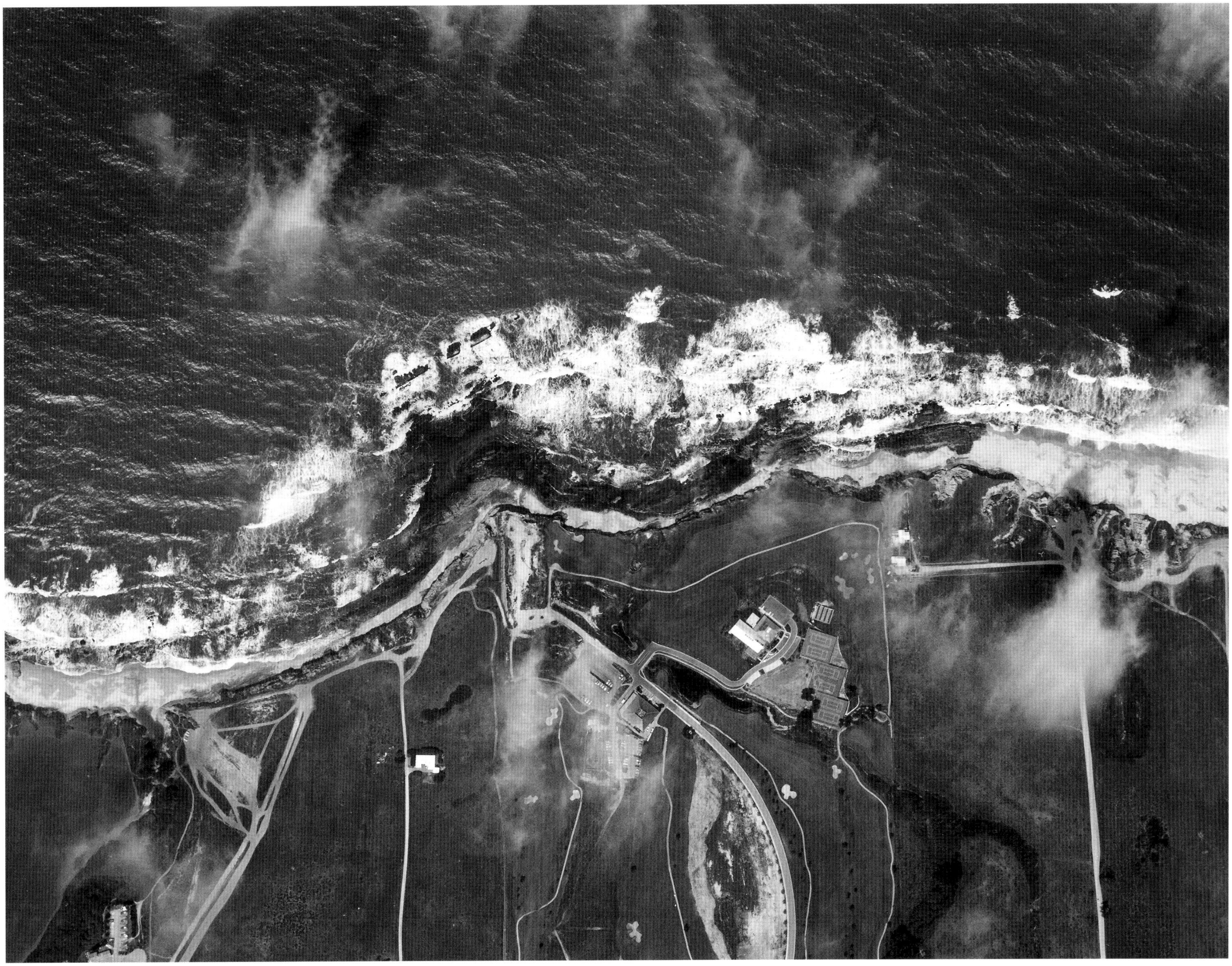

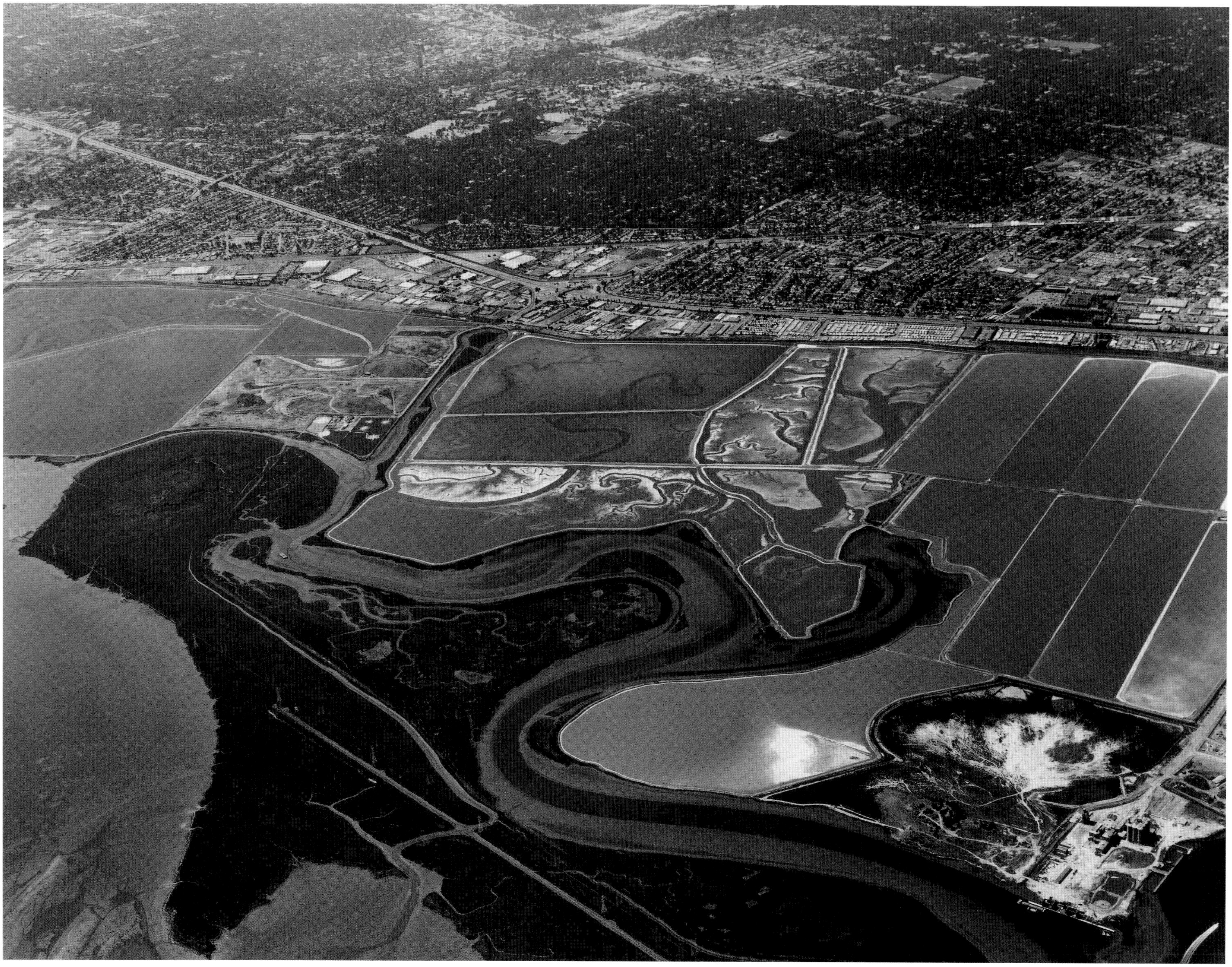

49. Redwood City, Atherton und Menlo Park.
50. Newark. Blick von oberhalb des Central Park in Fremont in Richtung Palo Alto, rechts die Dumbarton Bridge.

S. 60/61
51. Moffet Field, südliche Bucht von San Francisco. Im Vordergrund Prielsysteme.

S. 62/63
52. Palo Alto und Stanford University. In der Mitte der Bibliotheksturm der Universität.

49. Redwood City, Atherton und Menlo Park.
50. Newark. View from above of Central Park in Fremont towards Palo Alto, on the right Dumbarton Bridge.

p. 60/61
51. Moffet Field, southern San Francisco Bay. Network of tidal channels in the foreground.

p. 62/63
52. Palo Alto and Stanford University. In the centre the library tower of the university.

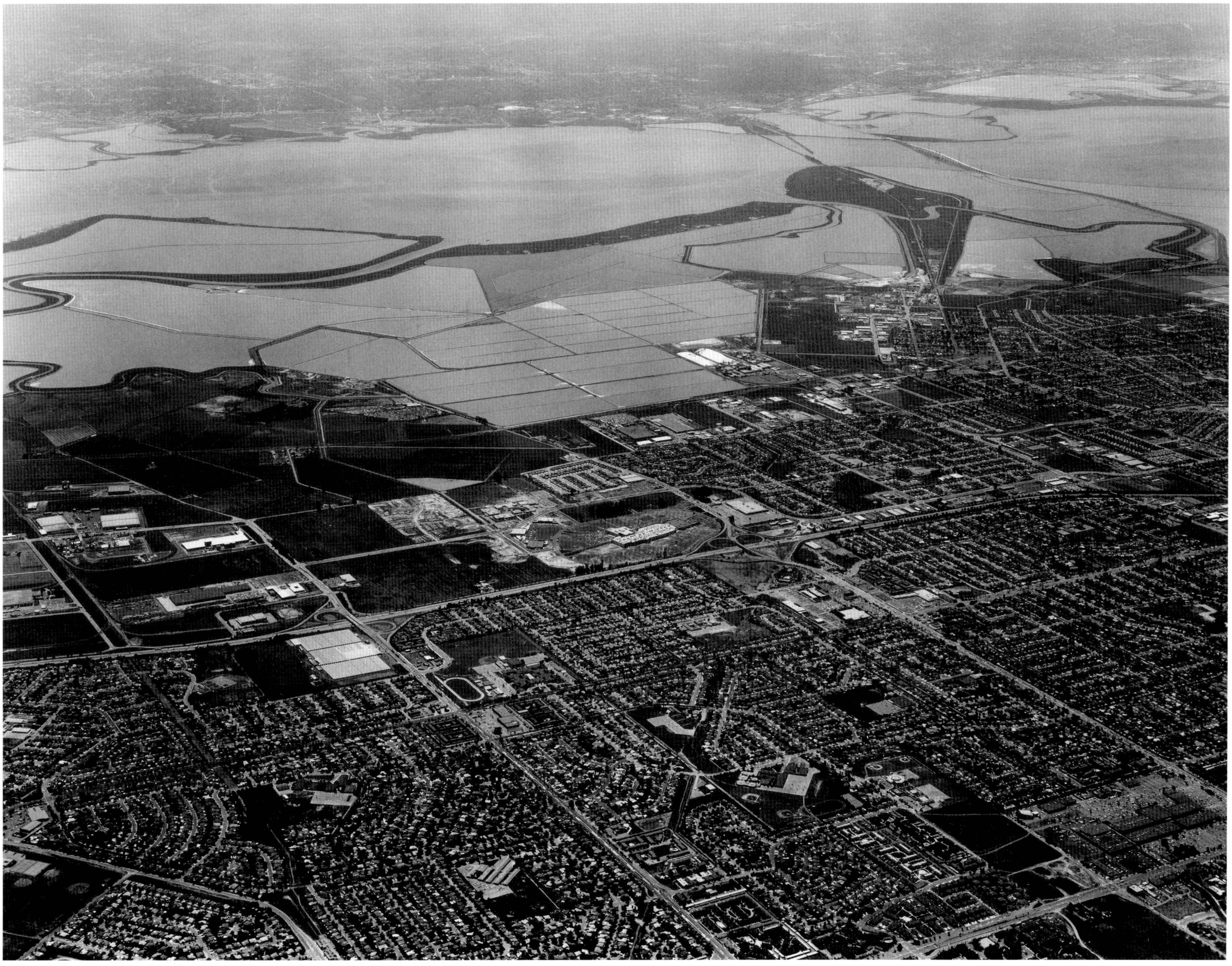

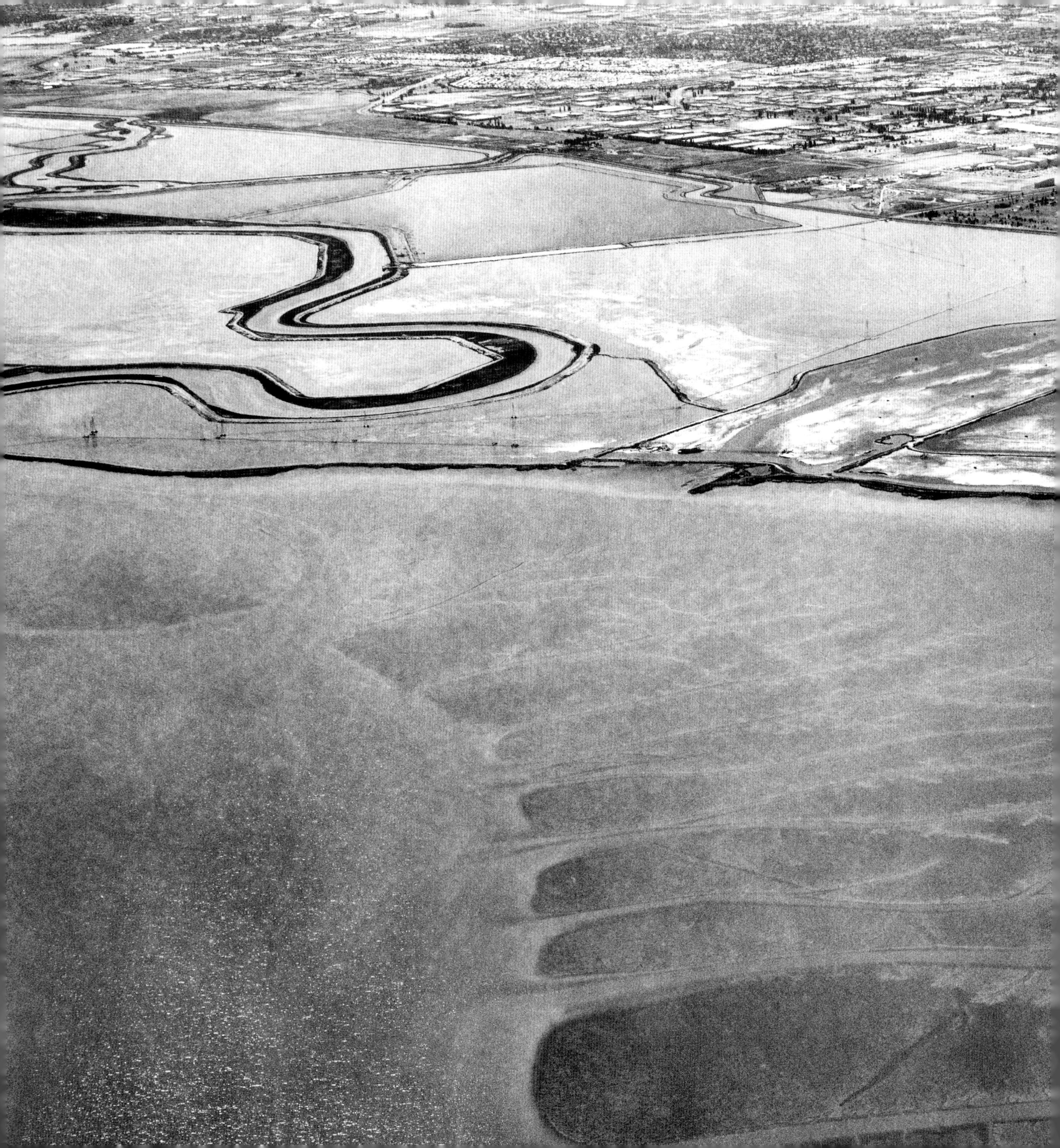

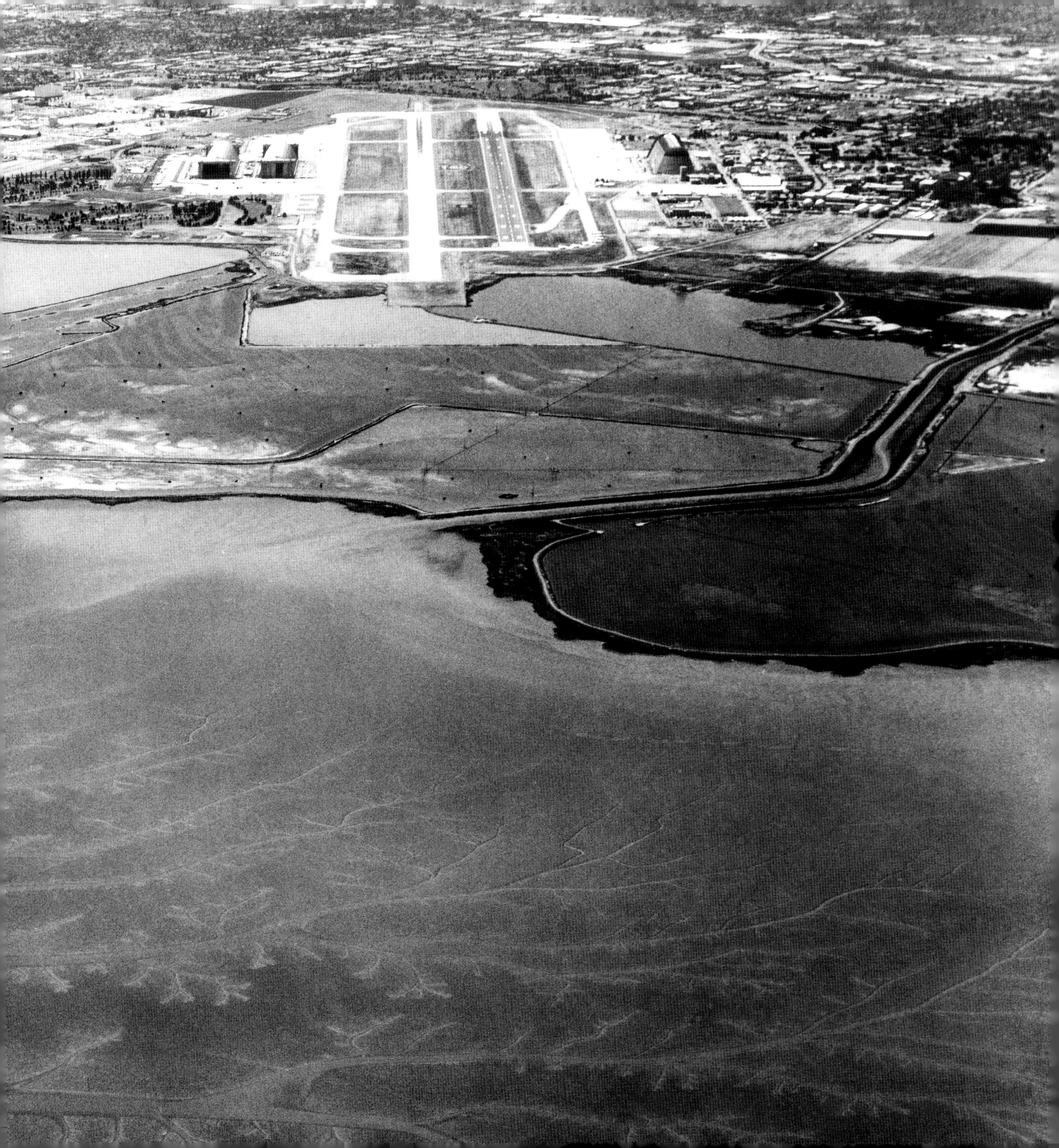

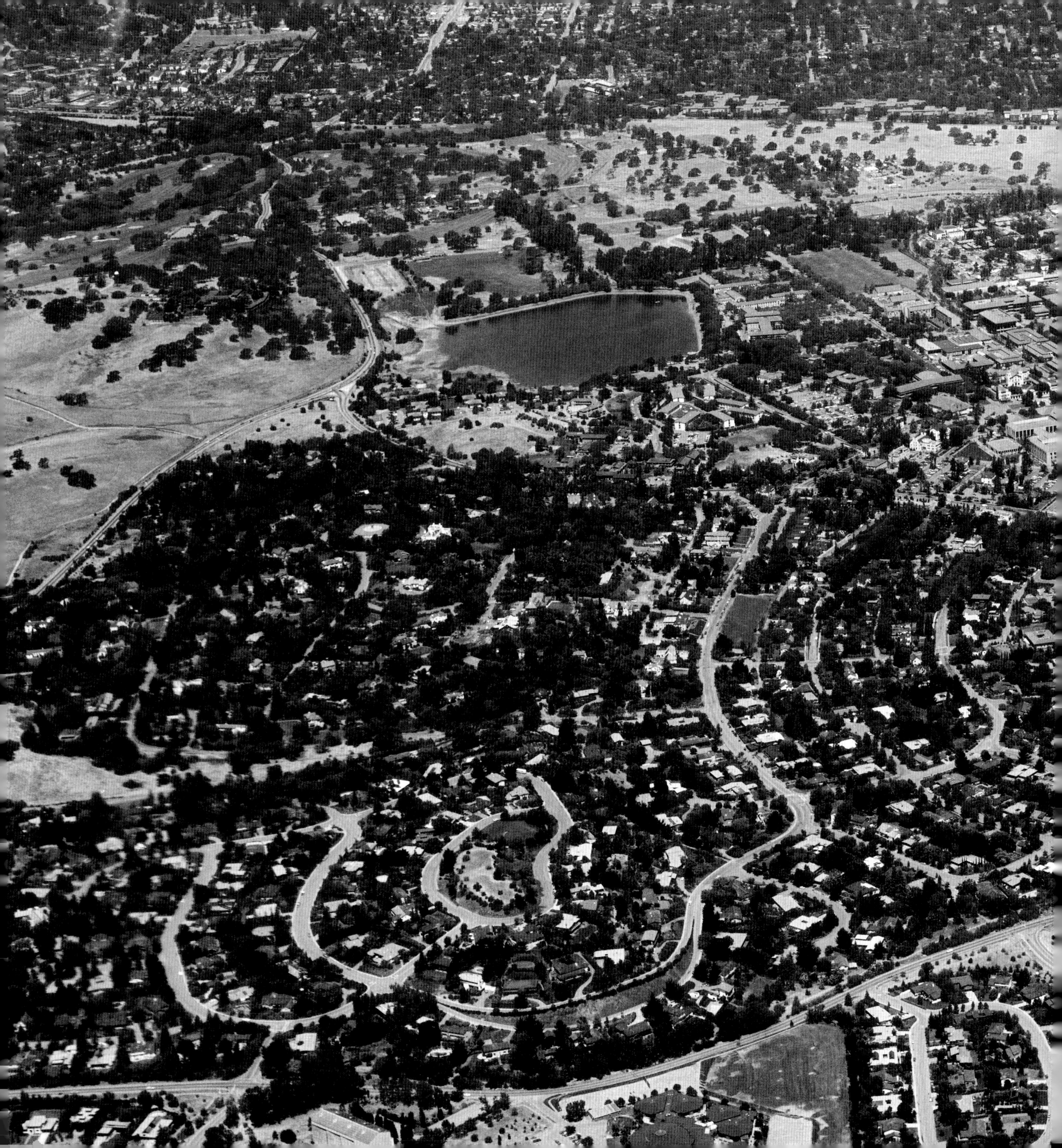

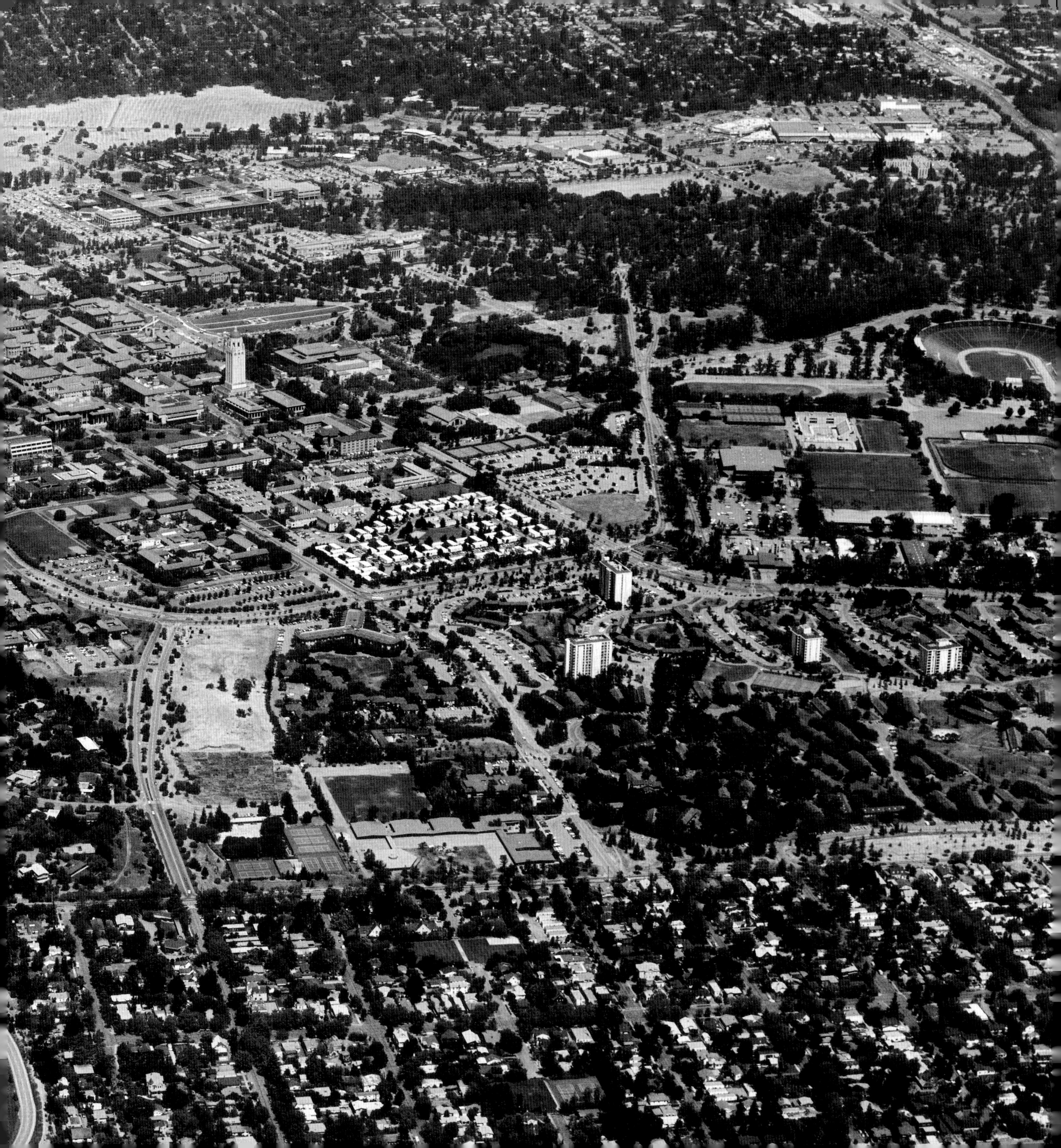

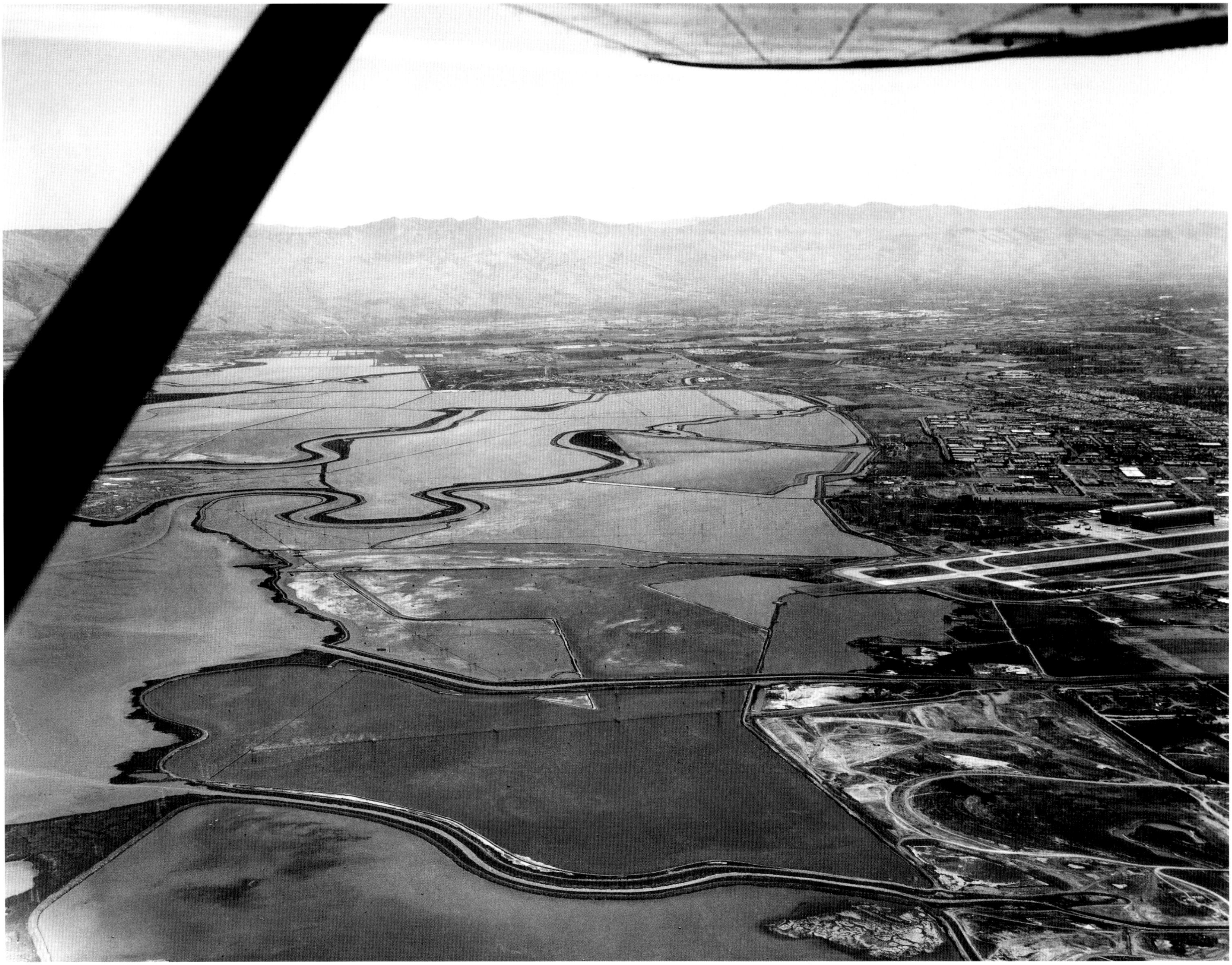

53. Moffet Field.
54. Bair Island südlich der San Mateo Bridge.

53. Moffet Field.
54. Bair Island south of San Mateo Bridge.

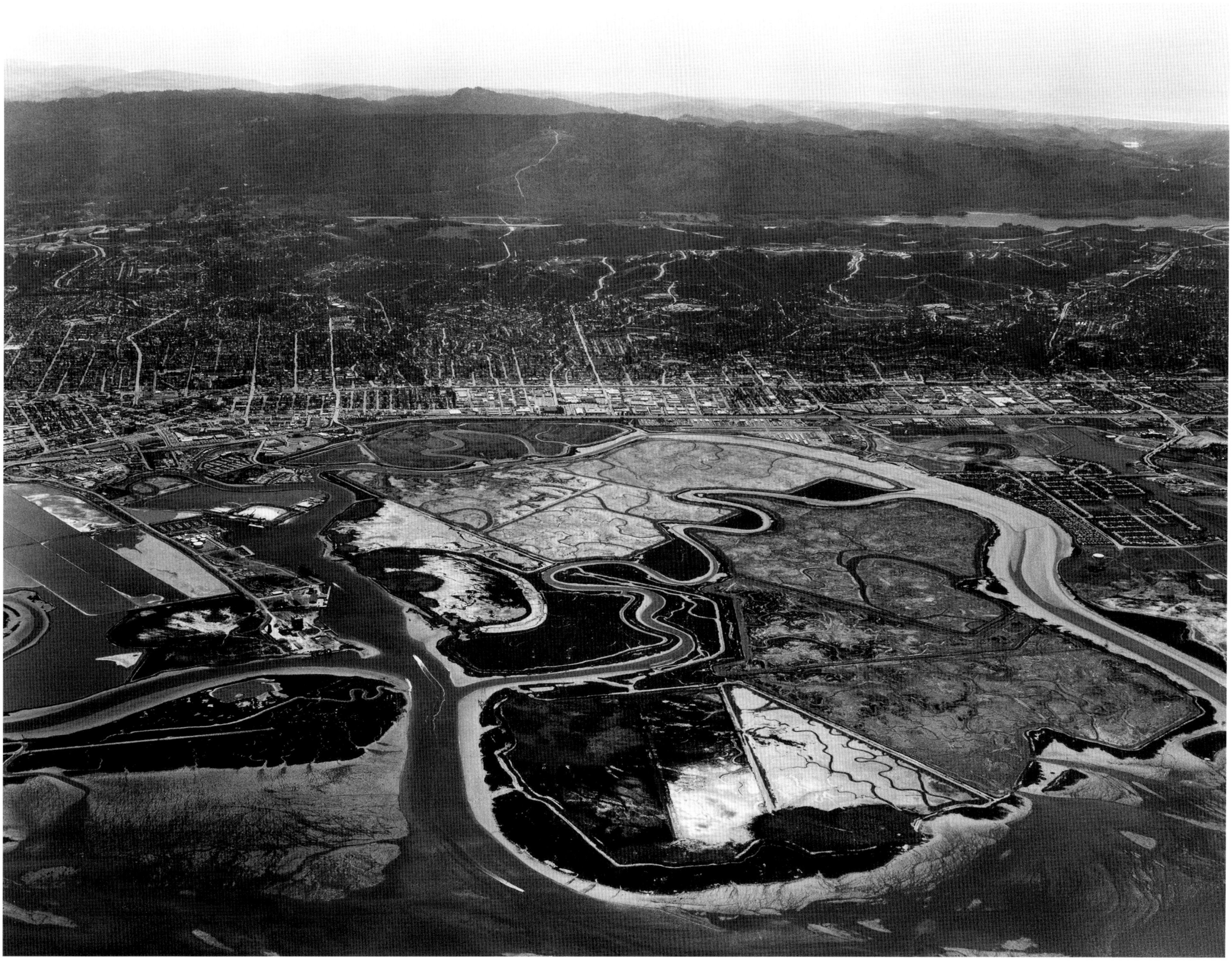

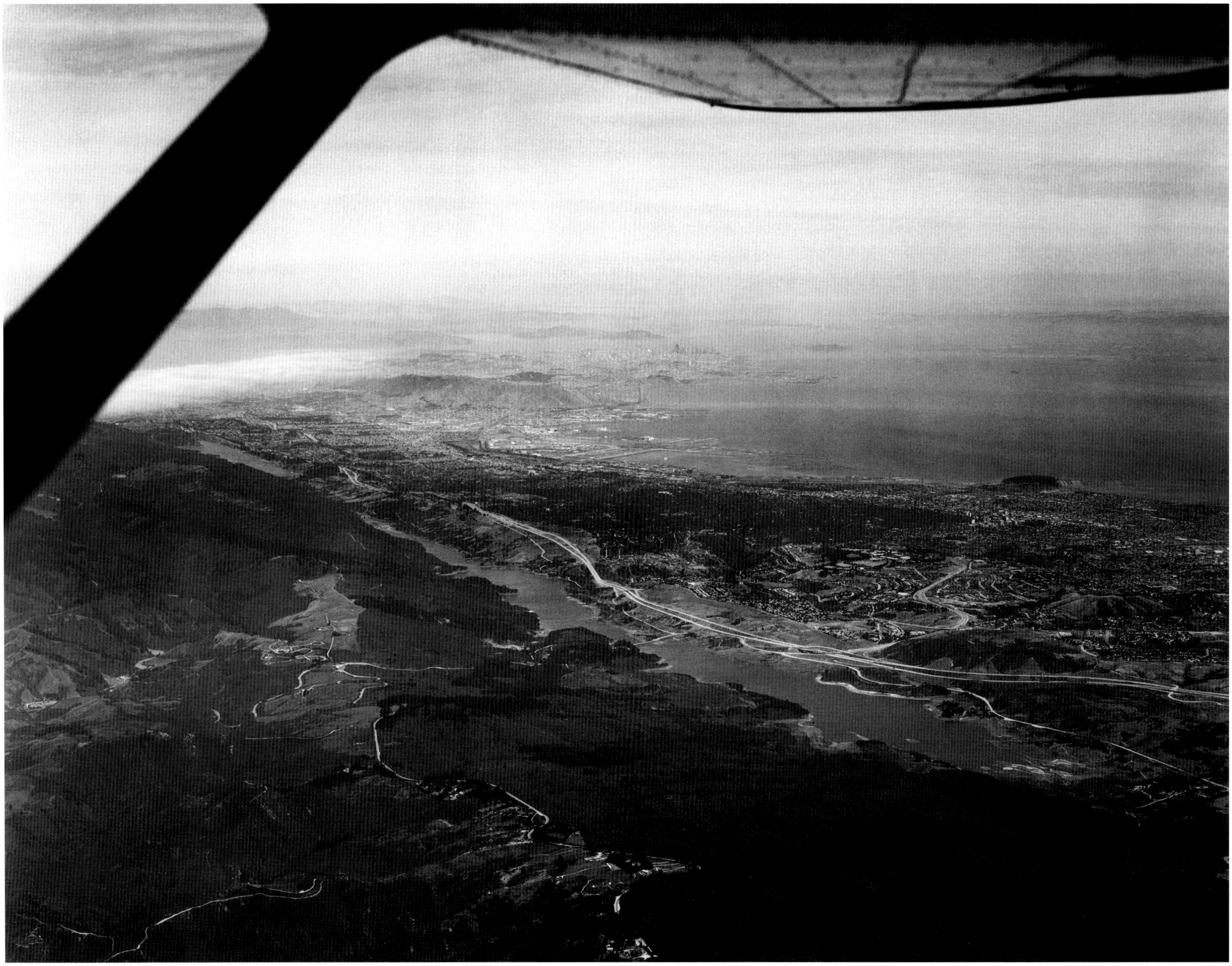

55. Blick über das Crystal Springs Reservoir mit San Francisco im Hintergrund.
56. Crystal Springs Reservoir. Die Seen markieren die San-Andreas-Störung.

55. View across Crystal Springs Reservoir with San Francisco in the background.
56. Crystal Springs Reservoir. The lakes mark the San Andreas Fault.

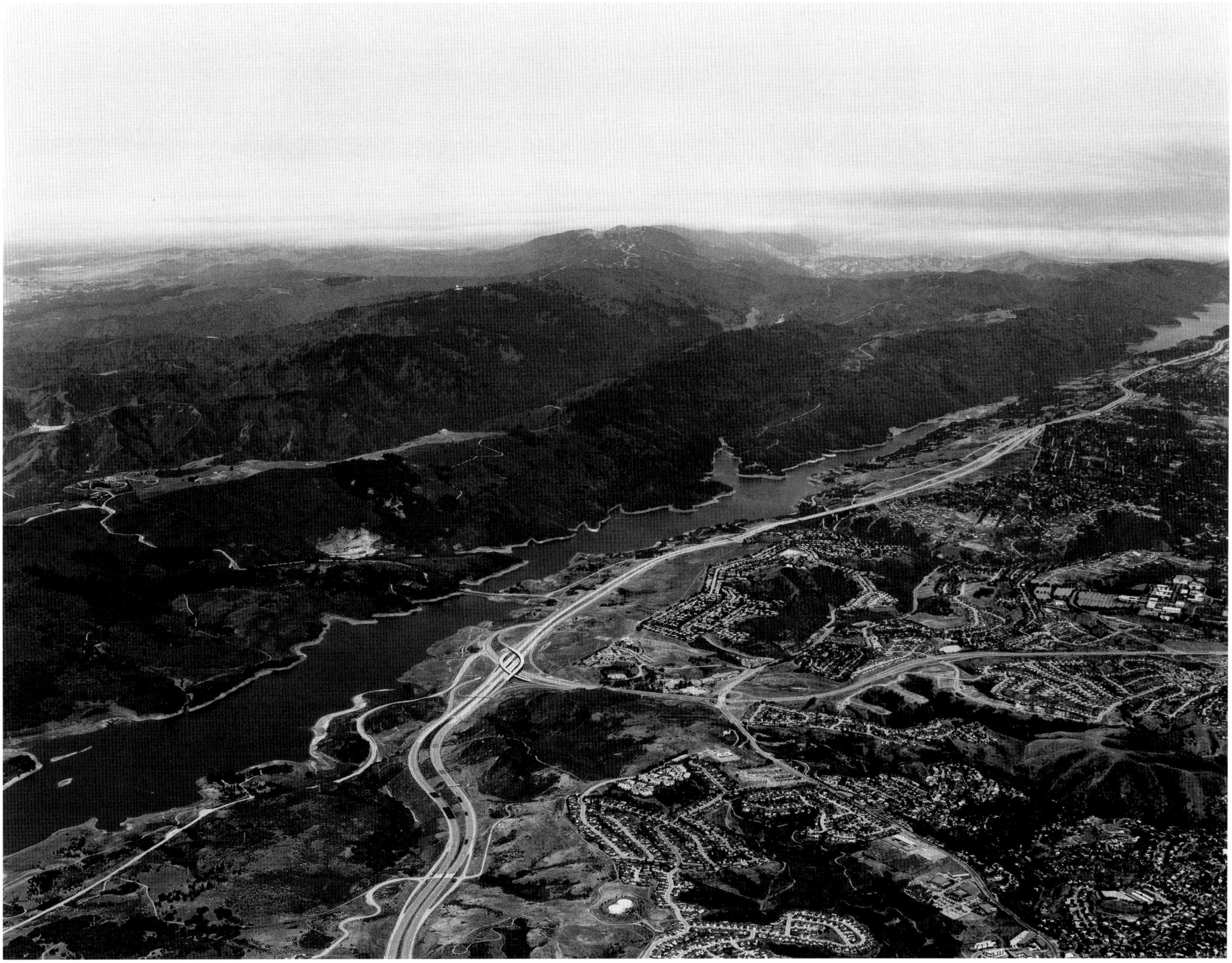

57, 58. Kings Canyon National Park. North Dome am östlichen Ende der Parkstraße.

57, 58. Kings Canyon National Park. North Dome at the eastern end of the park road.

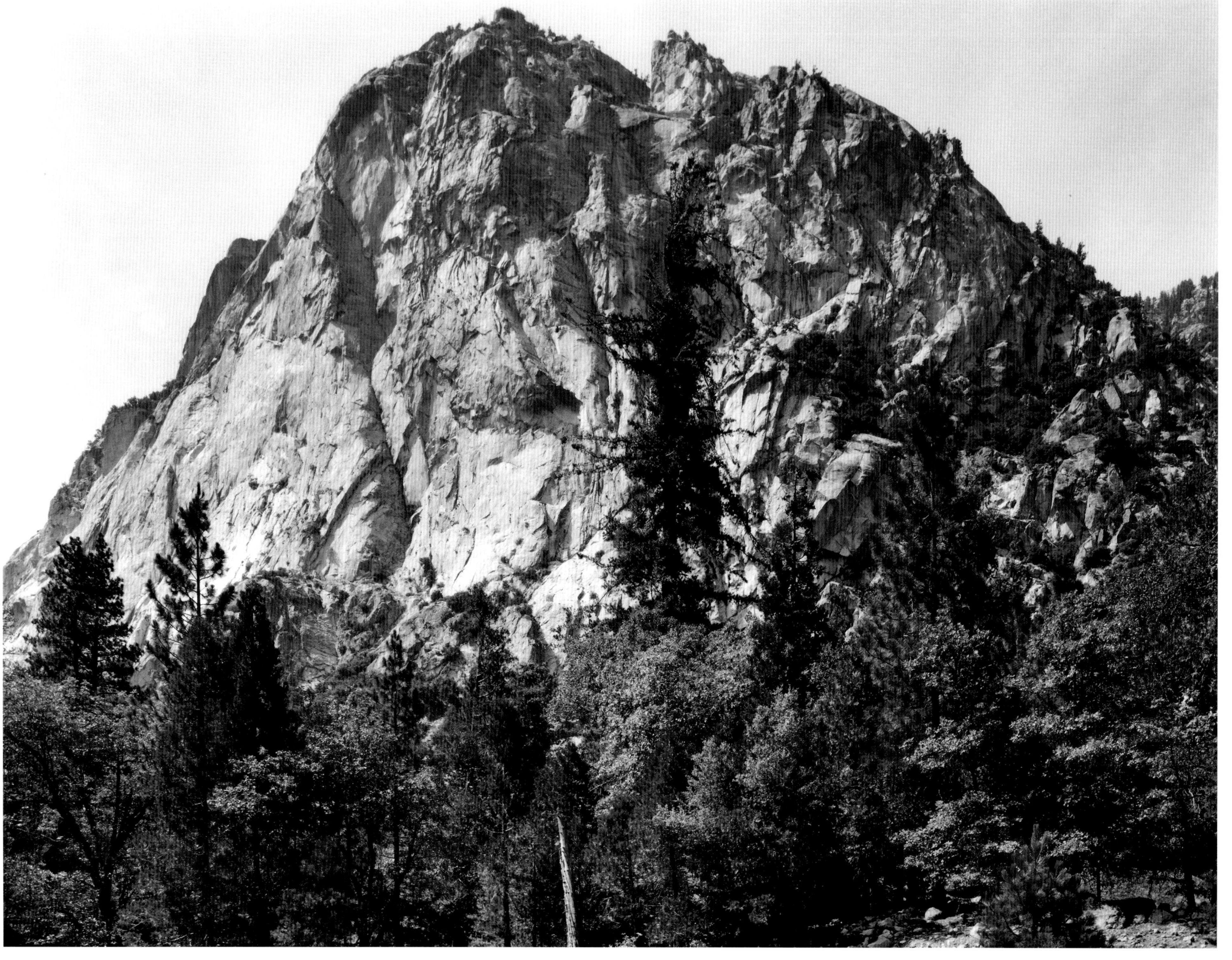

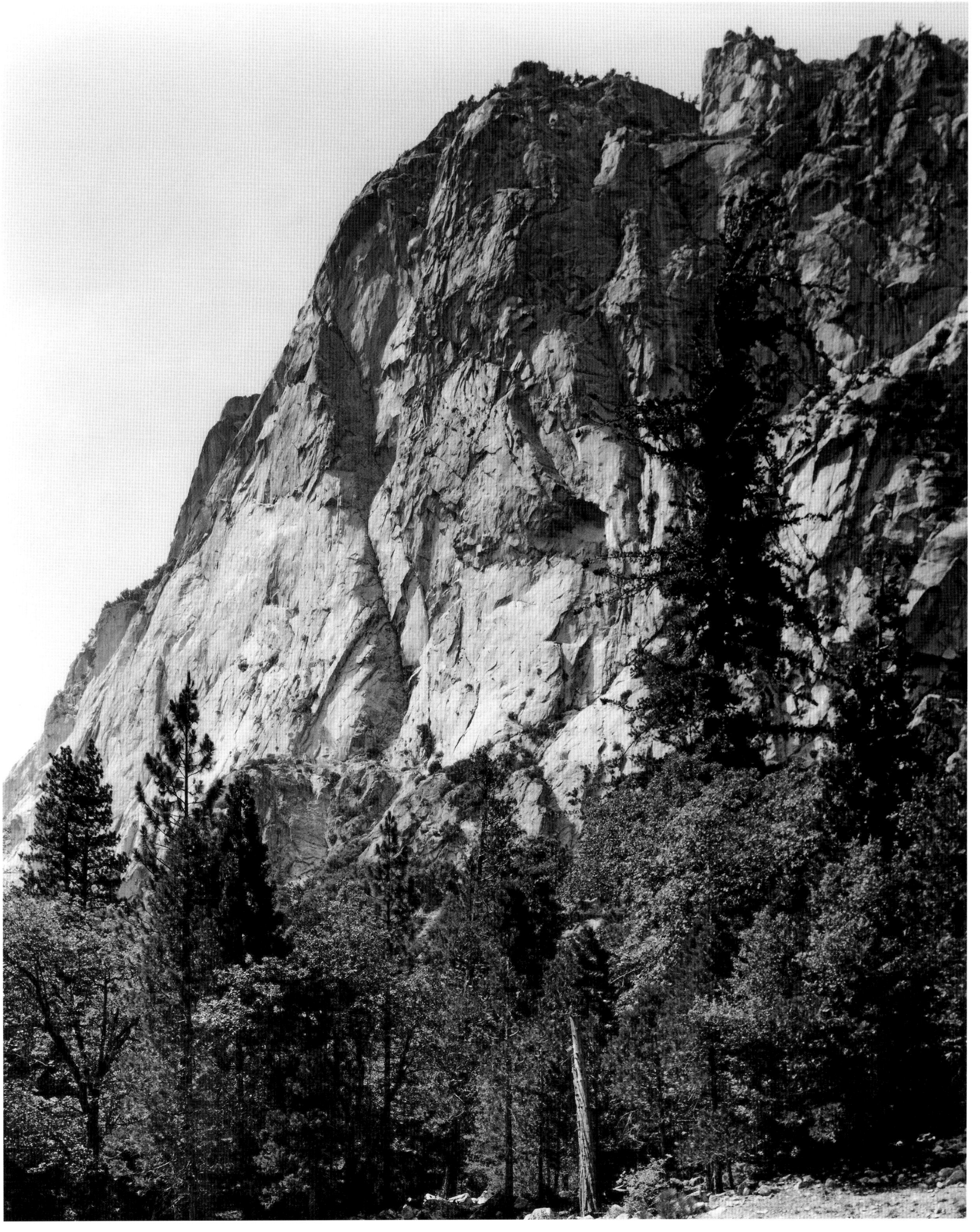

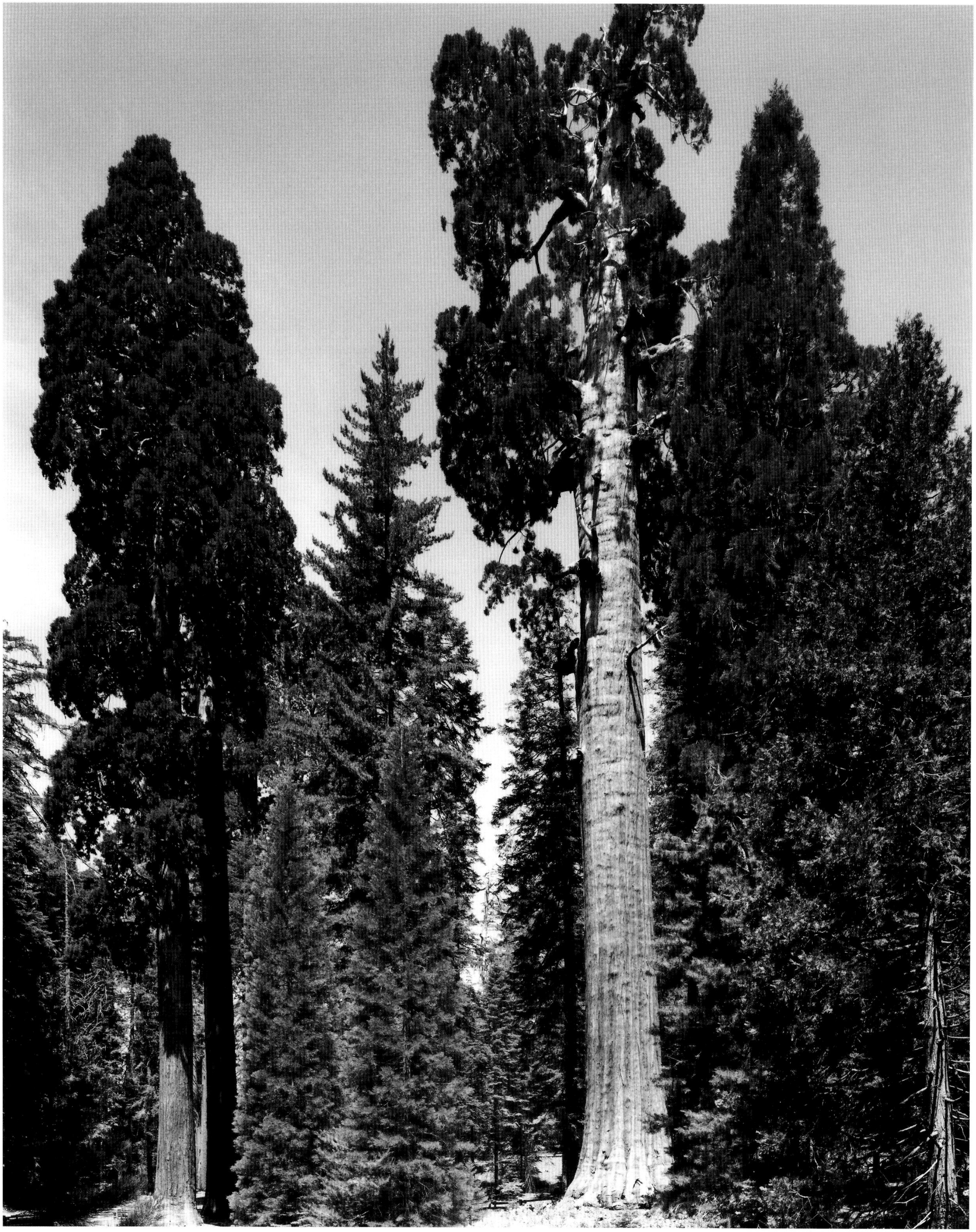

59. Kings Canyon National Park. Der über 80 m hohe Sequoia General Grant Tree im General Grant Grove.

59. Kings Canyon National Park. The Sequoia General Grant Tree more than 80 m high in General Grant Grove.

60. Kings Canyon National Park. Sequoias im General Grant Grove.

60. Kings Canyon National Park. Sequoias in General Grant Grove.

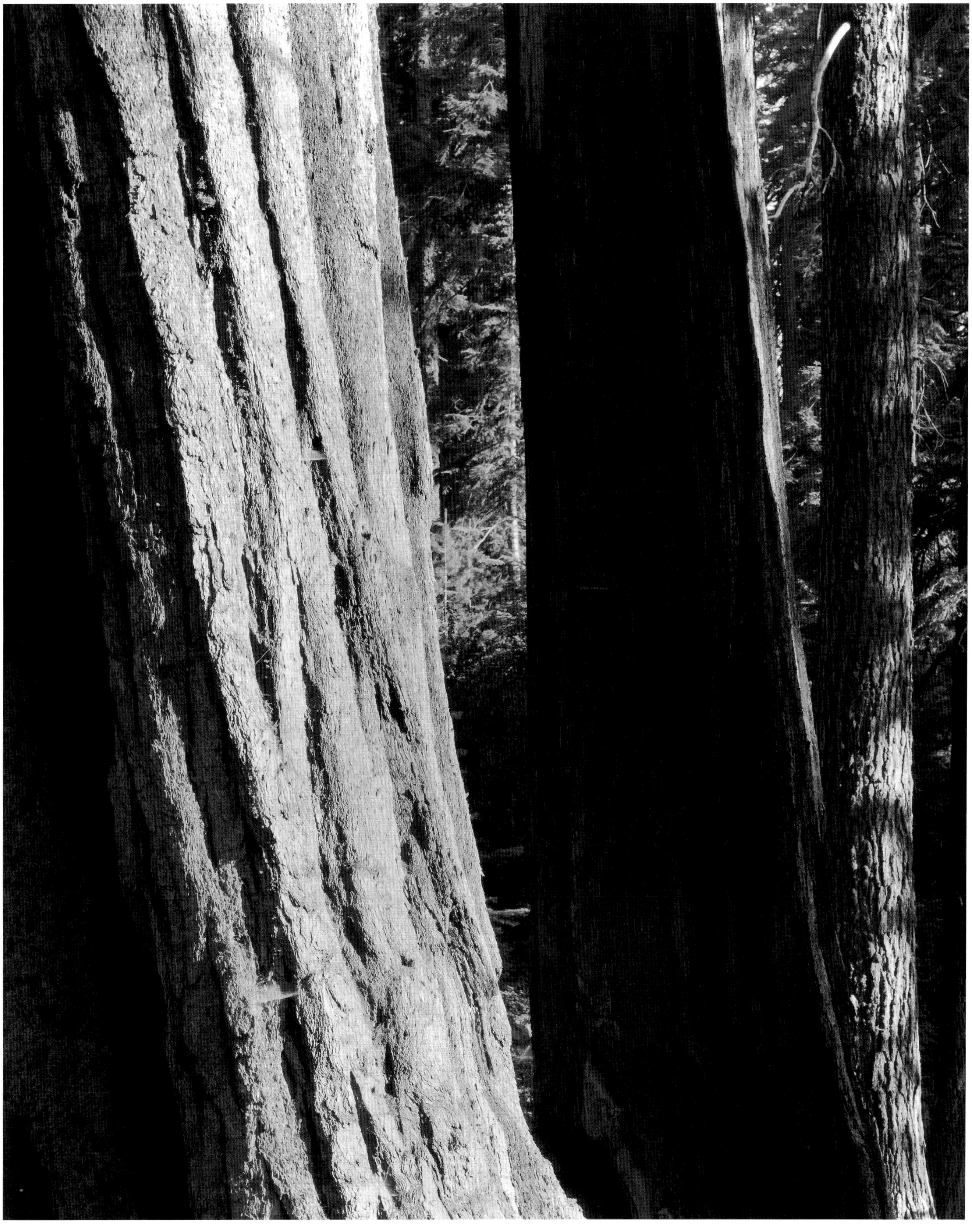

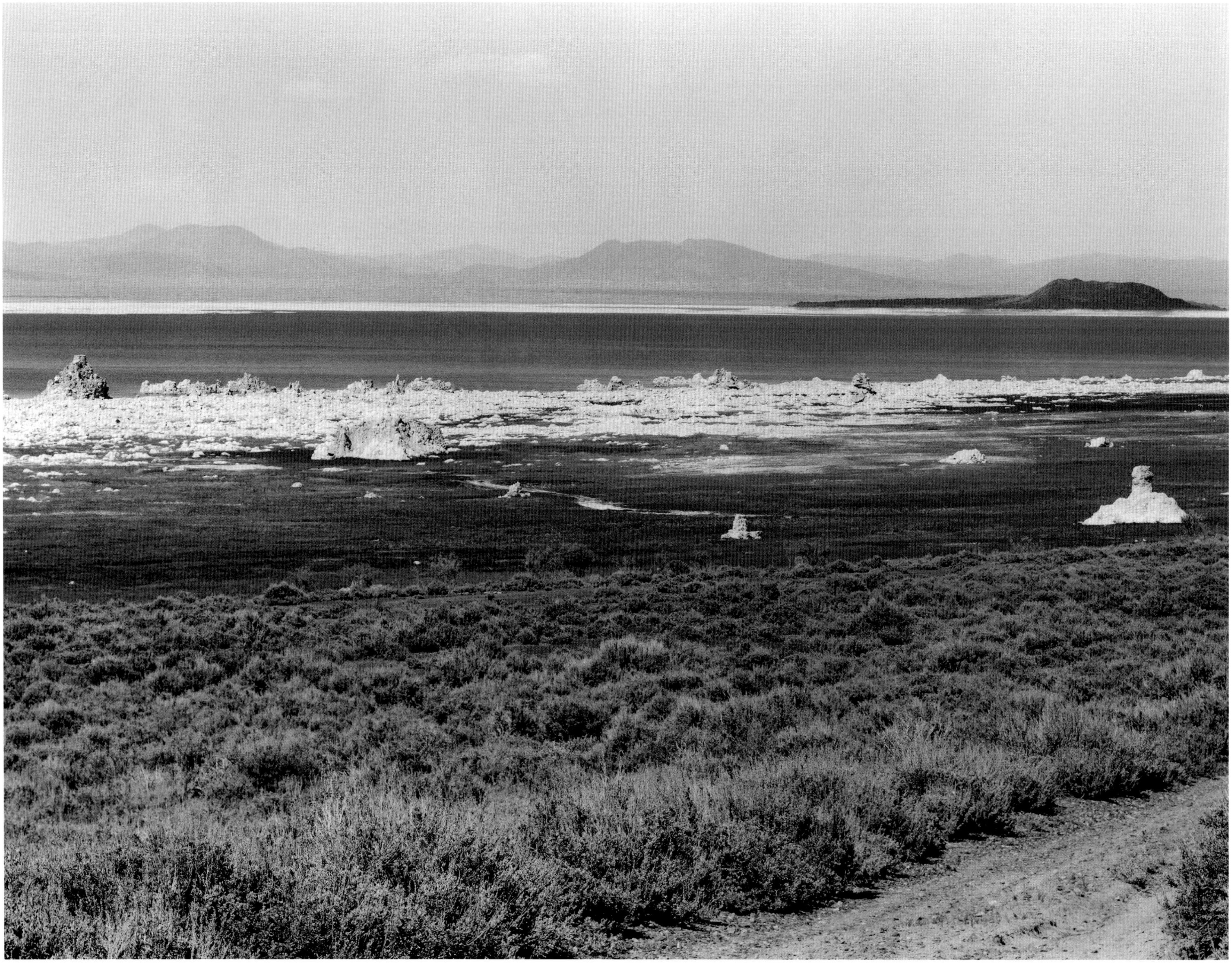

61, 62. Mono Lake. Kalkreiches Wasser tritt am Boden des Sees aus und reagiert mit dem Seewasser. Es bilden sich Schlote aus Kalk, die bei fallendem Wasserspiegel zutage treten.

61, 62. Mono Lake. Calcium bearing fresh-water wells up from the lake bottom and reacts with the lake water to form tufa towers, which appear when the water level drops.

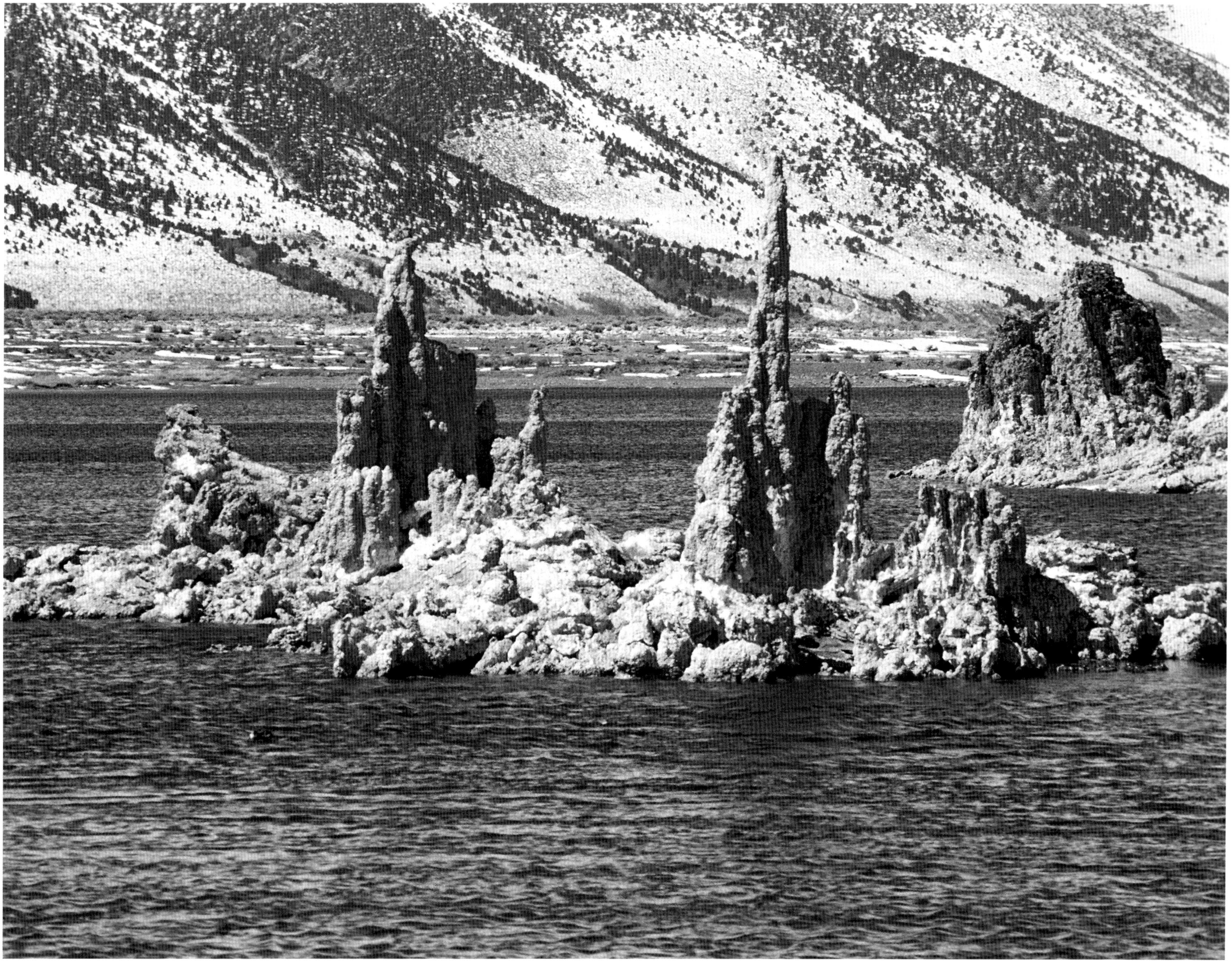

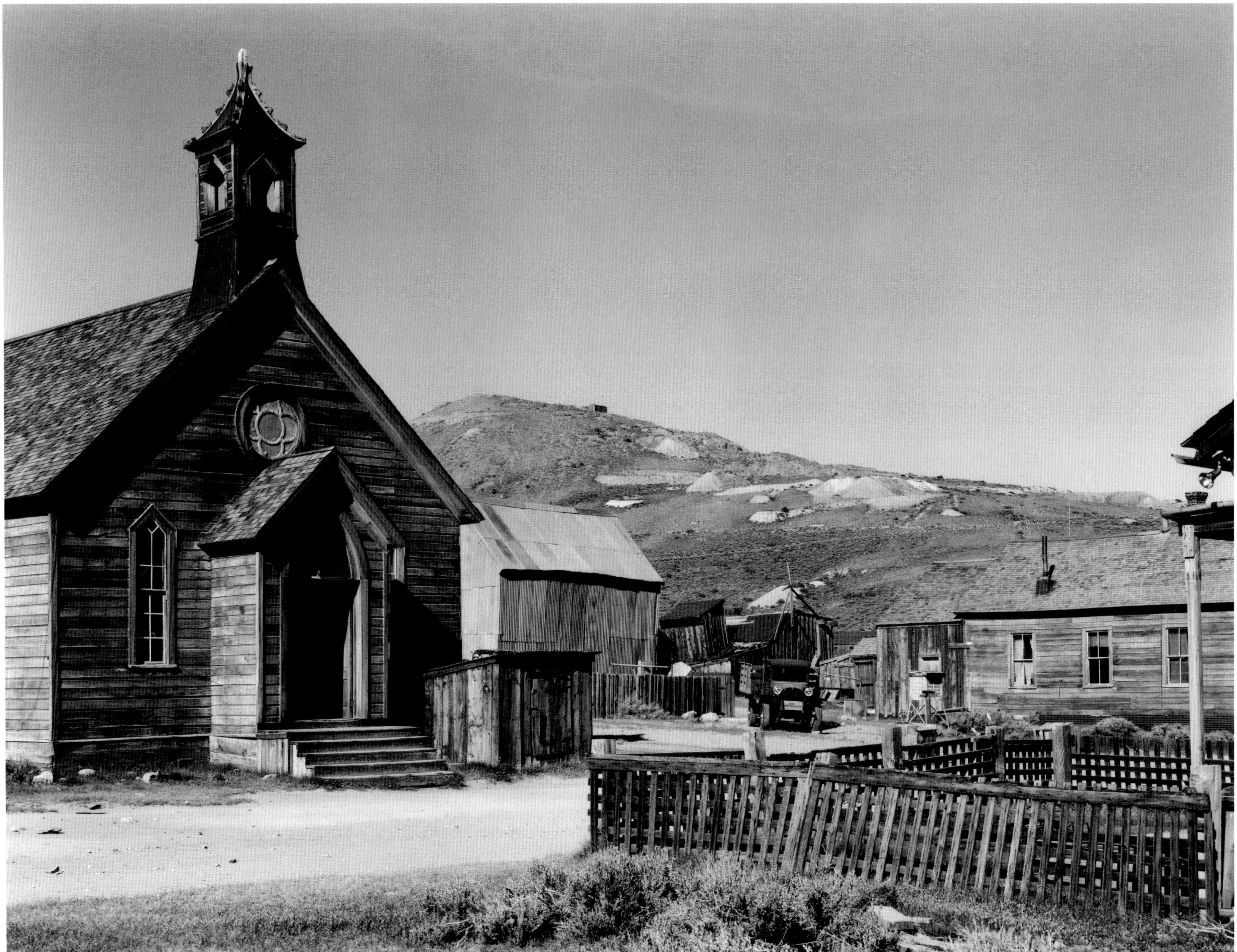

63. Bodie State Historic Park. Die Kirche der verlassenen Goldgräberstadt Bodie.
64. Bodie State Historic Park. Die Tankstelle aus dem frühen 20. Jahrhundert.

63. Bodie State Historic Park. The church of the abandoned goldmine town of Bodie.
64. Bodie State Historic Park. The early-20th century gas station.

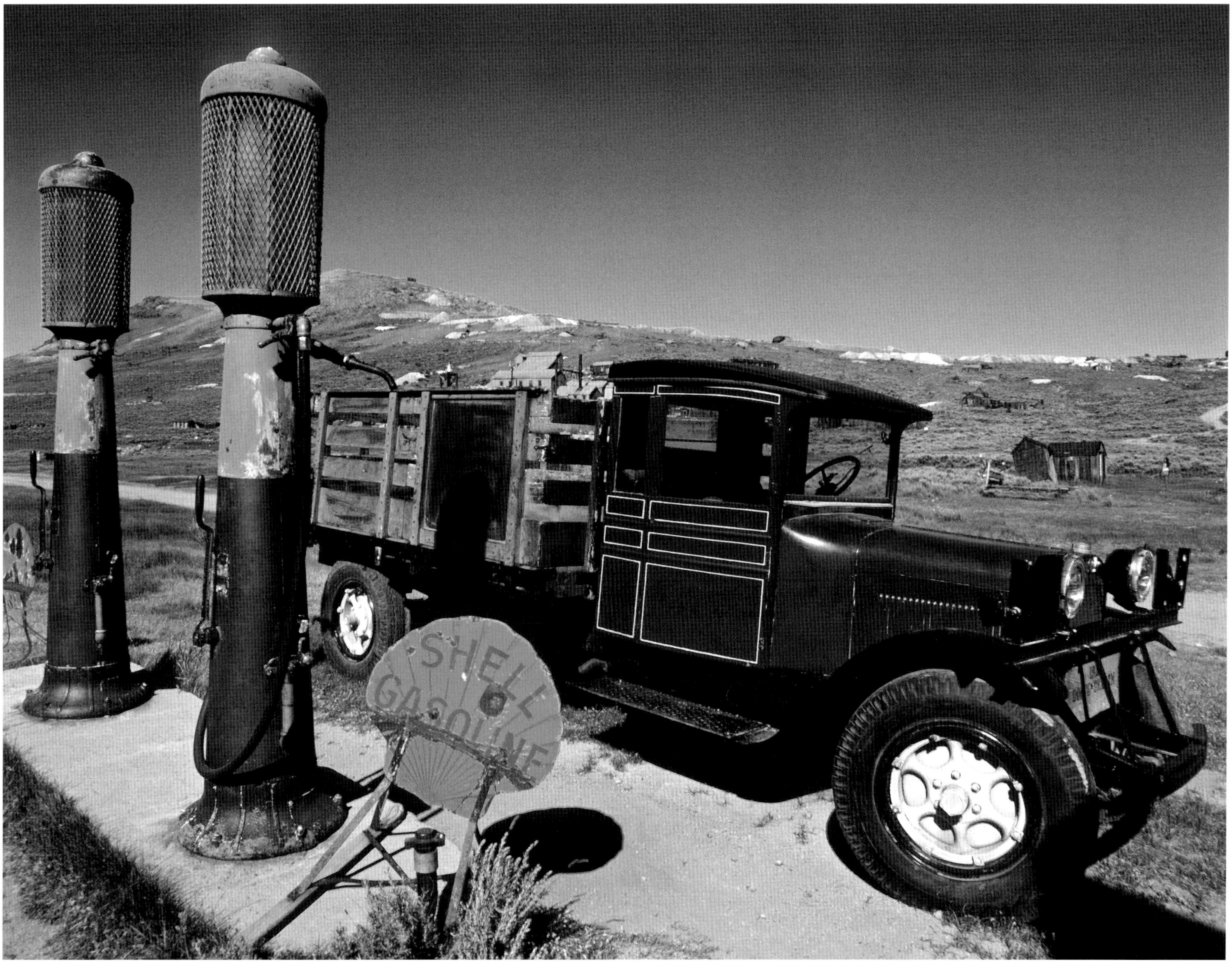

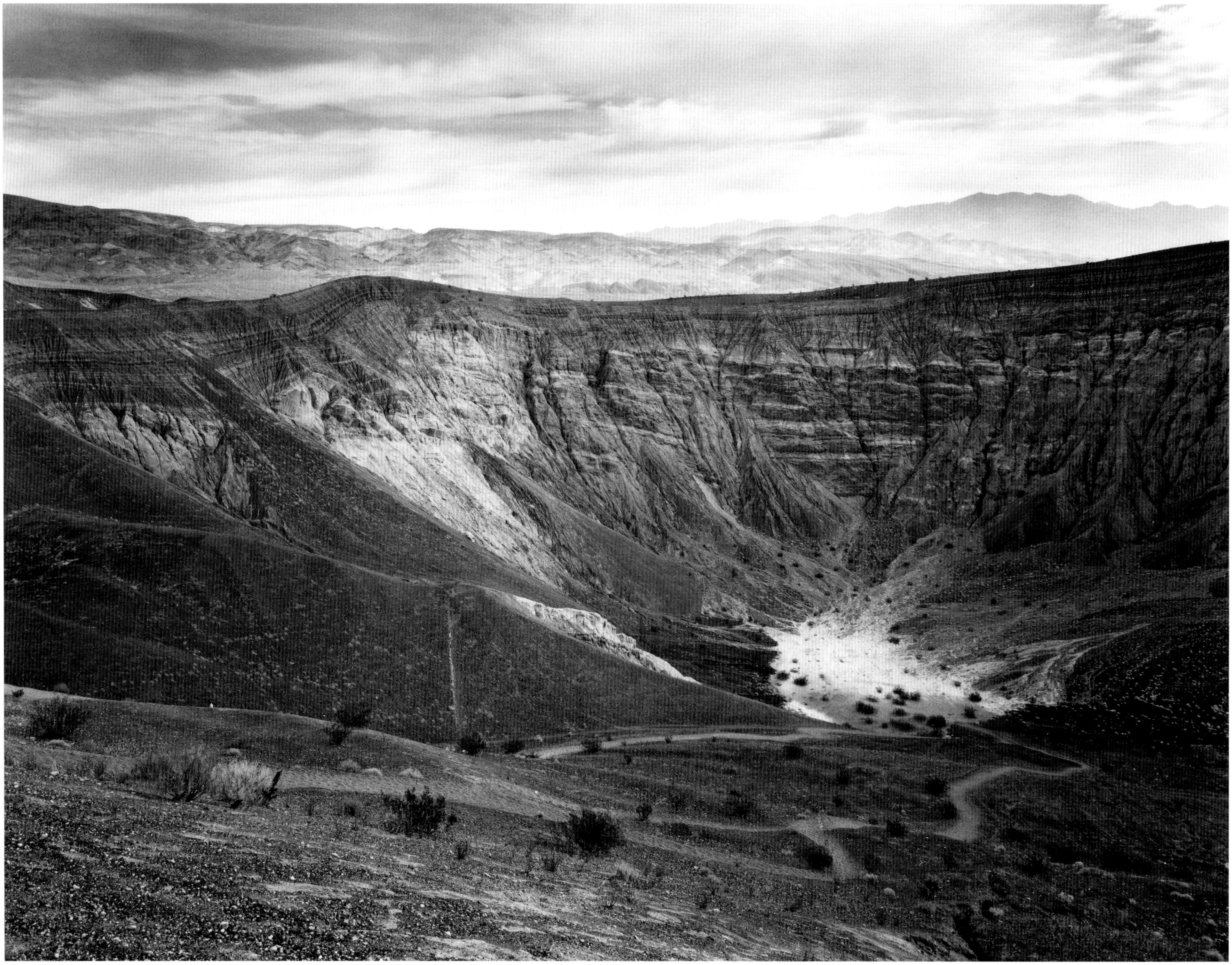

65, 66. Death Valley National Park. Ubehebe Crater im extremen Norden des Death Valley.

65, 66. Death Valley National Park. Ubehebe Crater in the extreme north of Death Valley.

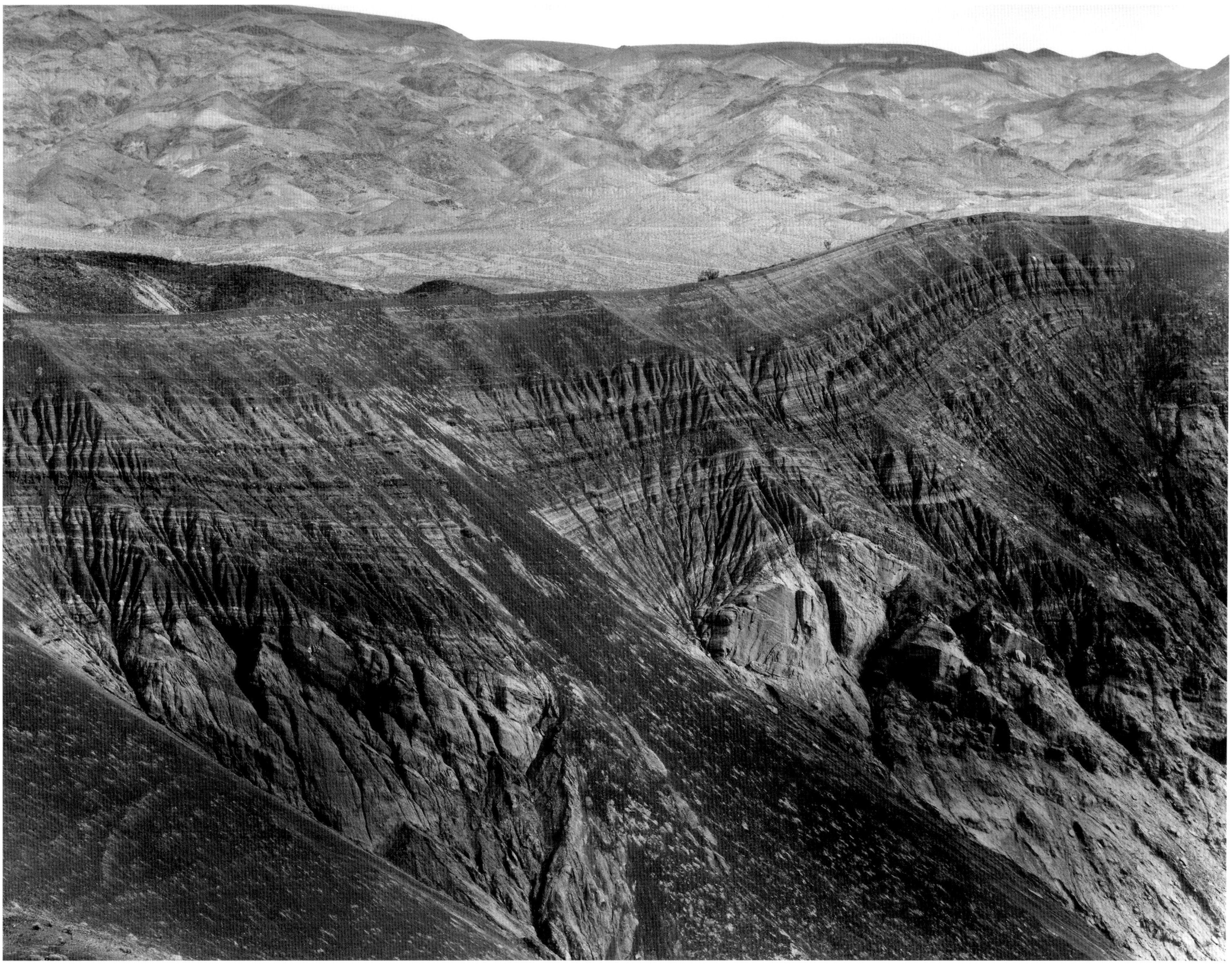

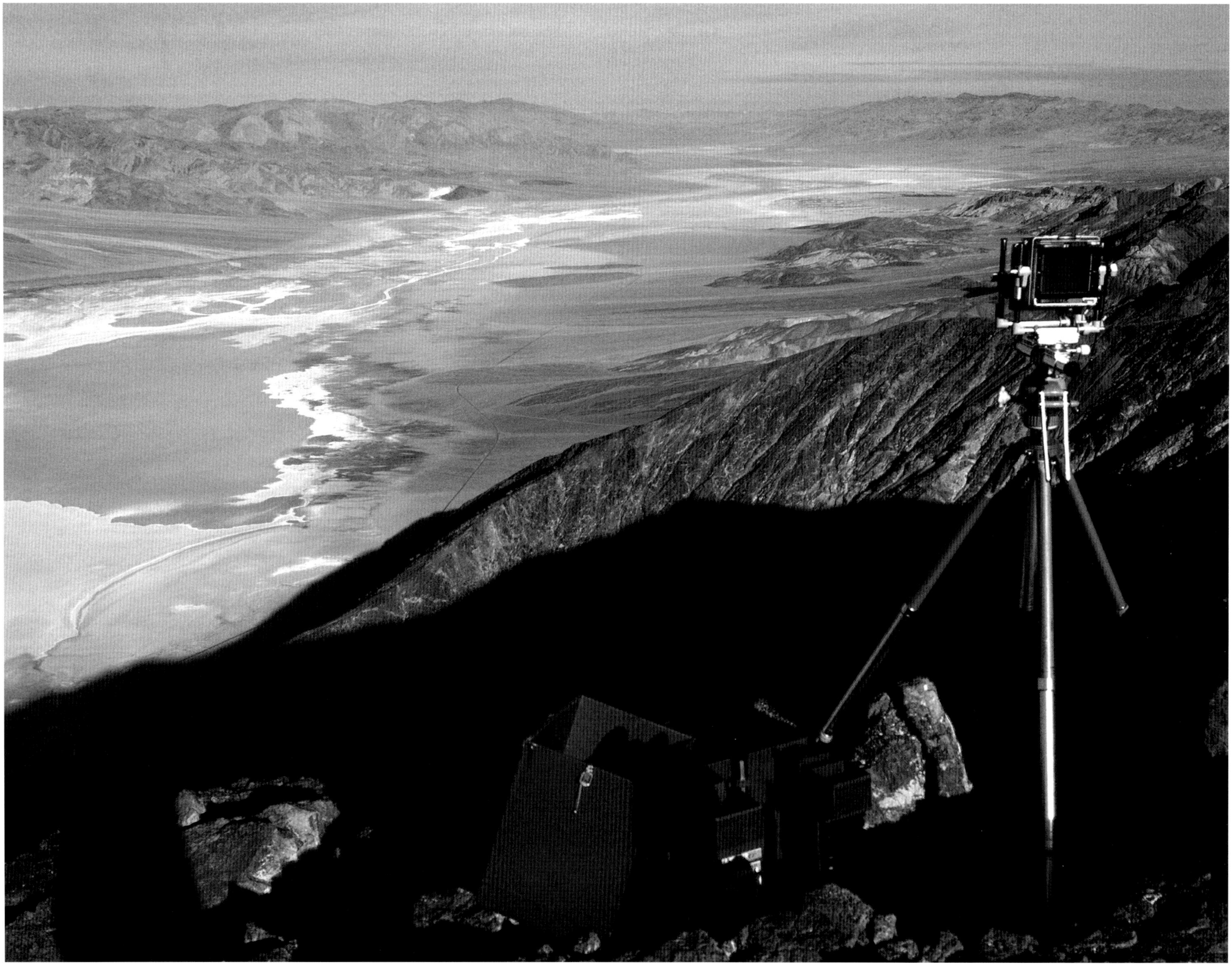

67. Death Valley National Park. Blick von Dante's View in das Death Valley.
68. Death Valley National Park. Blick von Dante's View auf den Hanaupah Fan (links), die Panamint Range mit dem Telescope Peak (3368 m) und die Sierra Nevada mit dem Mount Whitney (4418 m).

67. Death Valley National Park. View of Death Valley from Dante's View.
68. Death Valley National Park. View of the Hanaupah Fan (to the left), the Panamint Range with Telescope Peak (3368 m) and the Sierra Nevada with Mount Whitney (4418 m) from Dante's View.

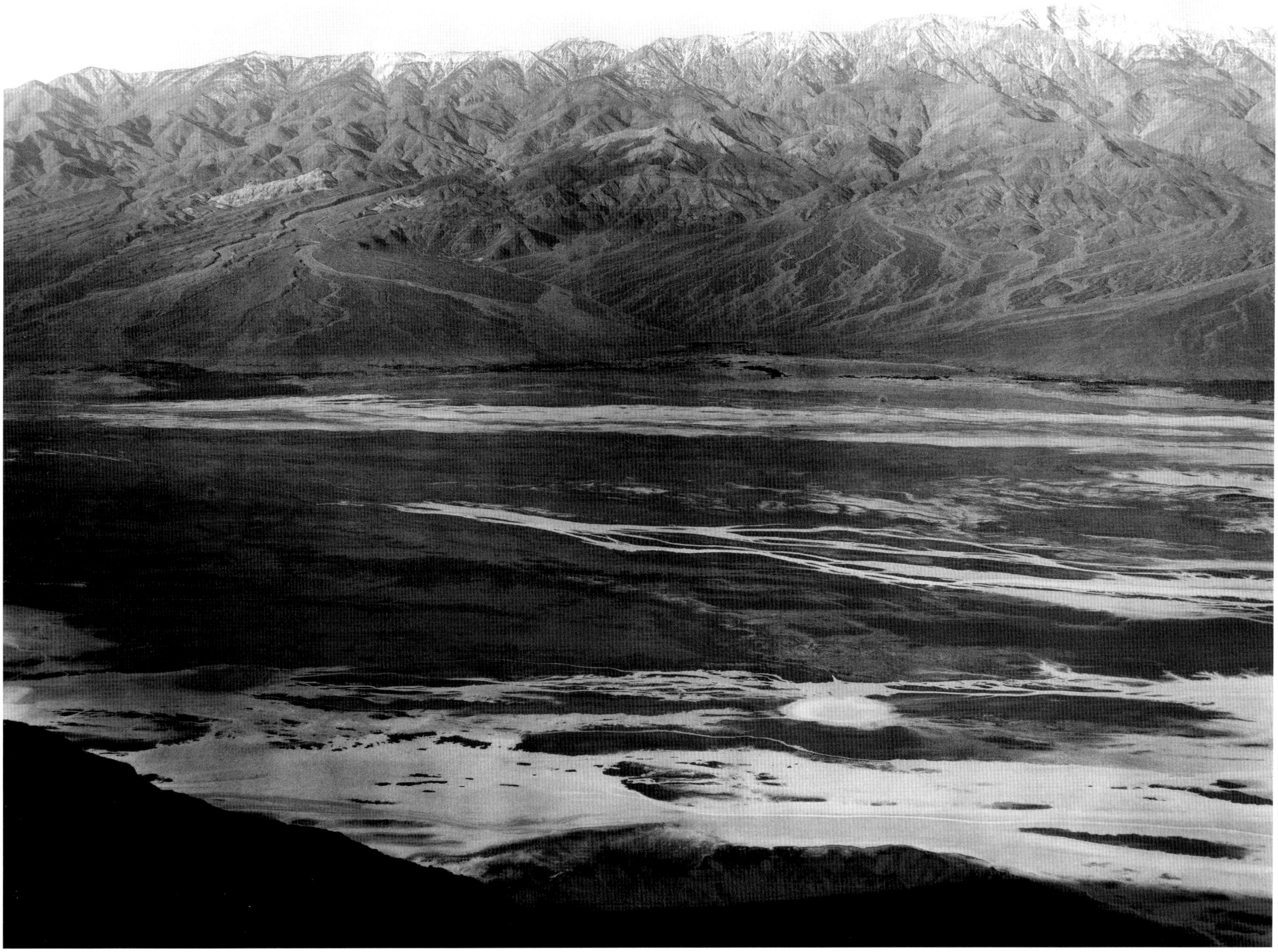

69. Death Valley National Park. Playa am nördlichen Ende der West Side Road.
70. Death Valley National Park. Devil's Golf Course. Niedrigster Punkt der Vereinigten Staaten (–86 m).

69. Death Valley National Park. Playa at the northern End of the West Side Road.
70. Death Valley National Park. Devil's Golf Course. Lowest point of the Unites States (–86 m).

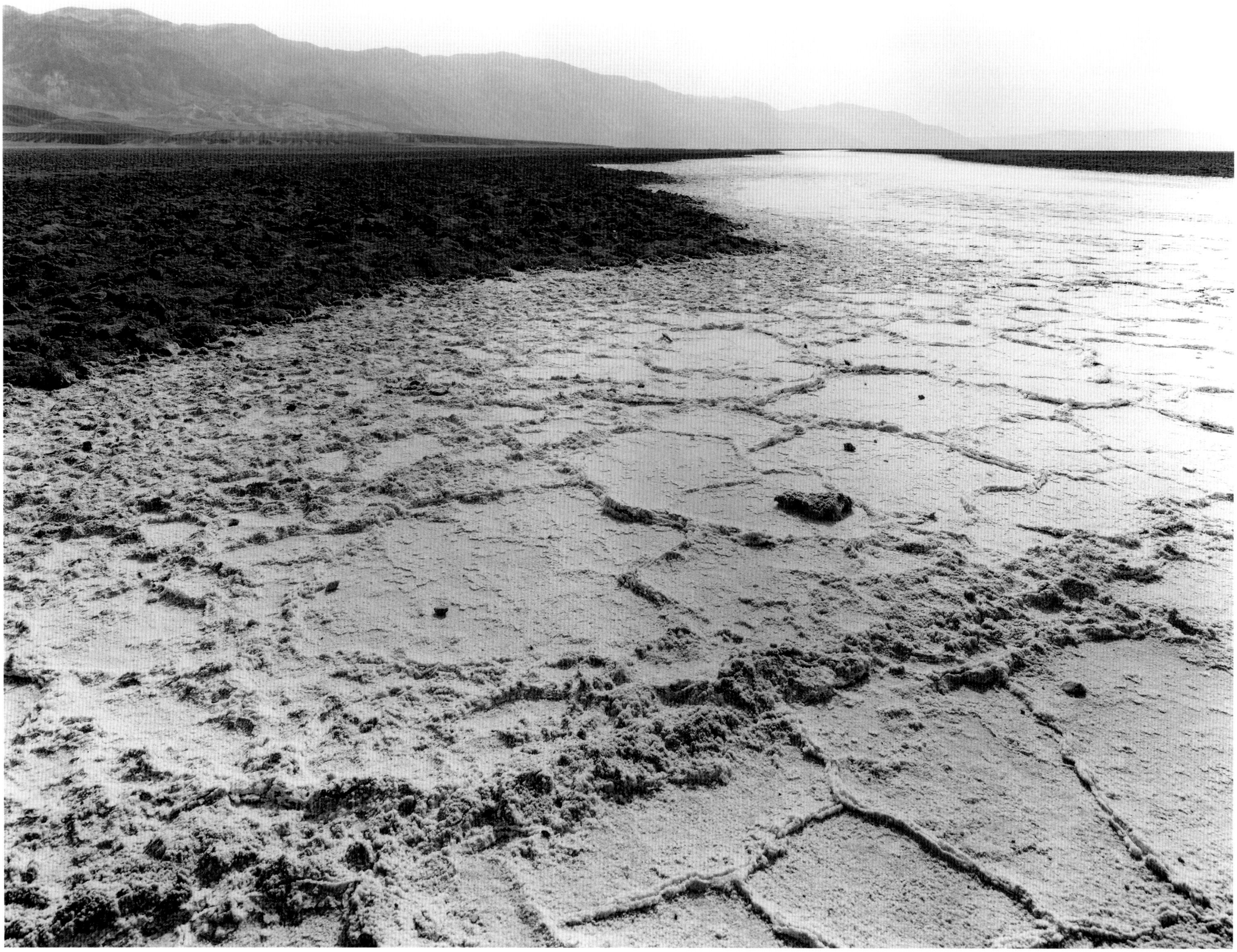

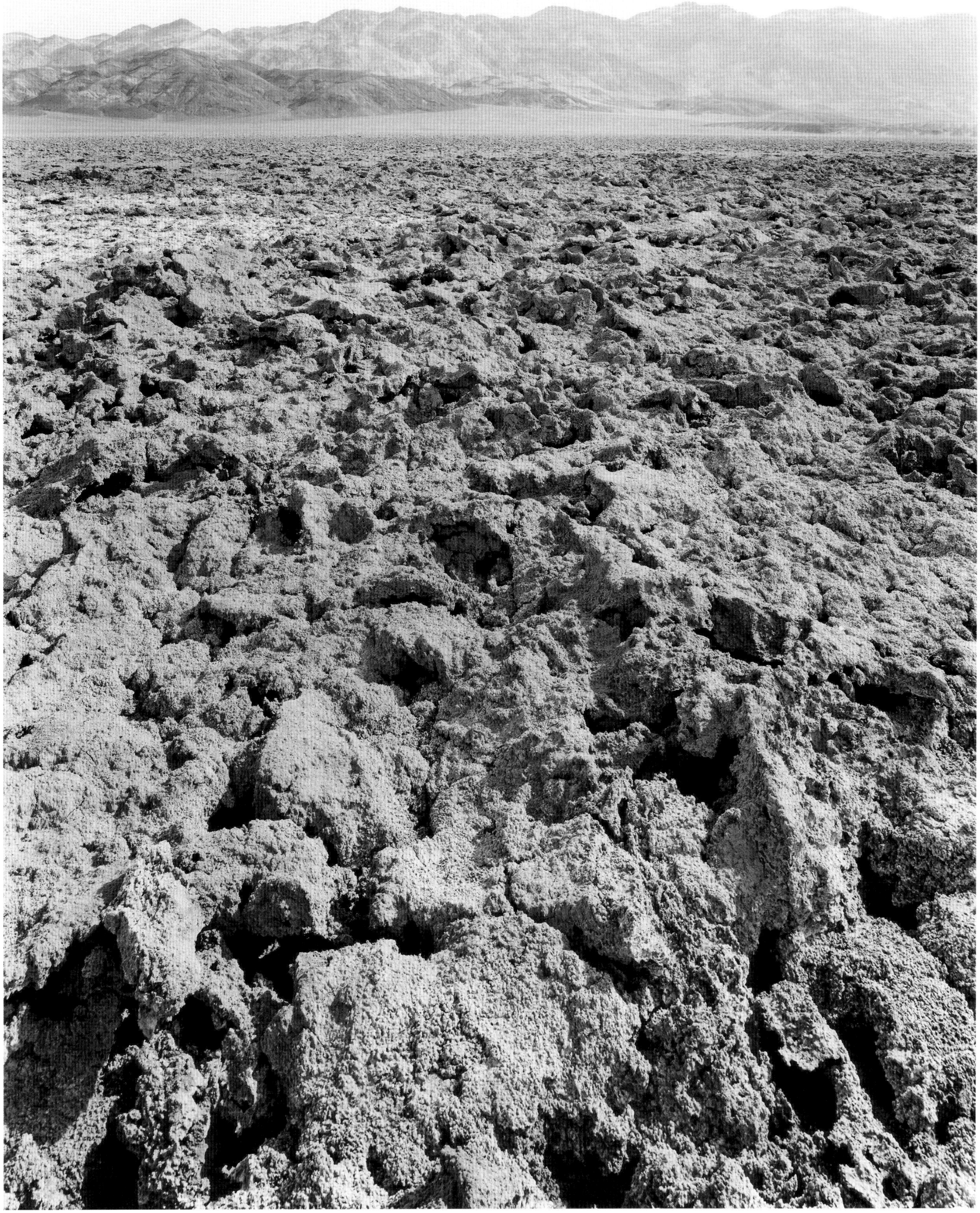

71. Death Valley National Park. Lavafelder am Ubehebe Crater mit Creosote-Büschen.
72. Death Valley National Park. Racetrack Playa, ein abflußloses Becken.

71. Death Valley National Park. Lava fields at the Ubehebe Crater with Creosote shrubs.
72. Death Valley National Park. Racetrack Playa, a basin without outlet.

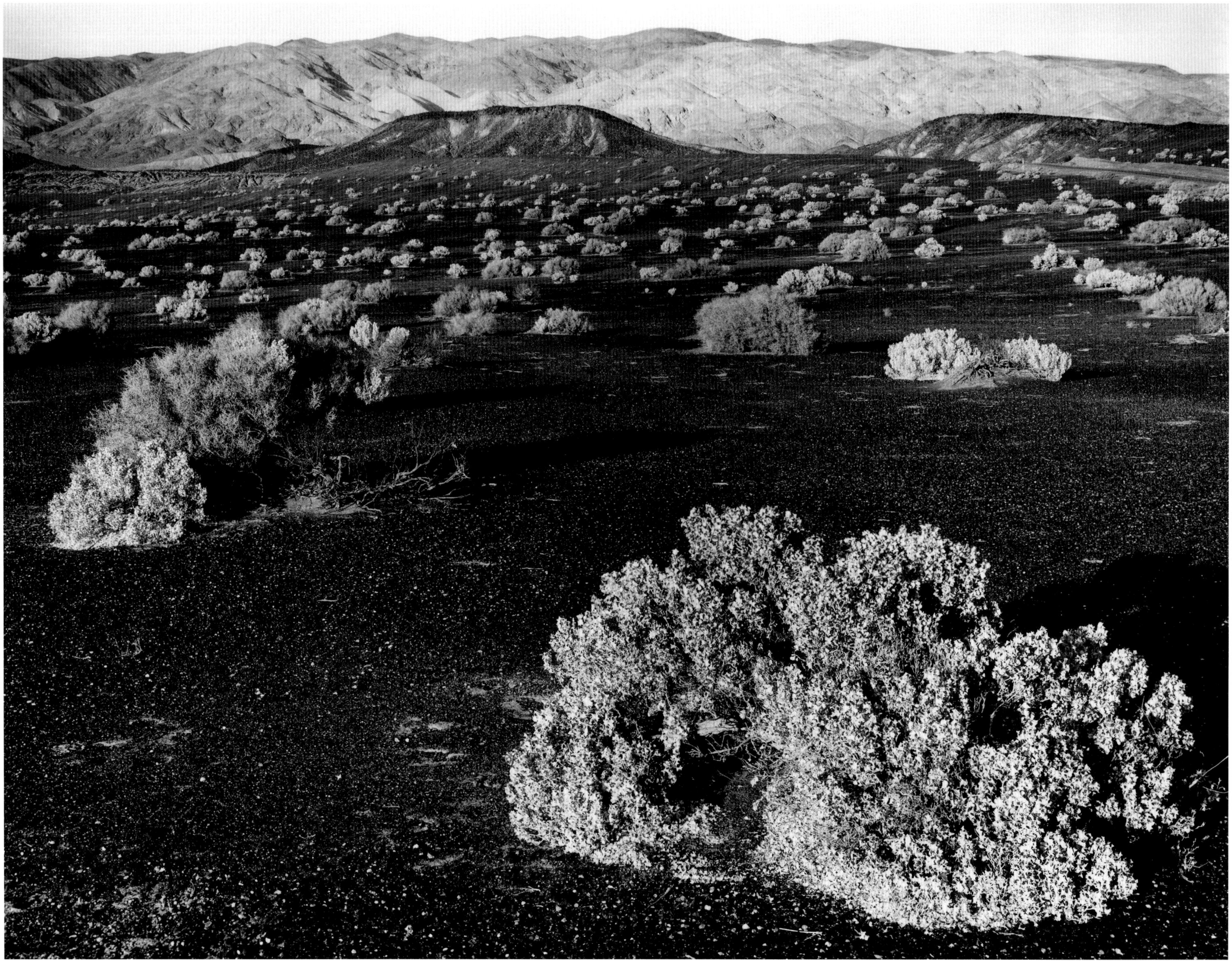

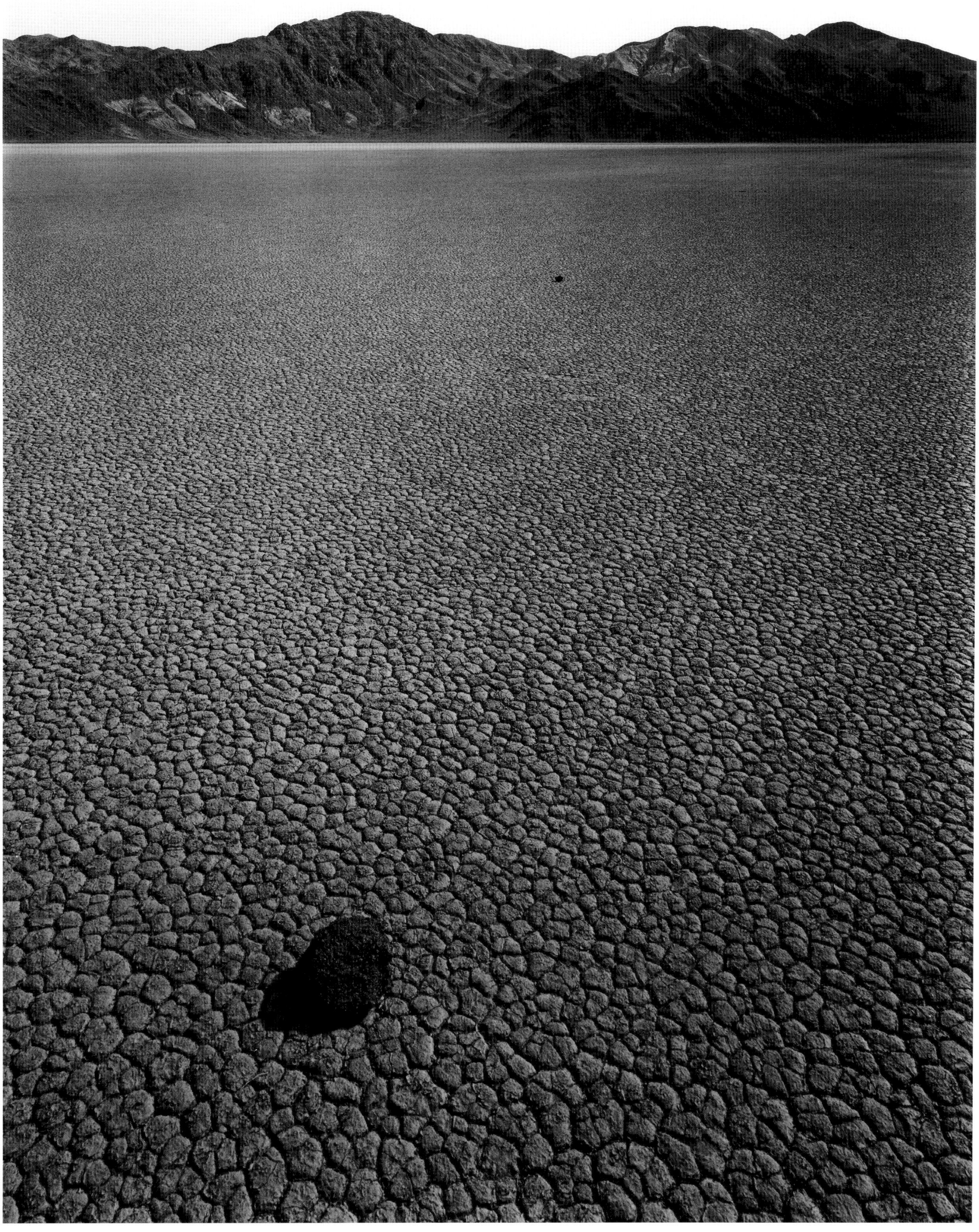

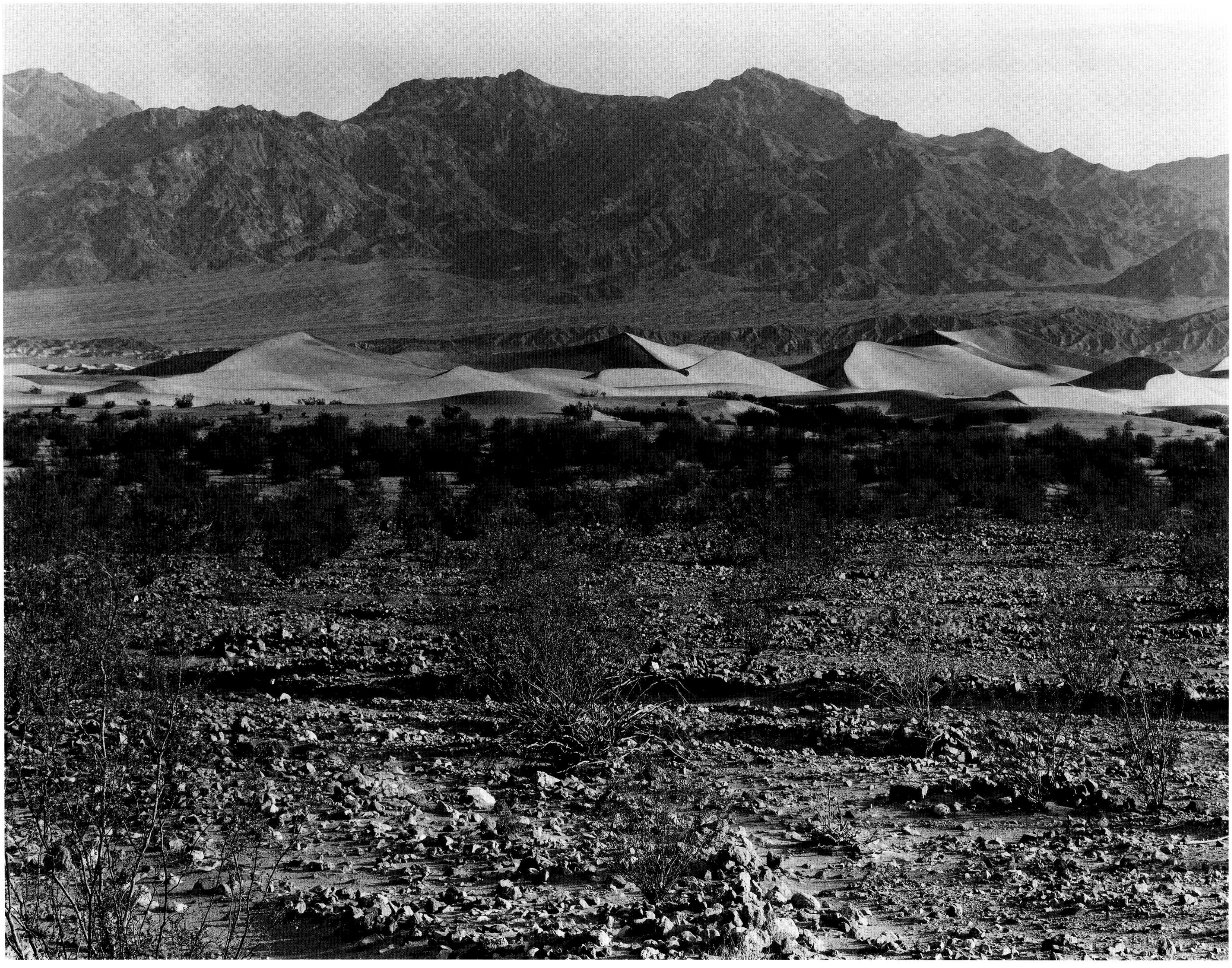

73. Death Valley National Park. Sanddünen, dahinter die Amargosa Range.
74. Death Valley National Park. Grape Vine Mountains zwischen Mud Canyon und Titus Canyon.

73. Death Valley National Park. Sand dunes, behind them the Amargosa Range.
74. Death Valley National Park. Grape Vine Mountains between Mud Canyon and Titus Canyon.

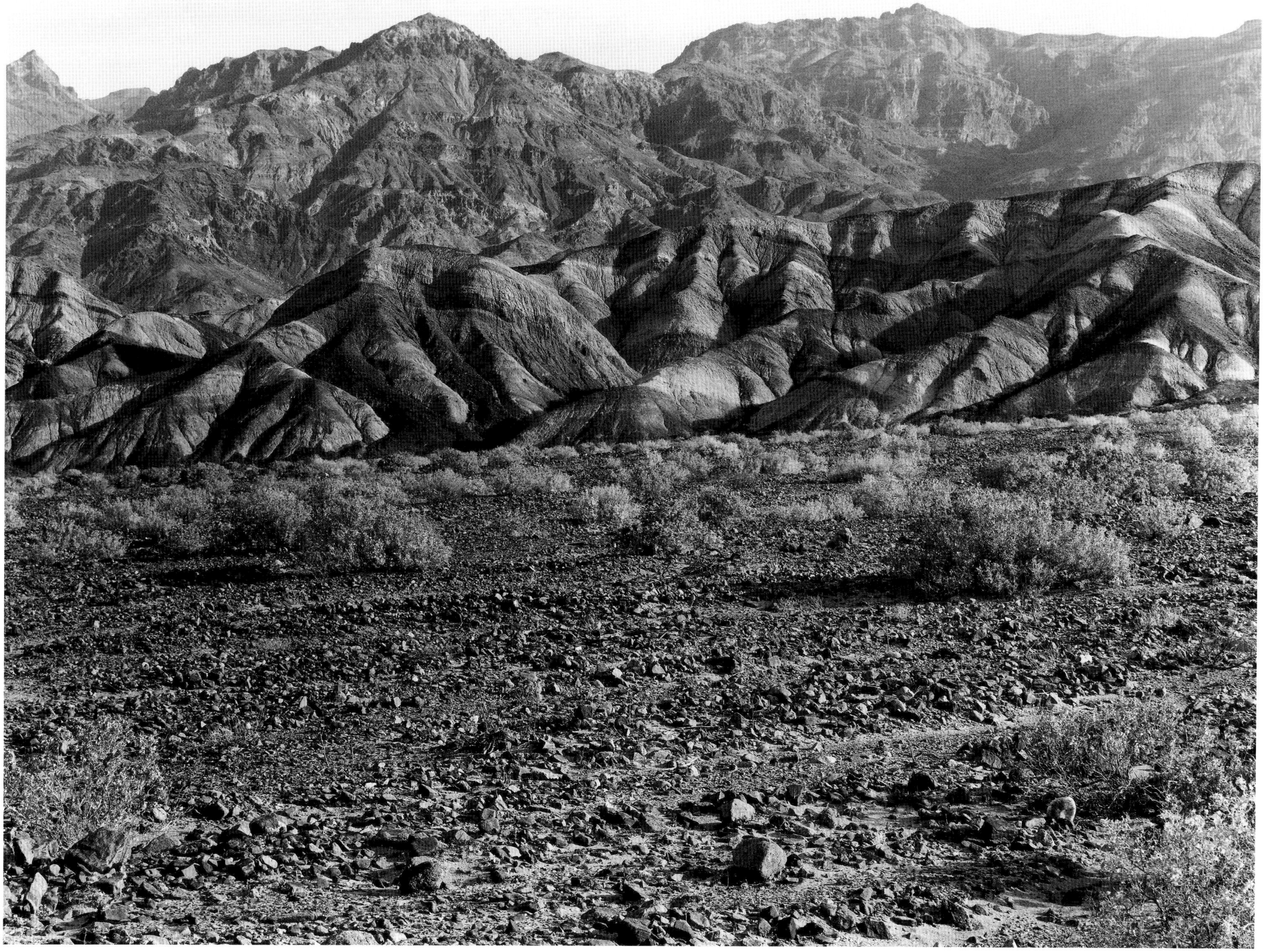

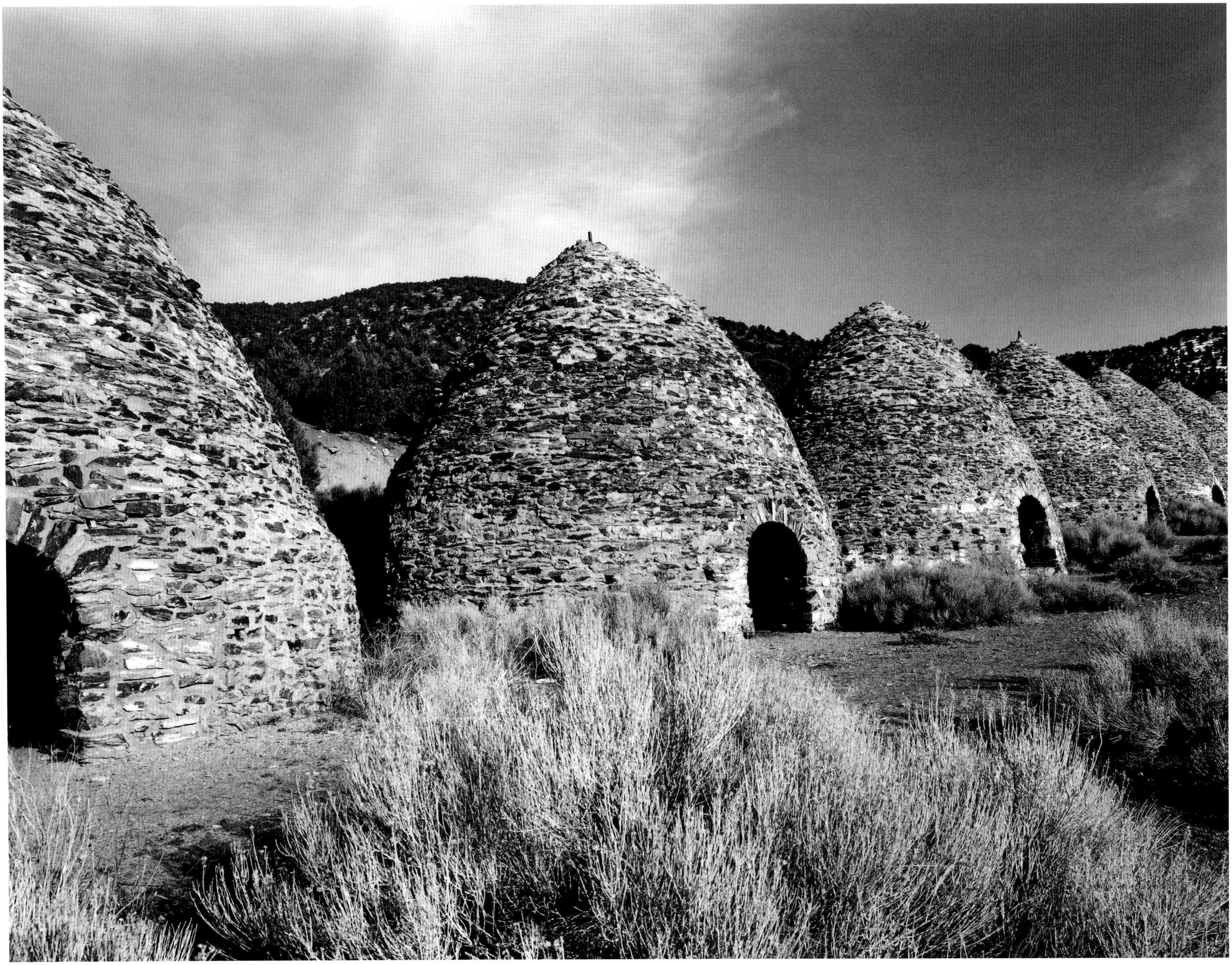

75. Death Valley National Park. Wildrose Charcoal Kilns nördlich des Telescope Peak. Hier wurde ab 1875 Holzkohle für die Minenbetriebe der Gegend gebrannt.
76. Rhyolite. Ruine des Bankgebäudes von 1908 in der am Ostrand des Death Valley gelegenen, heute verlassenen Goldgräberstadt.

75. Death Valley National Park. Wildrose Charcoal Kilns north of Telescope Peak. Here after 1875 charcoal was burned for he mining companies in the area.
76. Rhyolite. Ruin of the 1908 bank building in the mining town at the north edge of Death Valley, abandoned today.

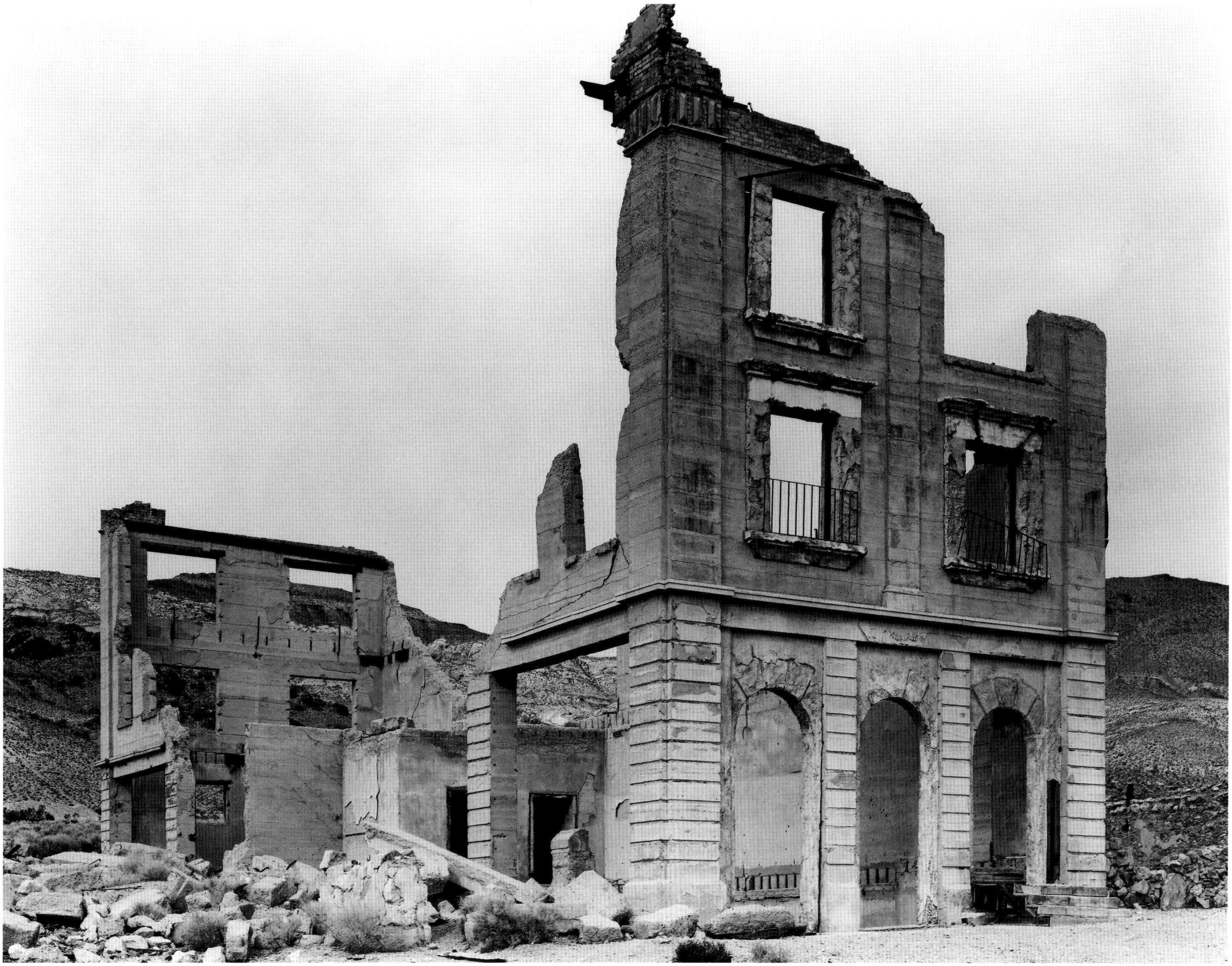

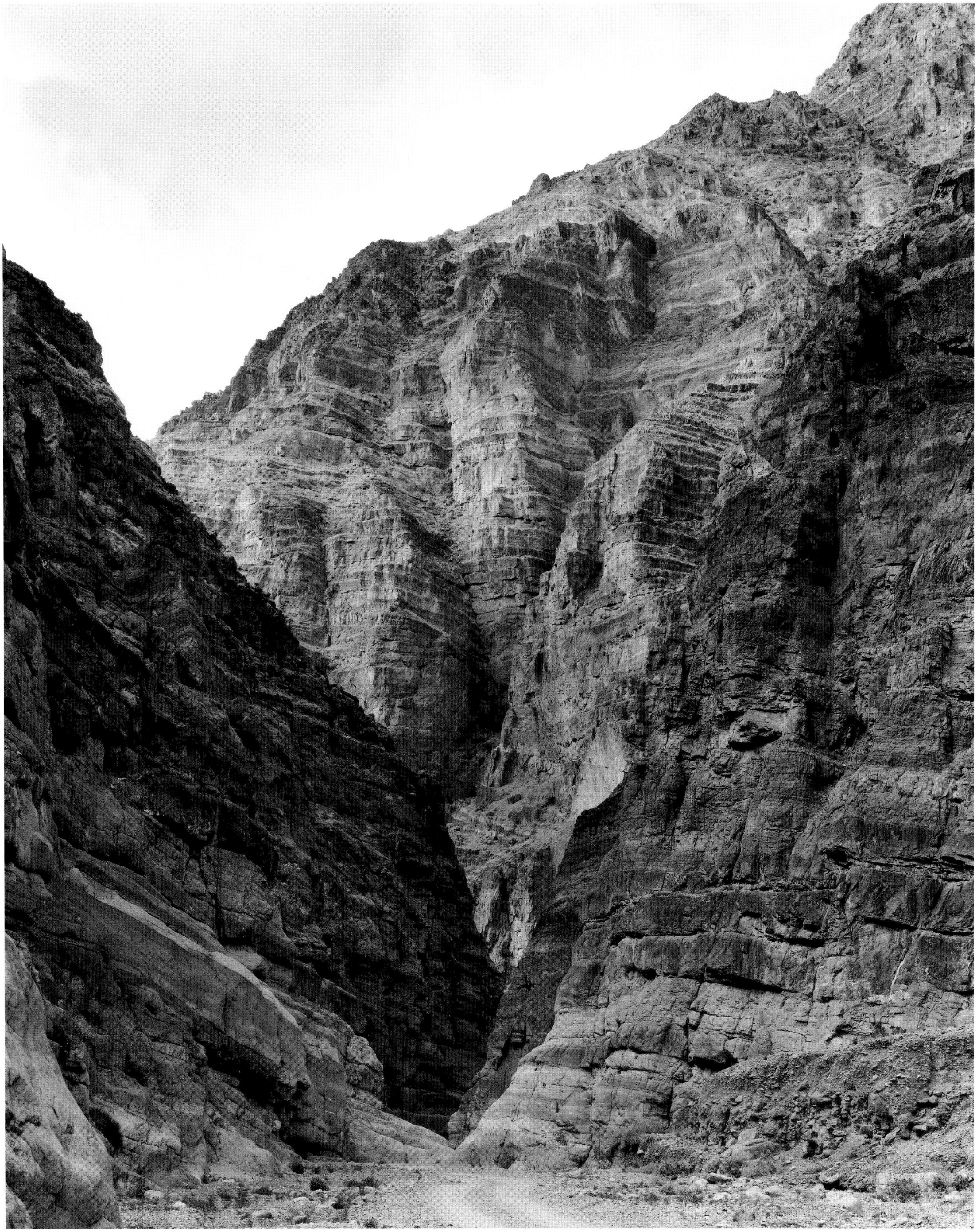

77. Death Valley National Park. Titus Canyon in den Grapevine Mountains.
78. Bizarrer Baum am Ostende des Isabella Lake.

S. 90/91
79. Grand Canyon National Park. Yava Point.

77. Death Valley National Park. Titus Canyon in the Grapevine Mountains.
78. Bizarre tree at the east end of Isabella Lake.

p. 90/91
79. Grand Canyon National Park. Yava Point.

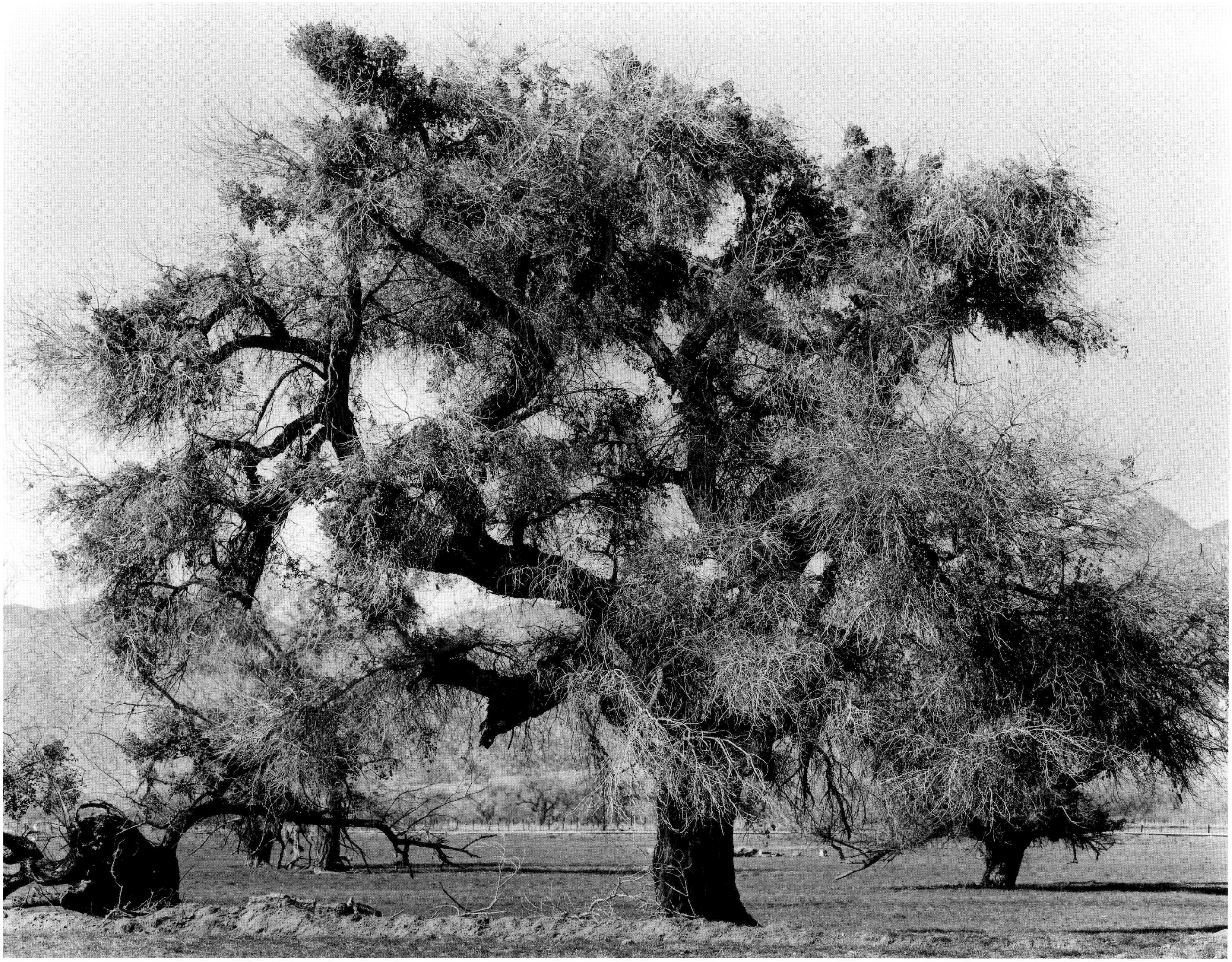

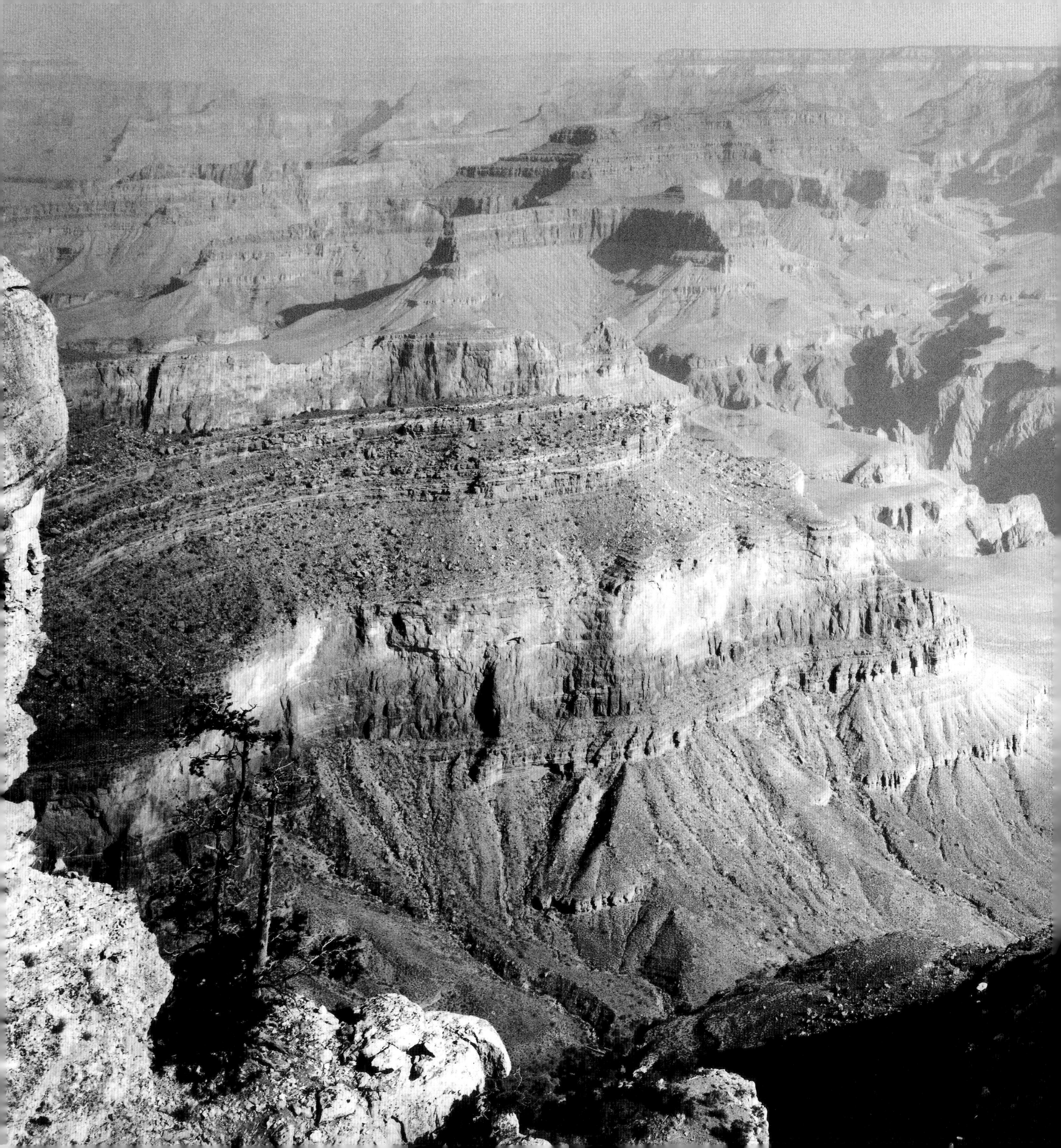

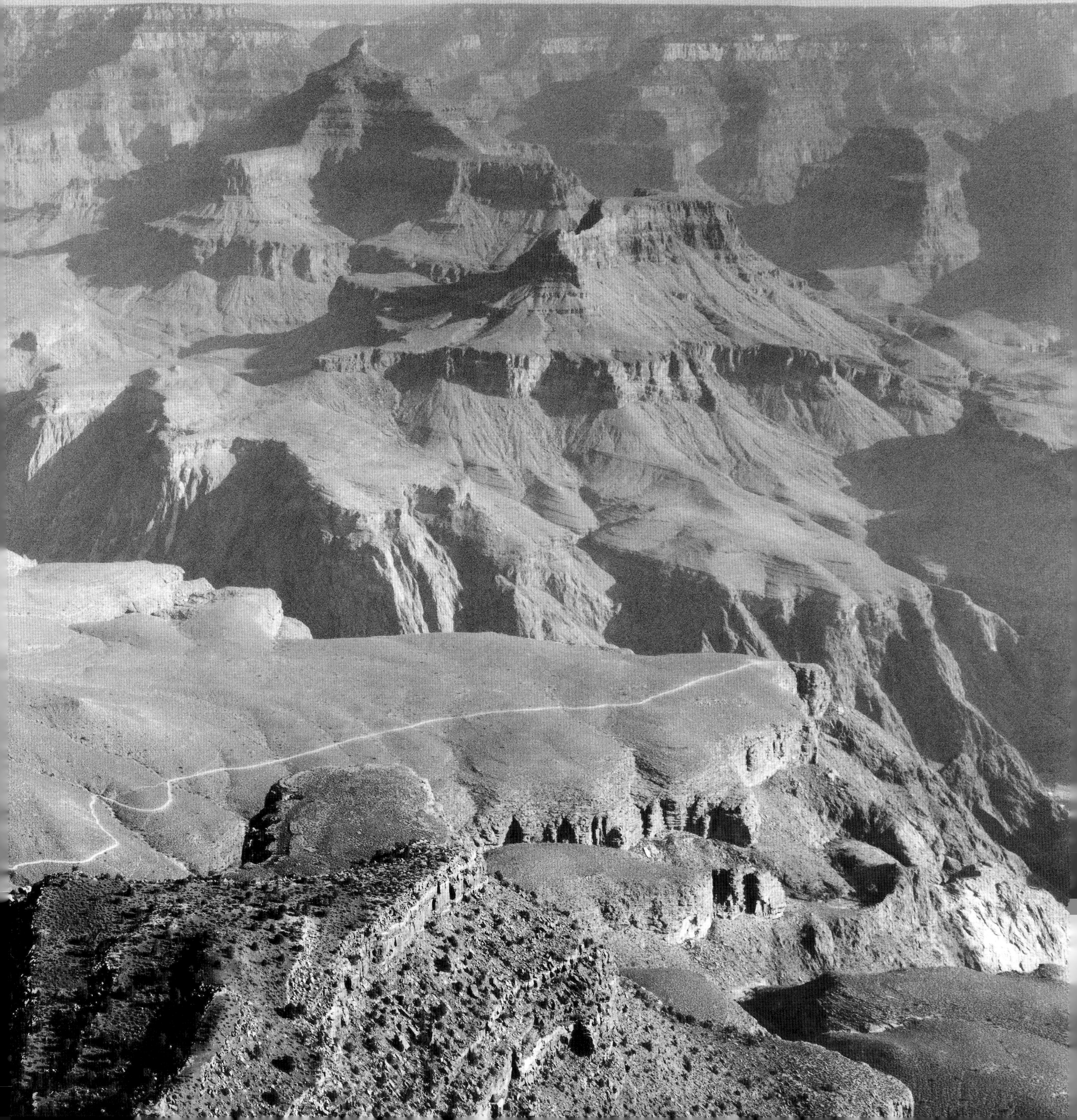

80, 81. Grand Canyon National Park. Desert View.

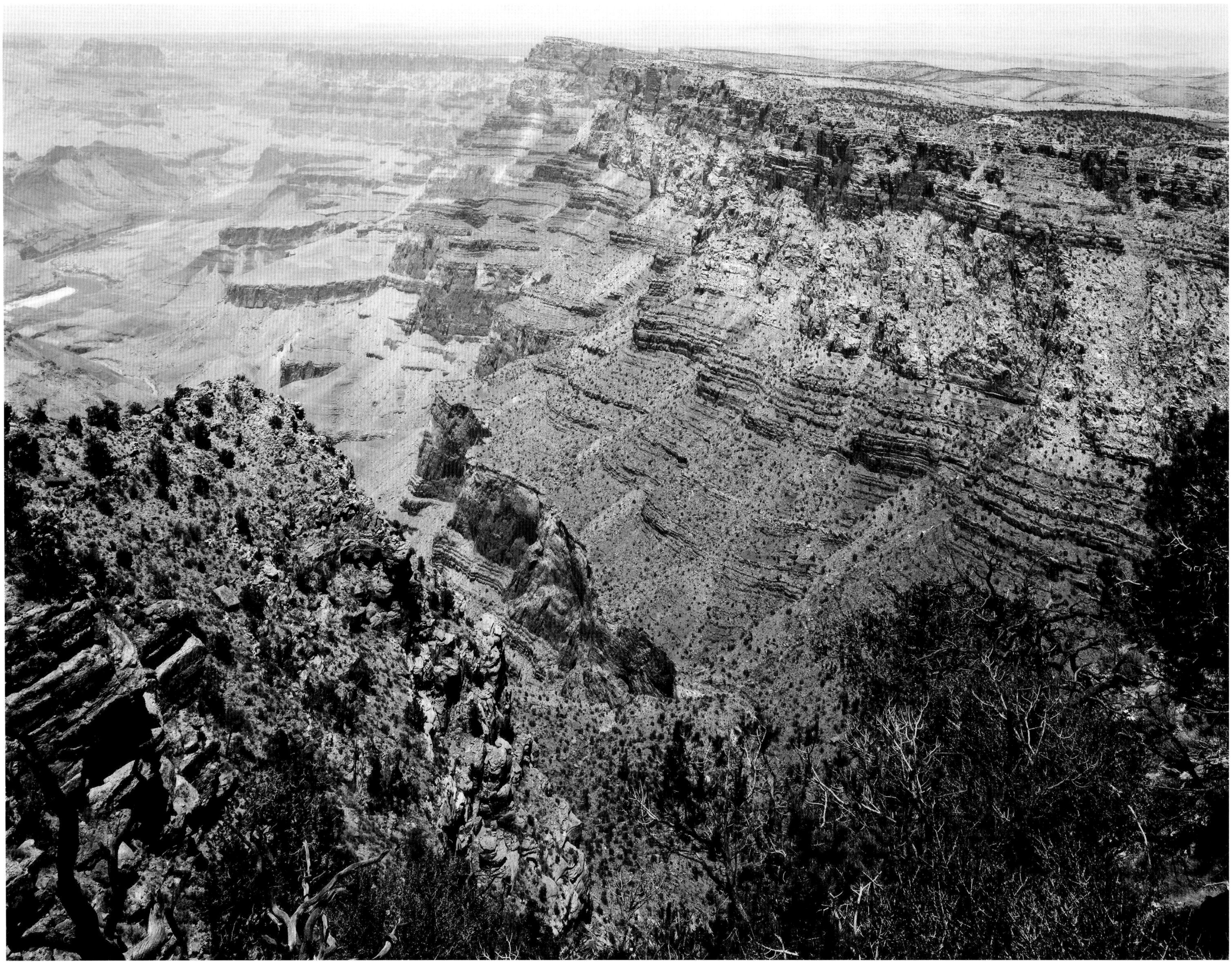

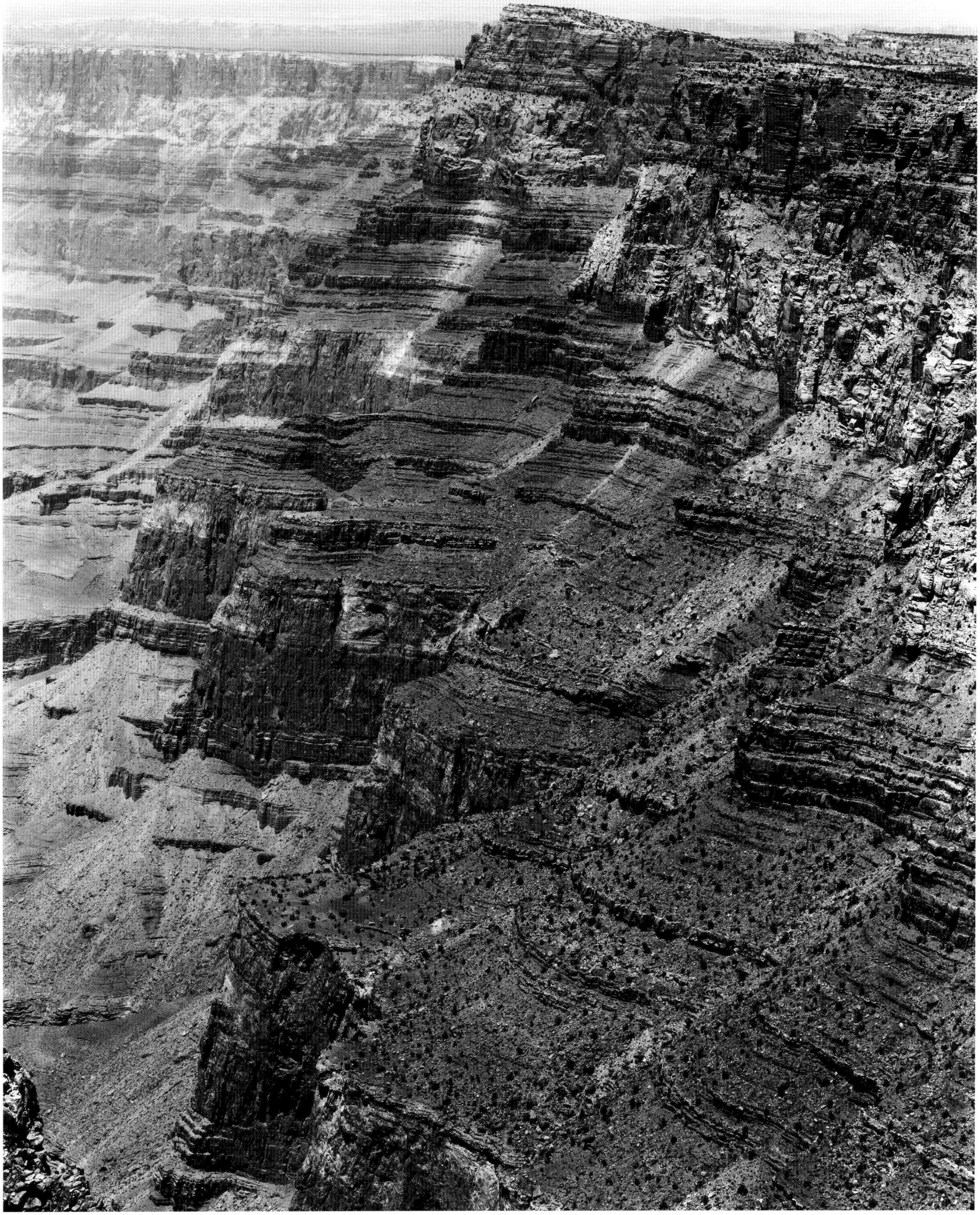

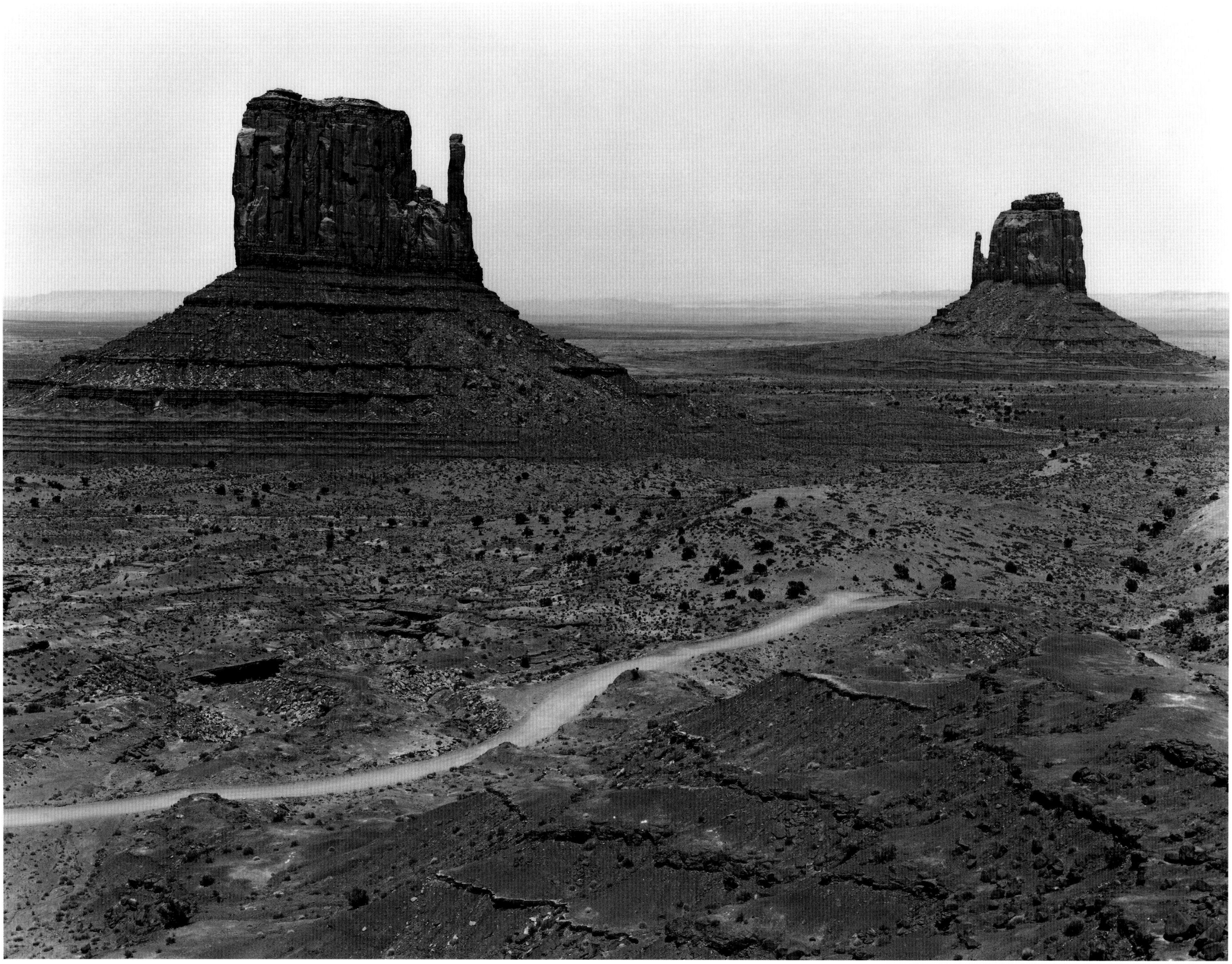

82. Monument Valley Navajo Tribal Park. West und East Mitten Butte.
83. Monument Valley Navajo Tribal Park. West Mitten Butte.

82. Monument Valley Navajo Tribal Park. West and East Mitten Butte.
83. Monument Valley Navajo Tribal Park. West Mitten Butte.

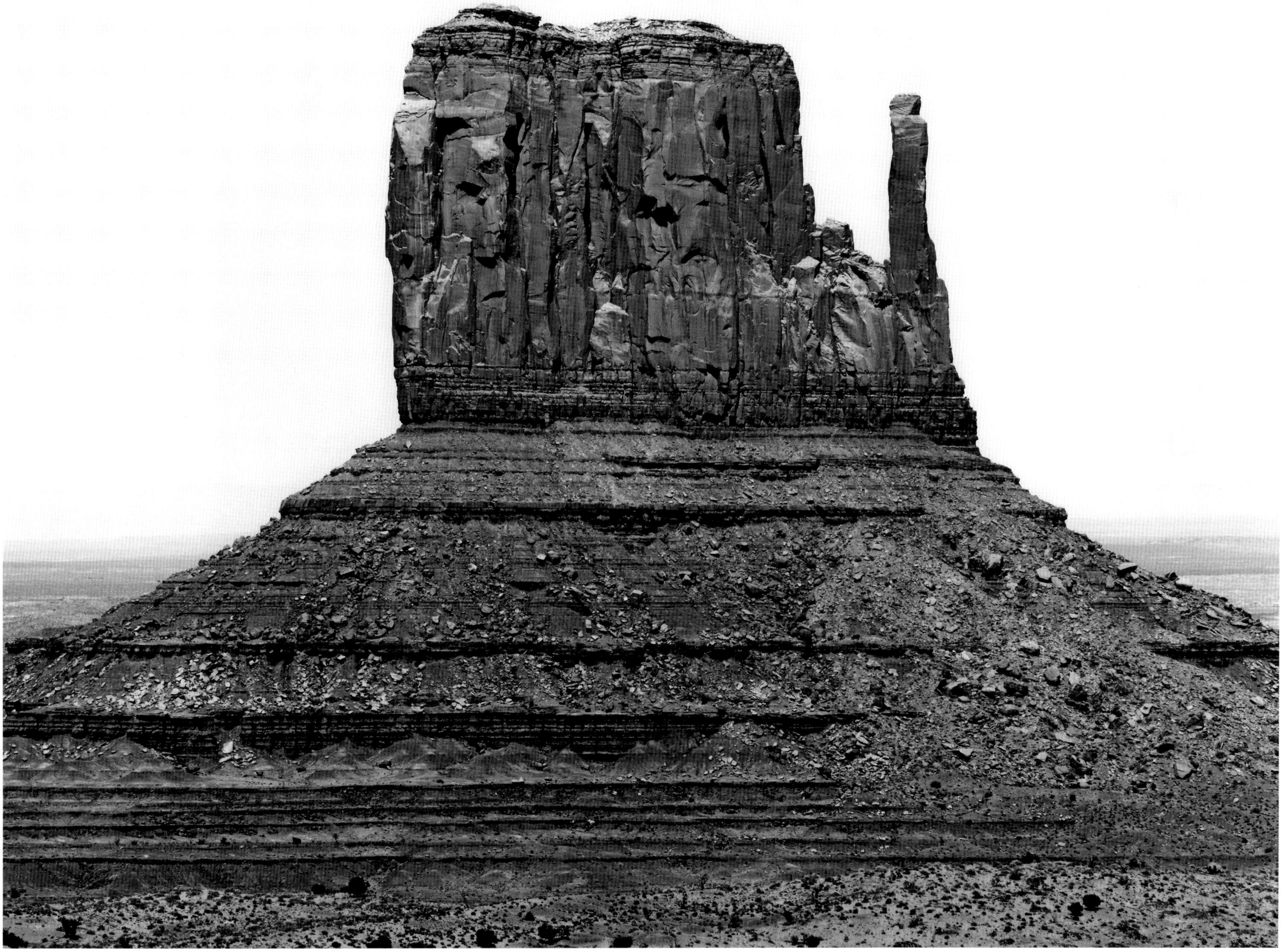

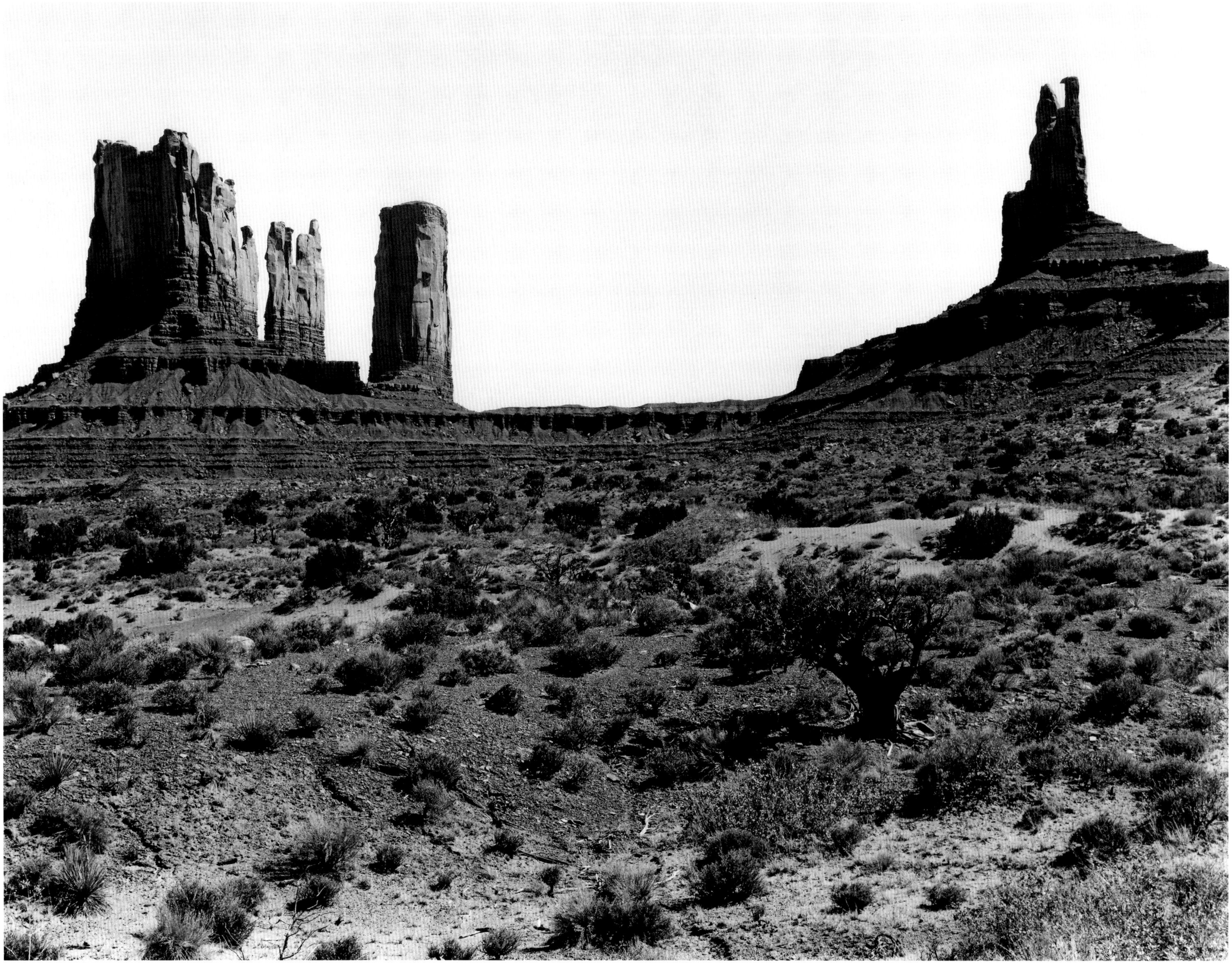

84. Monument Valley Navajo Tribal Park. Buttes.
85. Mexican Hat.

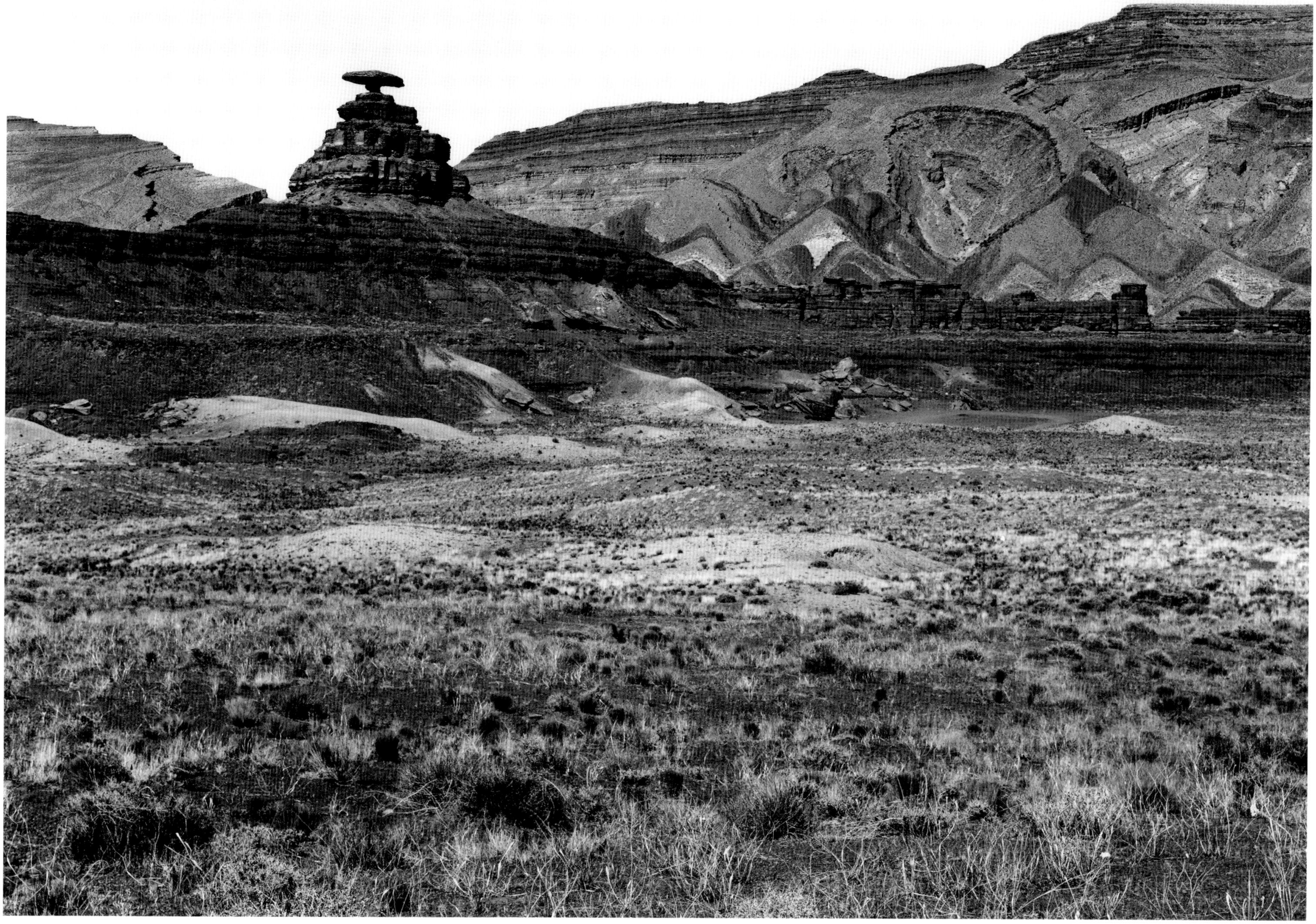

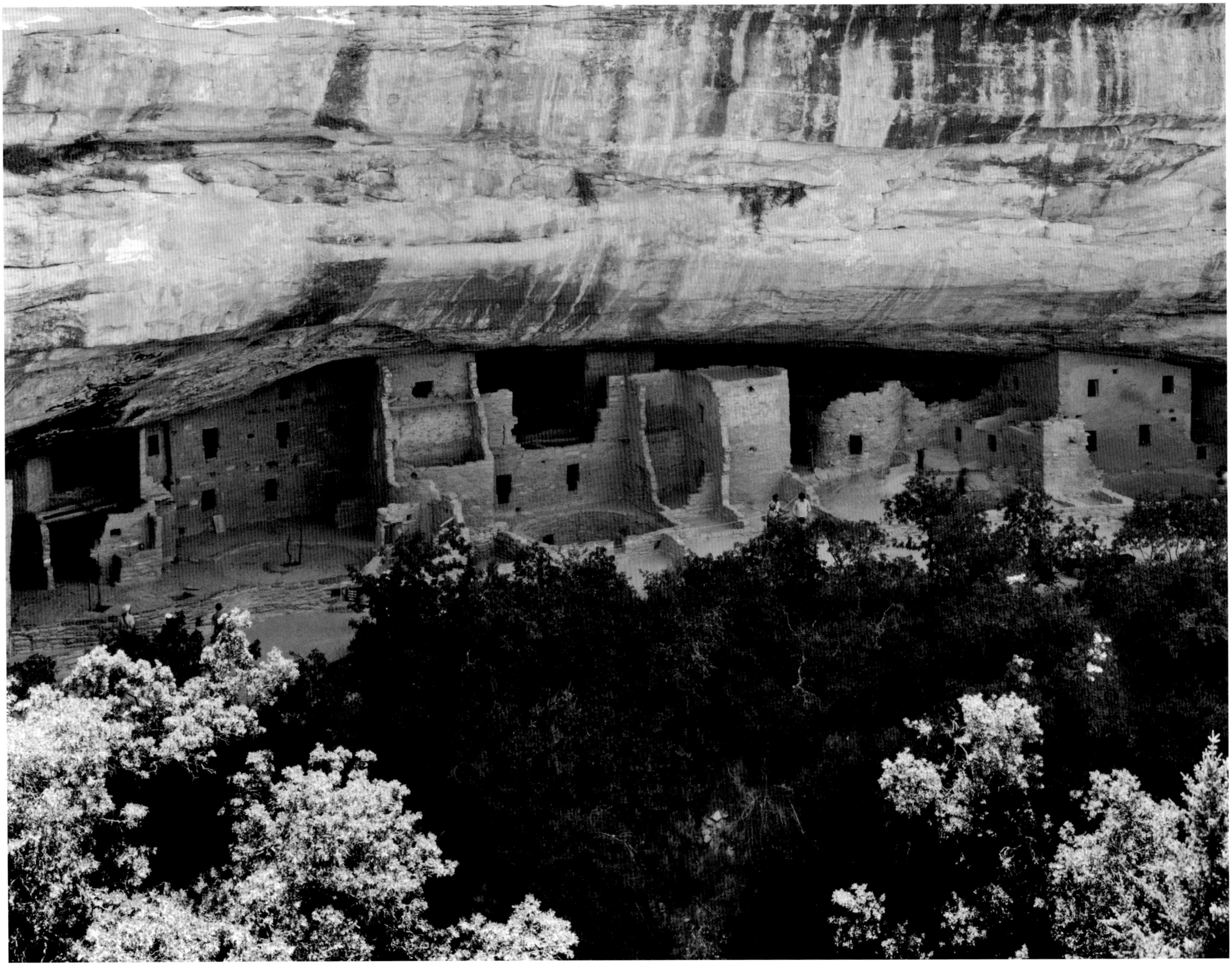

86. Mesa Verde National Park. Prähistorische Indianersiedlung.
87. Mesa Verde National Park. Cliff Palace, prähistorische Indianersiedlung.

S. 100/101
88. Bryce Canyon National Park. Erosionsformen in den Kalken der Charon-Formation.

86. Mesa Verde National Park. Prehistoric settlement of Indians.
87. Mesa Verde National Park. Cliff Palace, prehistoric Indian settlement.

p. 100/101
88. Bryce Canyon National Park. Eroded land forms in the limestones of the Charon formation.

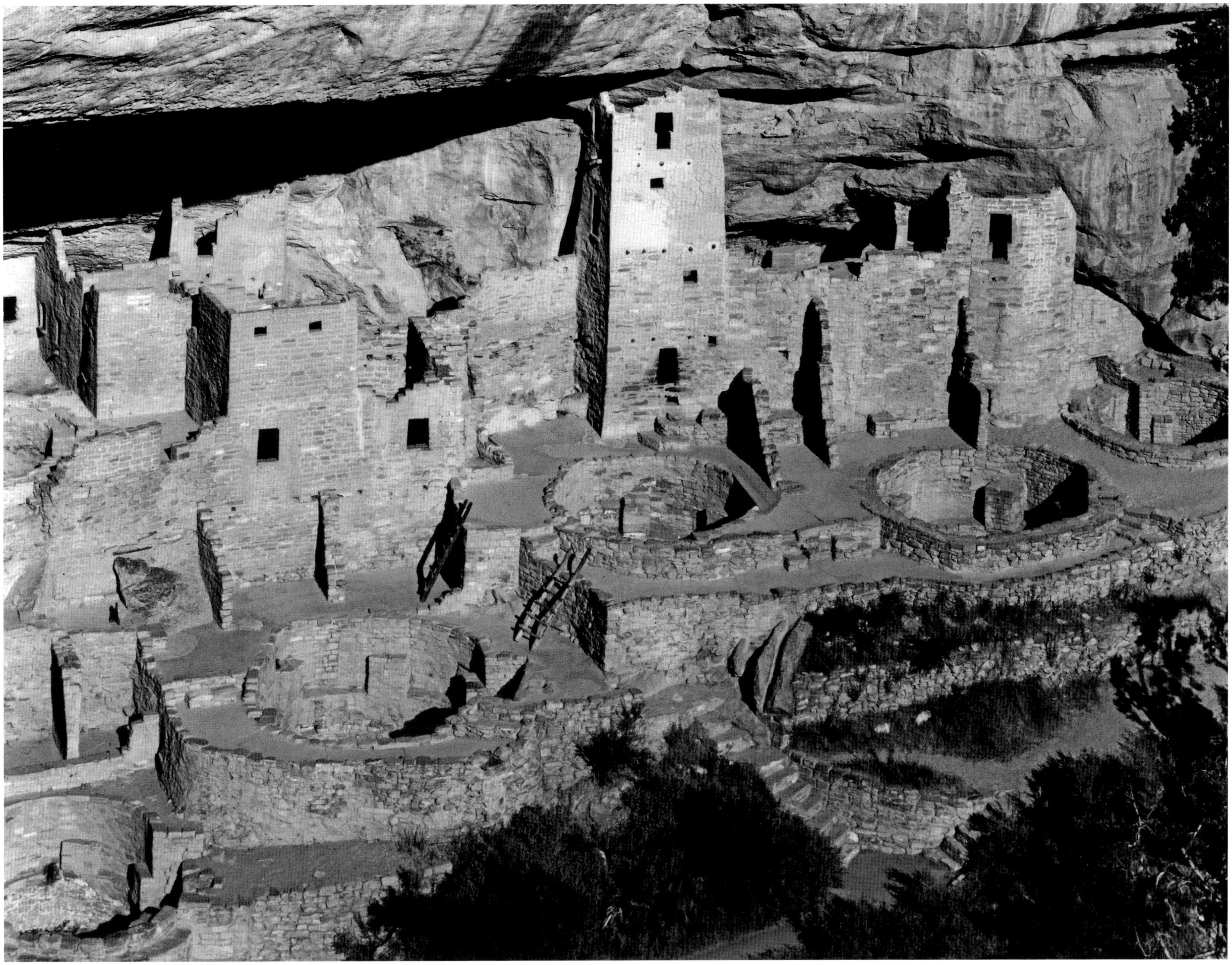

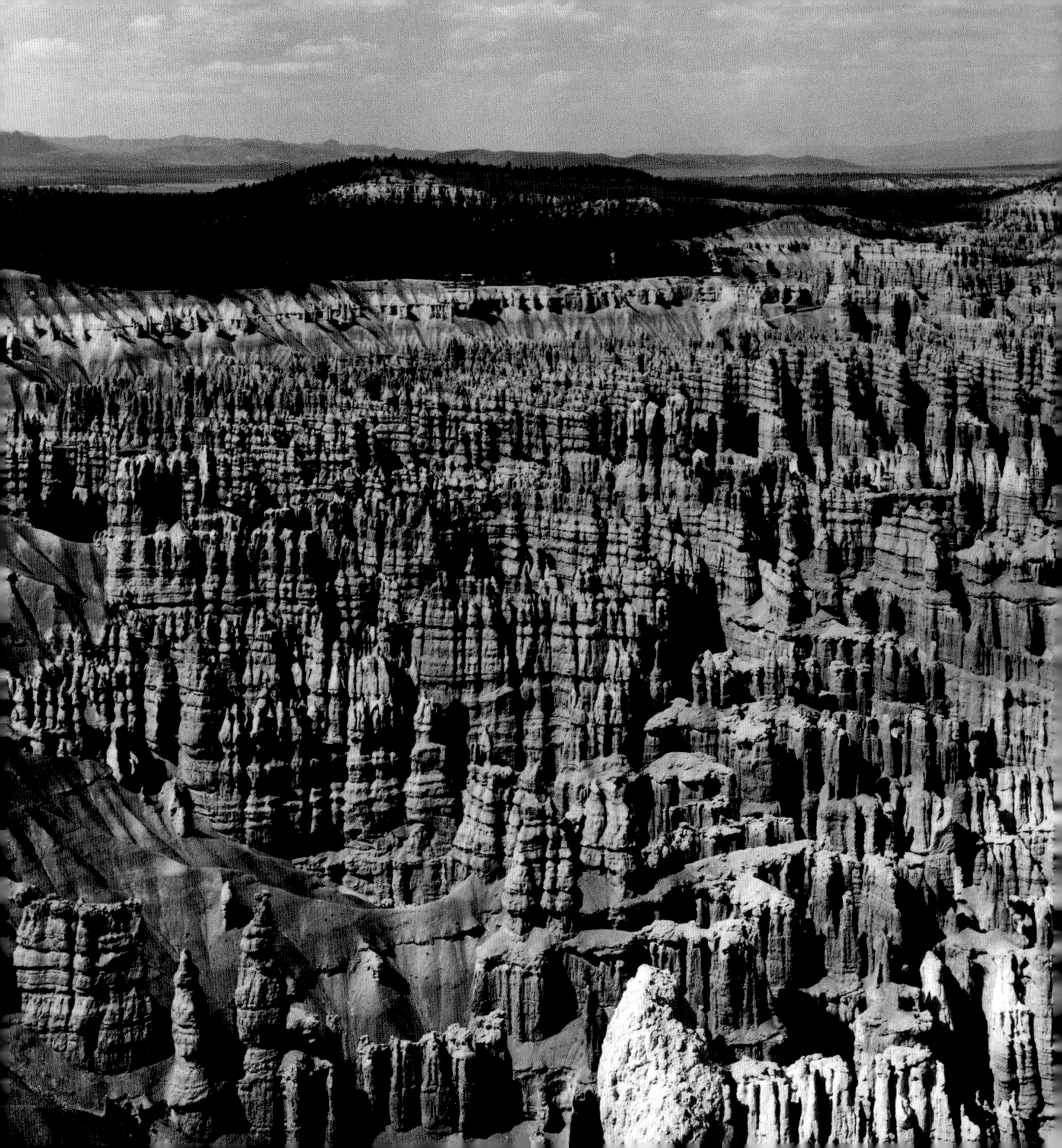

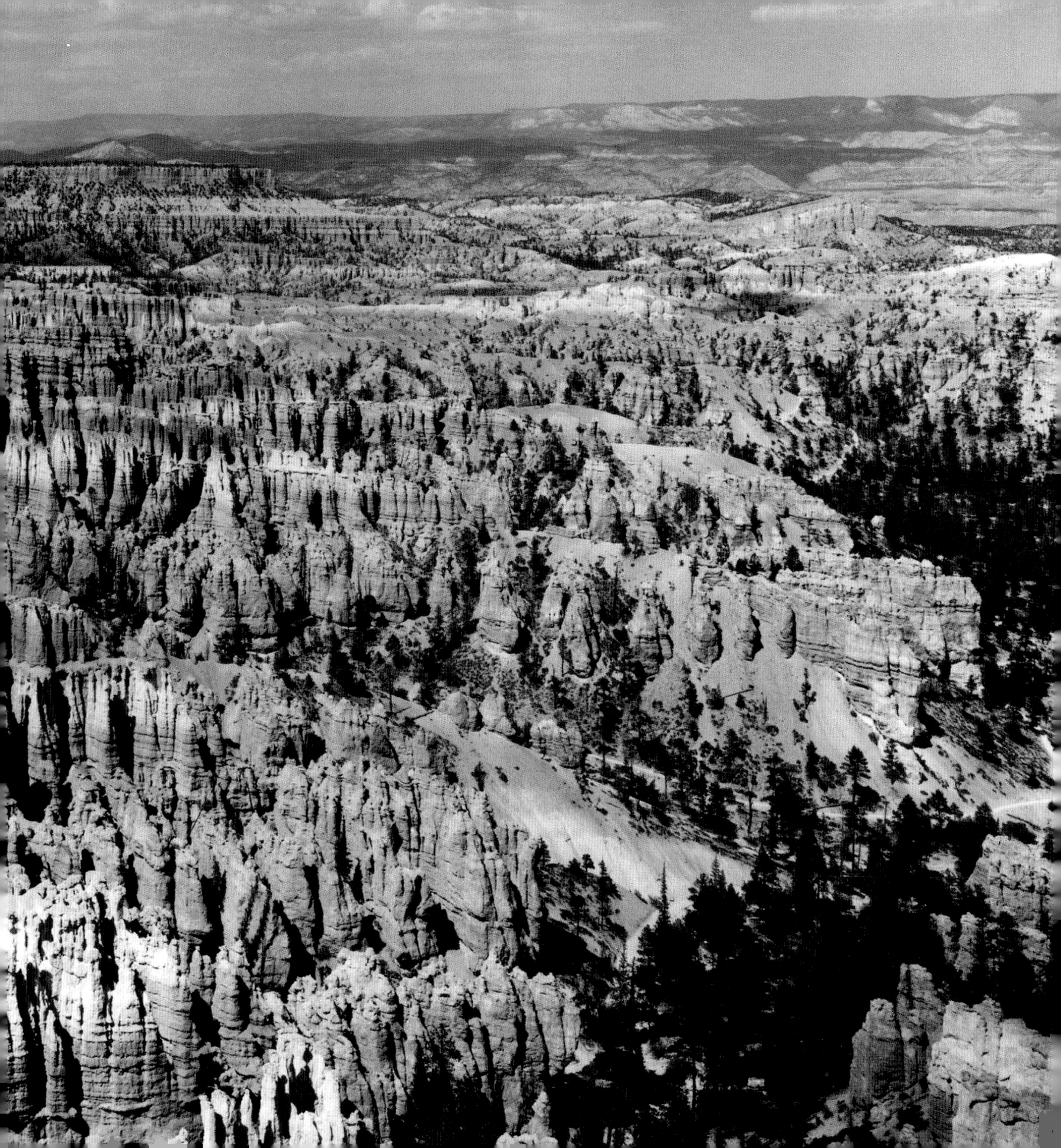

89. Craters of the Moon National Monument. Schweißschlackenkegel.
90. Craters of the Moon National Monument. Lava-Strom.

89. Craters of the Moon National Monument. Spatter cones.
90. Craters of the Moon National Monument. Lava flow.

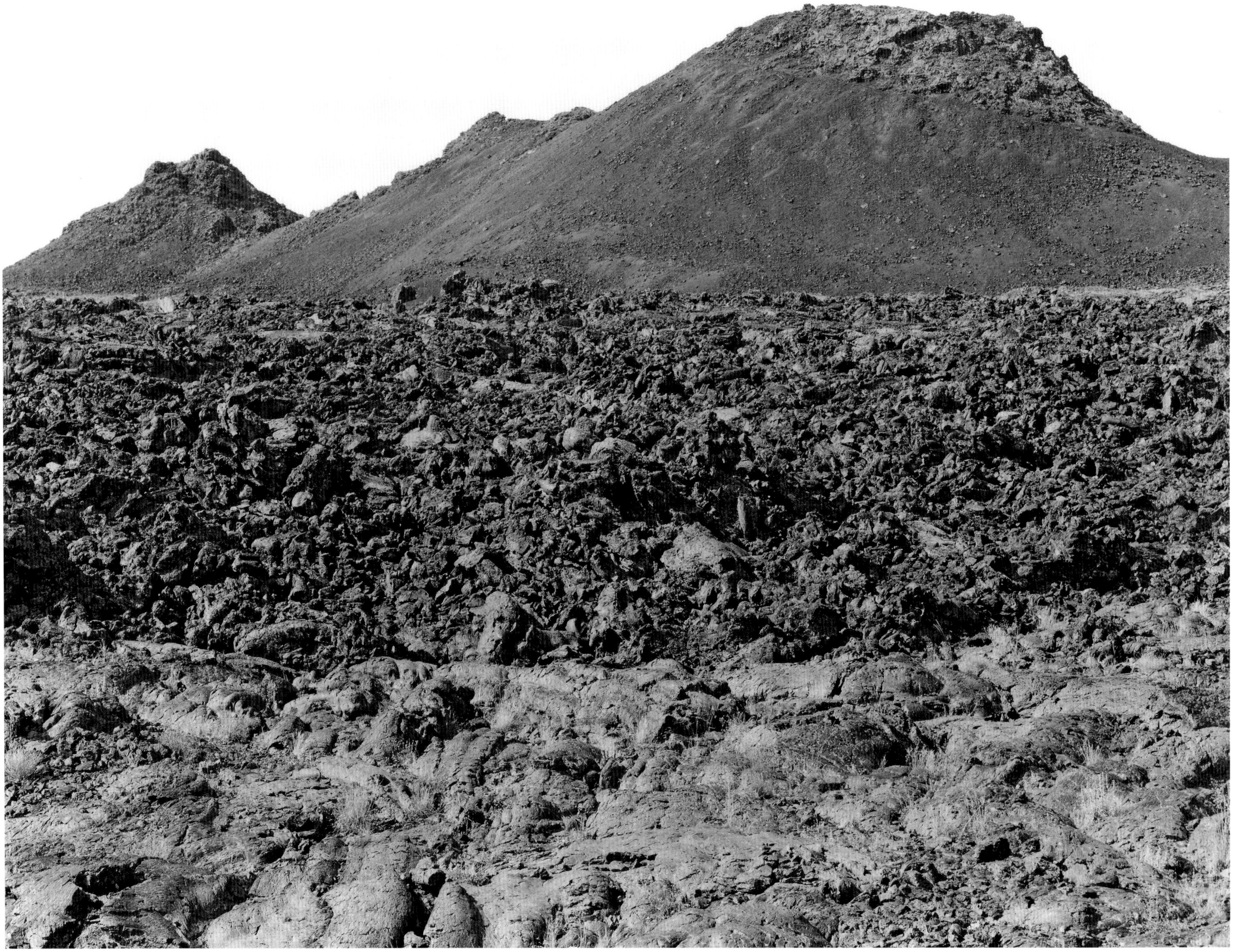

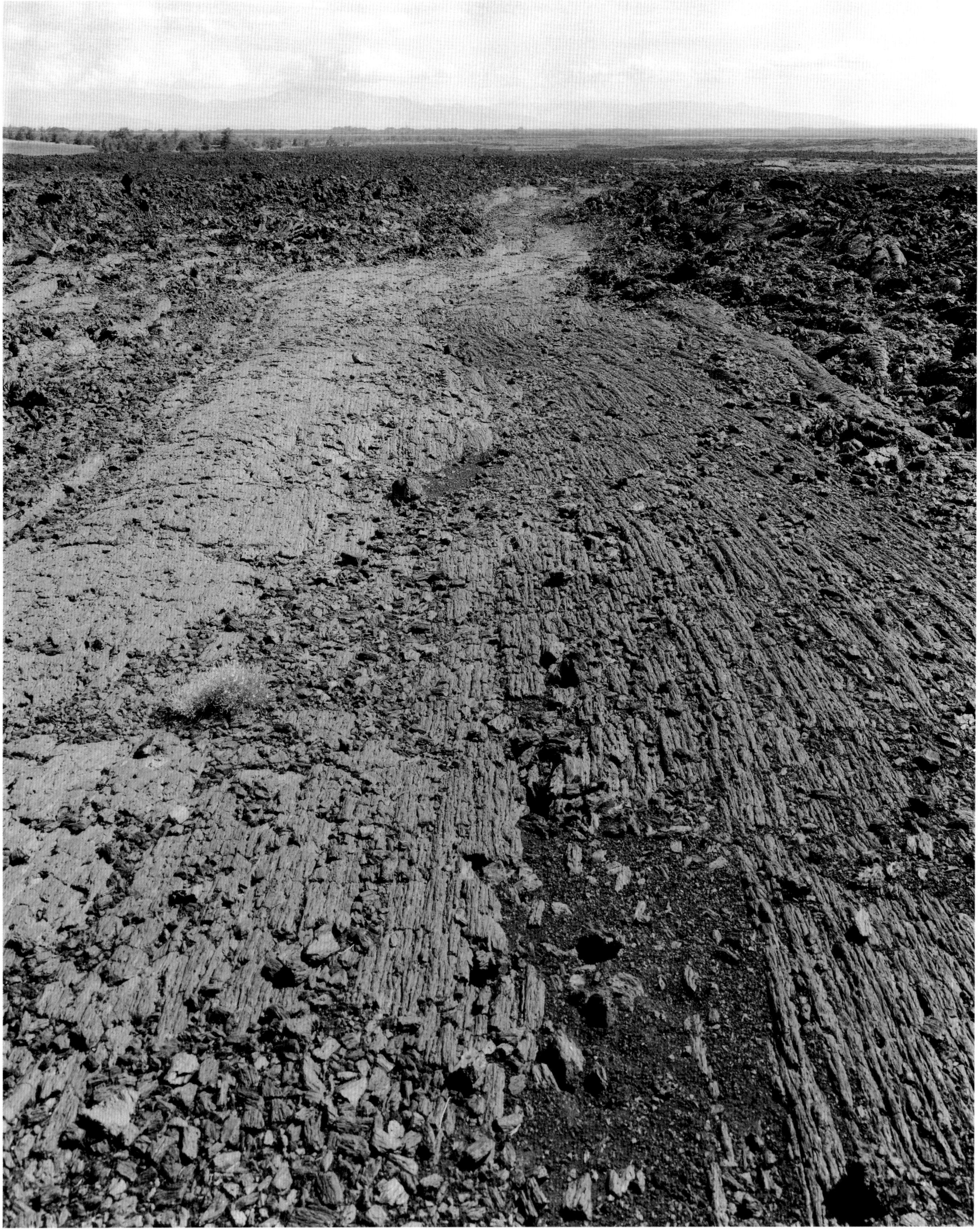

91. Yellowstone National Park. Mammoth Hot Springs. White Elephant Back Terrace.
92. Yellowstone National Park. Lower Fall des Yellowstone River (etwa 100 m hoch).

91. Yellowstone National Park. Mammoth Hot Springs. White Elephant Back Terrace.
92. Yellowstone National Park. Lower Fall of the Yellowstone River (approx. 100 m high).

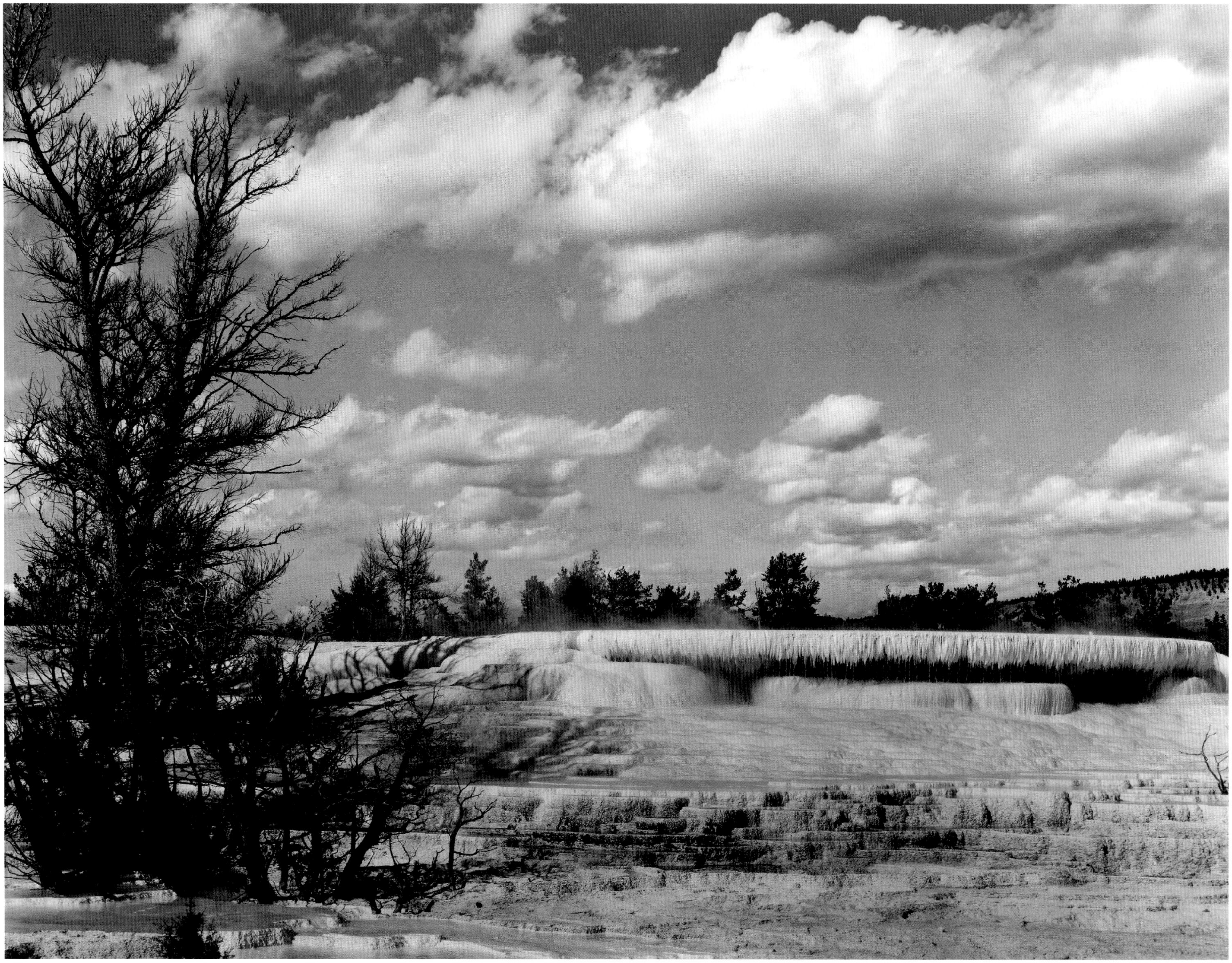

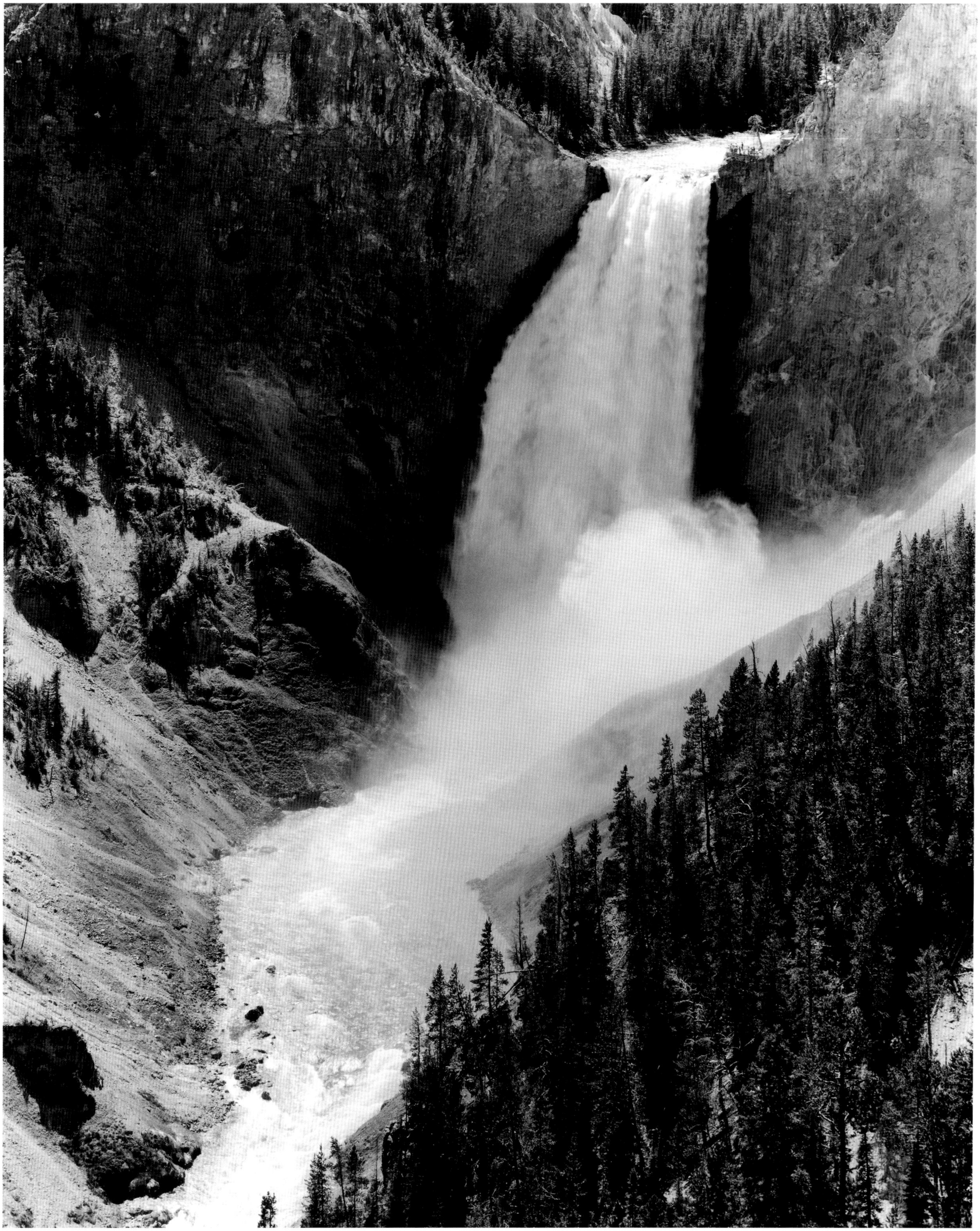

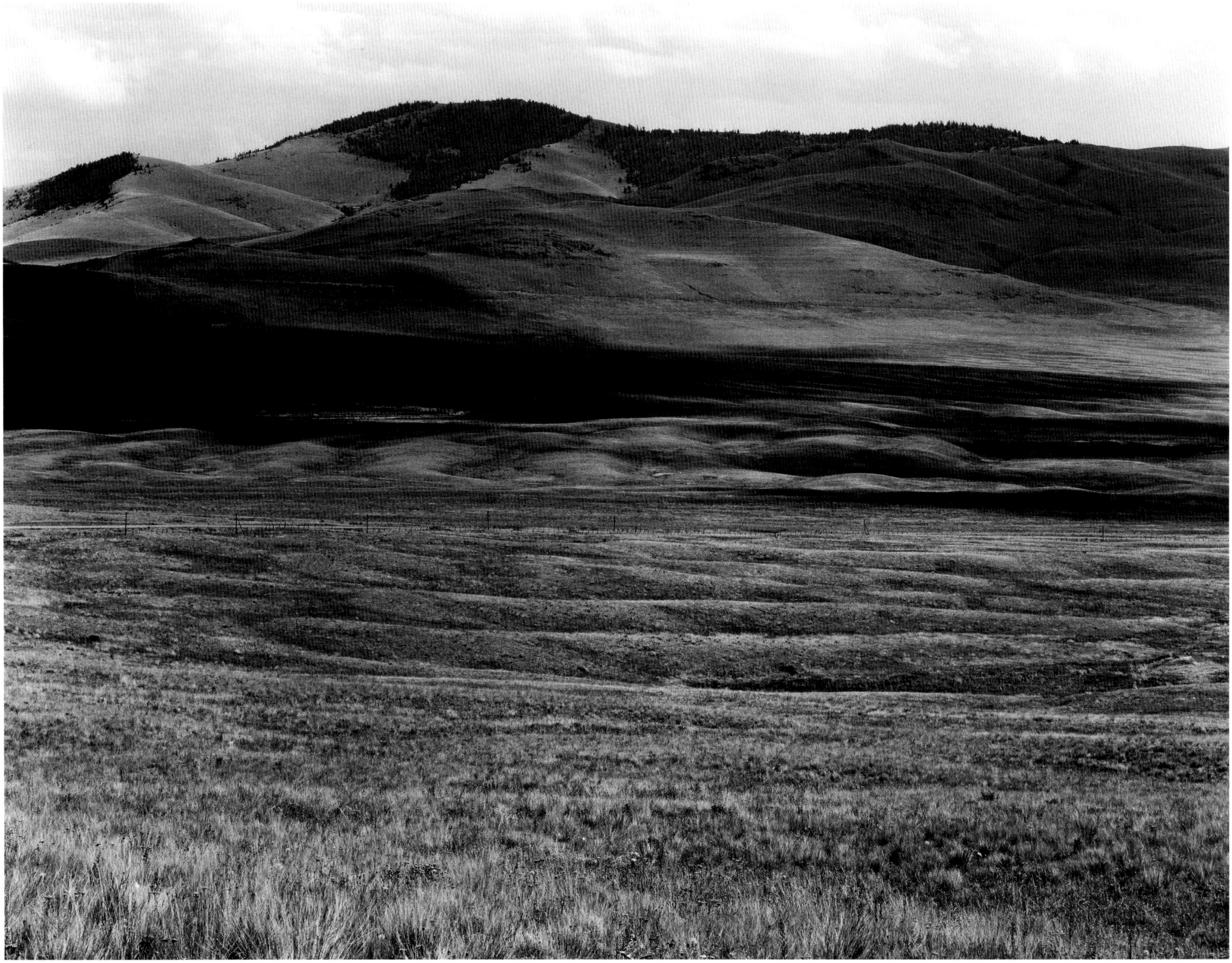

93. Markle Pass bei Camas Hot Springs nördlich von Perma, Montana.
94. Alte Silbermine bei Prichard nördlich von Wallace, Idaho.

93. Markle Pass near Camas Hot Springs north of Perma, Montana.
94. Old silver mine near Prichard north of Wallace, Idaho.

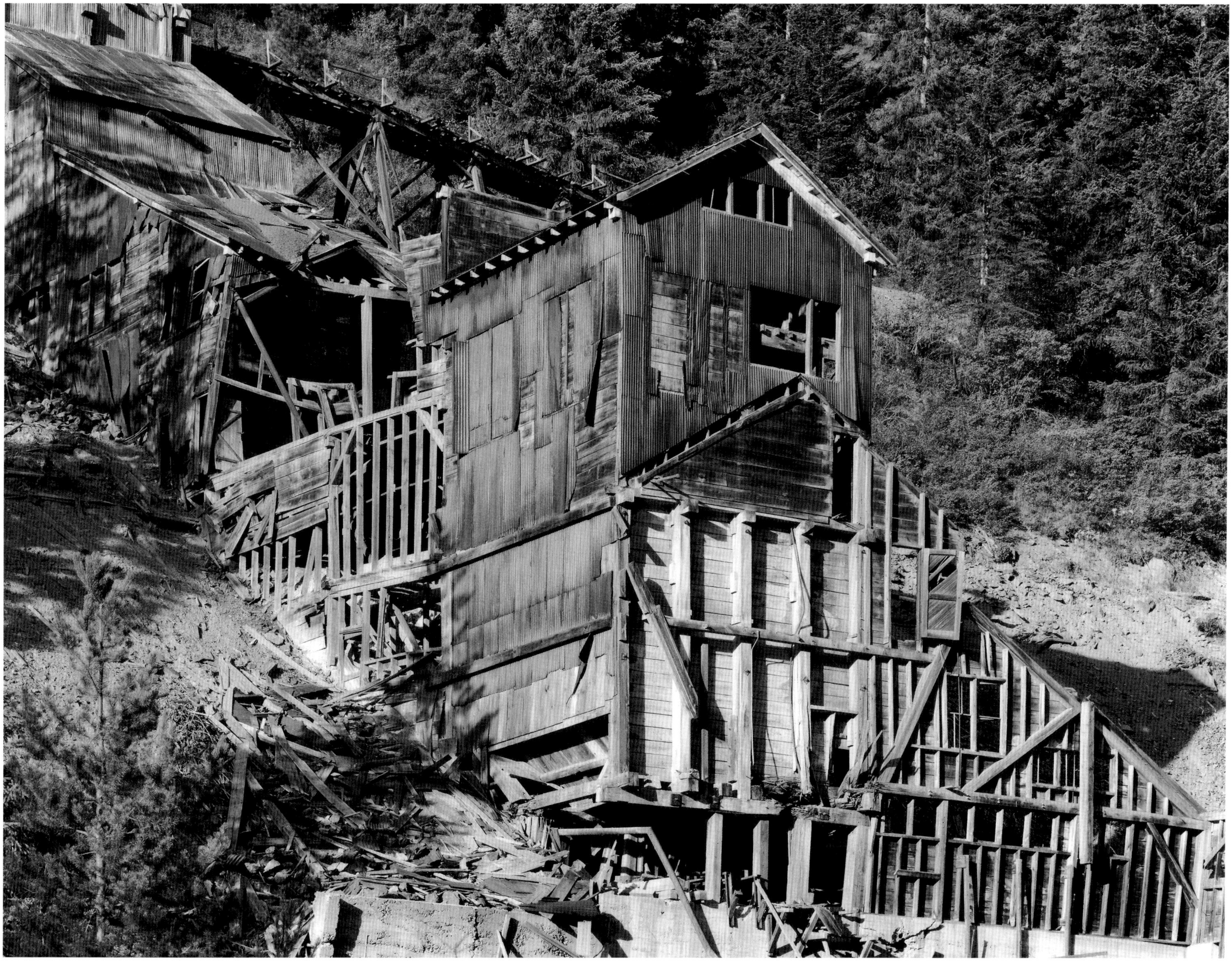

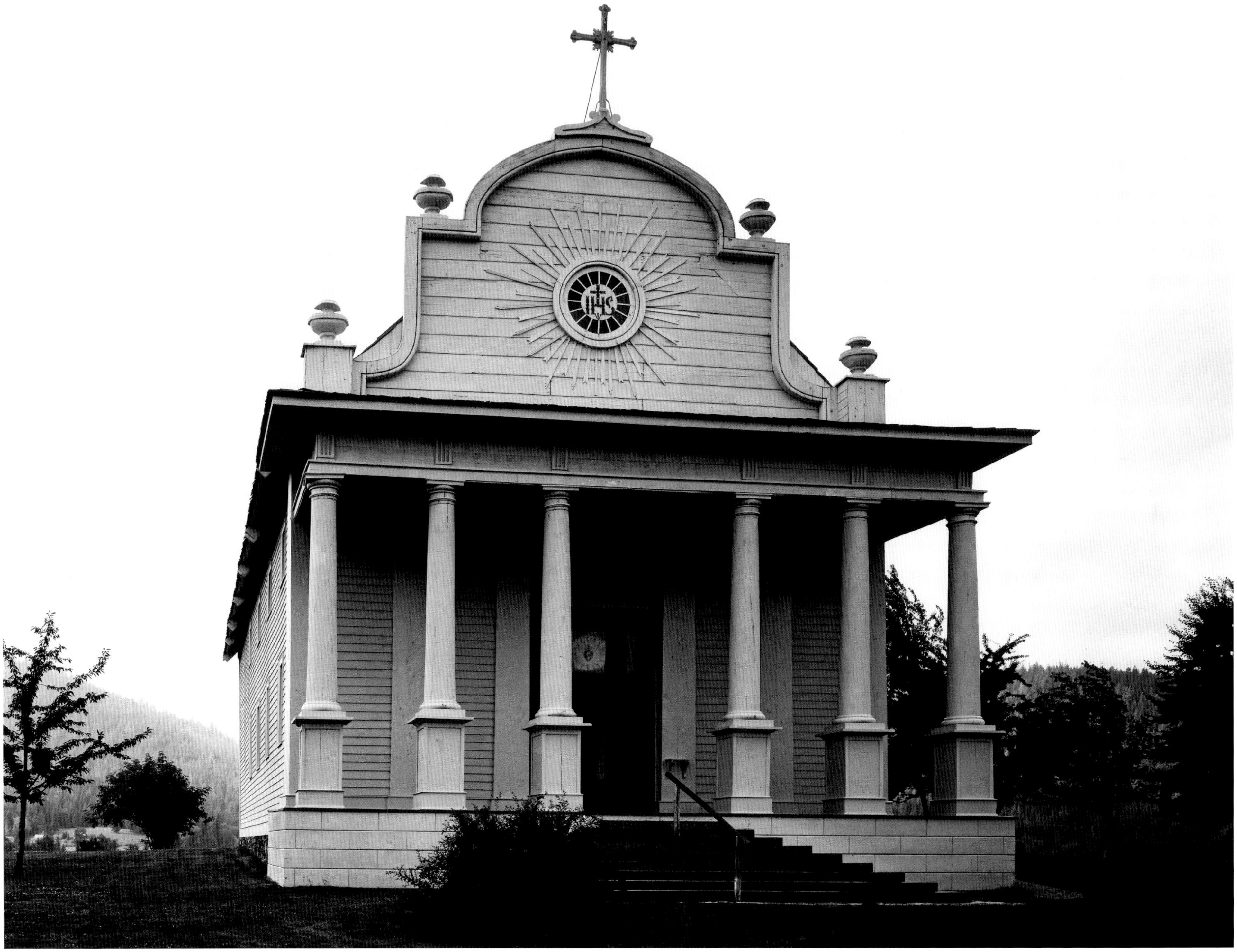

95, 96. Coeur D'Alene, Idaho. Old Mission (1850–53).

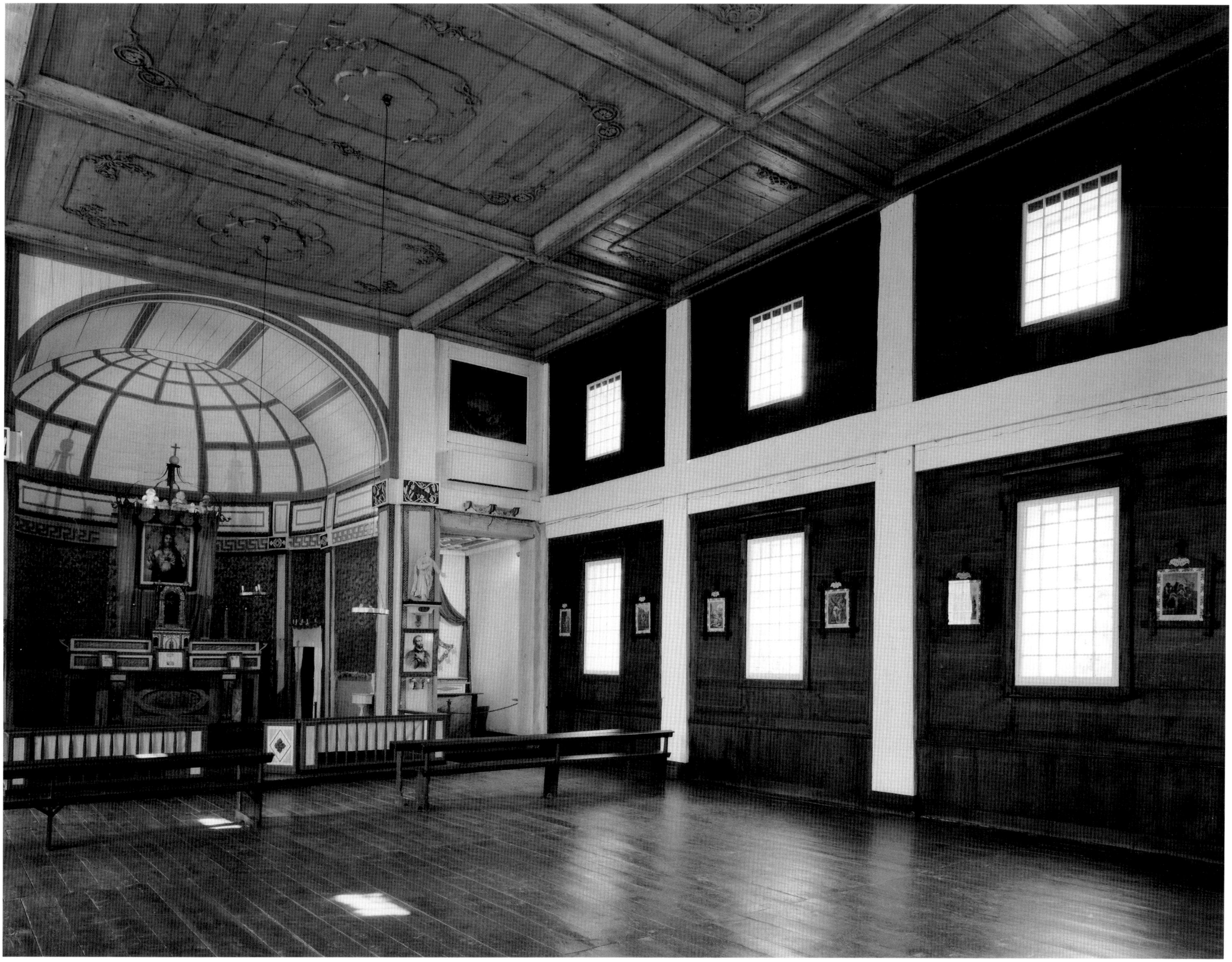

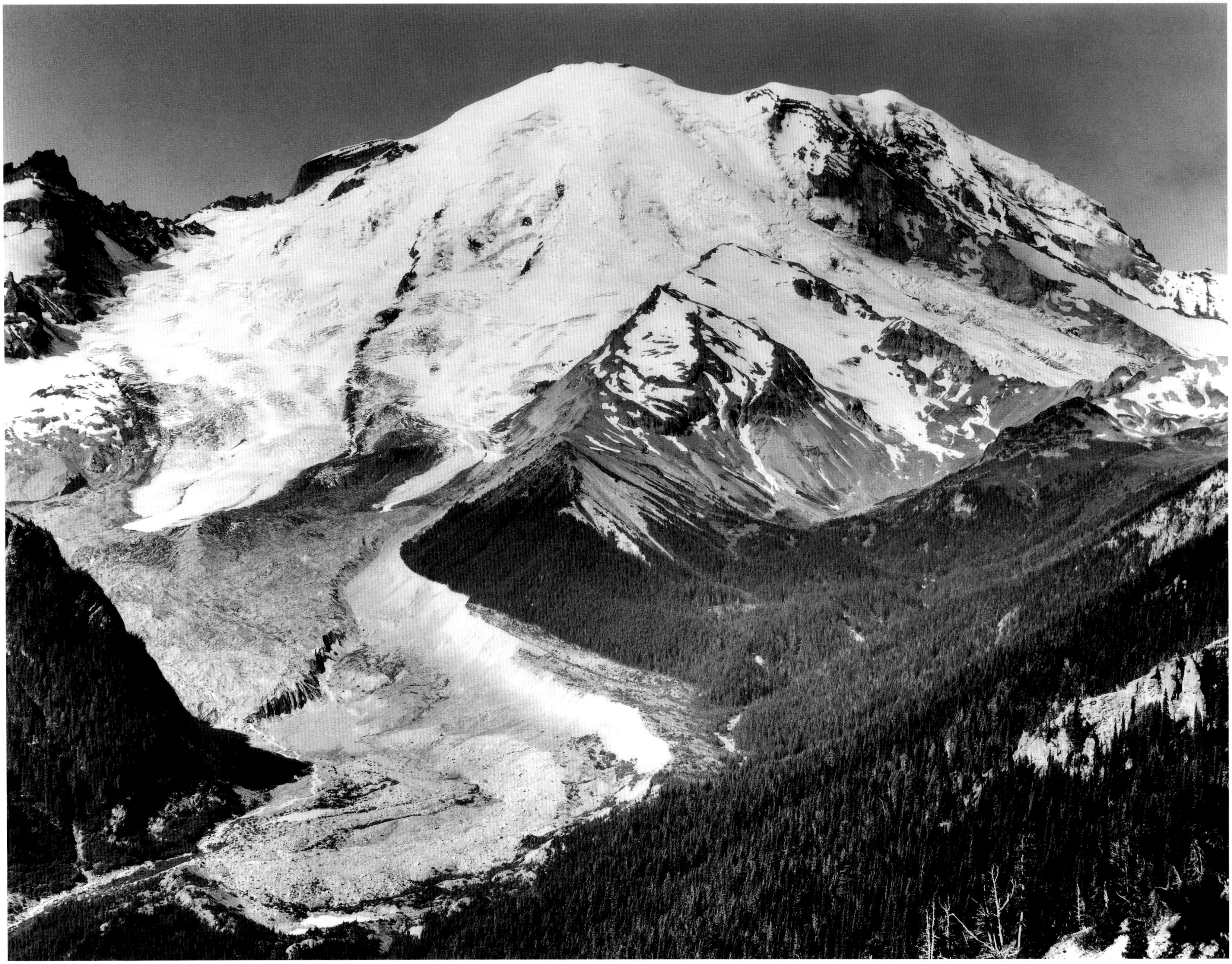

97. Mount Rainier National Park. Mount Rainier.
98. Mount St. Helens National Park. Blick auf den bei dem Ausbruch am 18. Mai 1980 entstandenen Krater des Mount St. Helens.

97. Mount Rainier National Park. Mount Rainier.
98. Mount St. Helens National Park. View of the crater of Mount St. Helens, which came into being during the eruption on 18 May 1980.

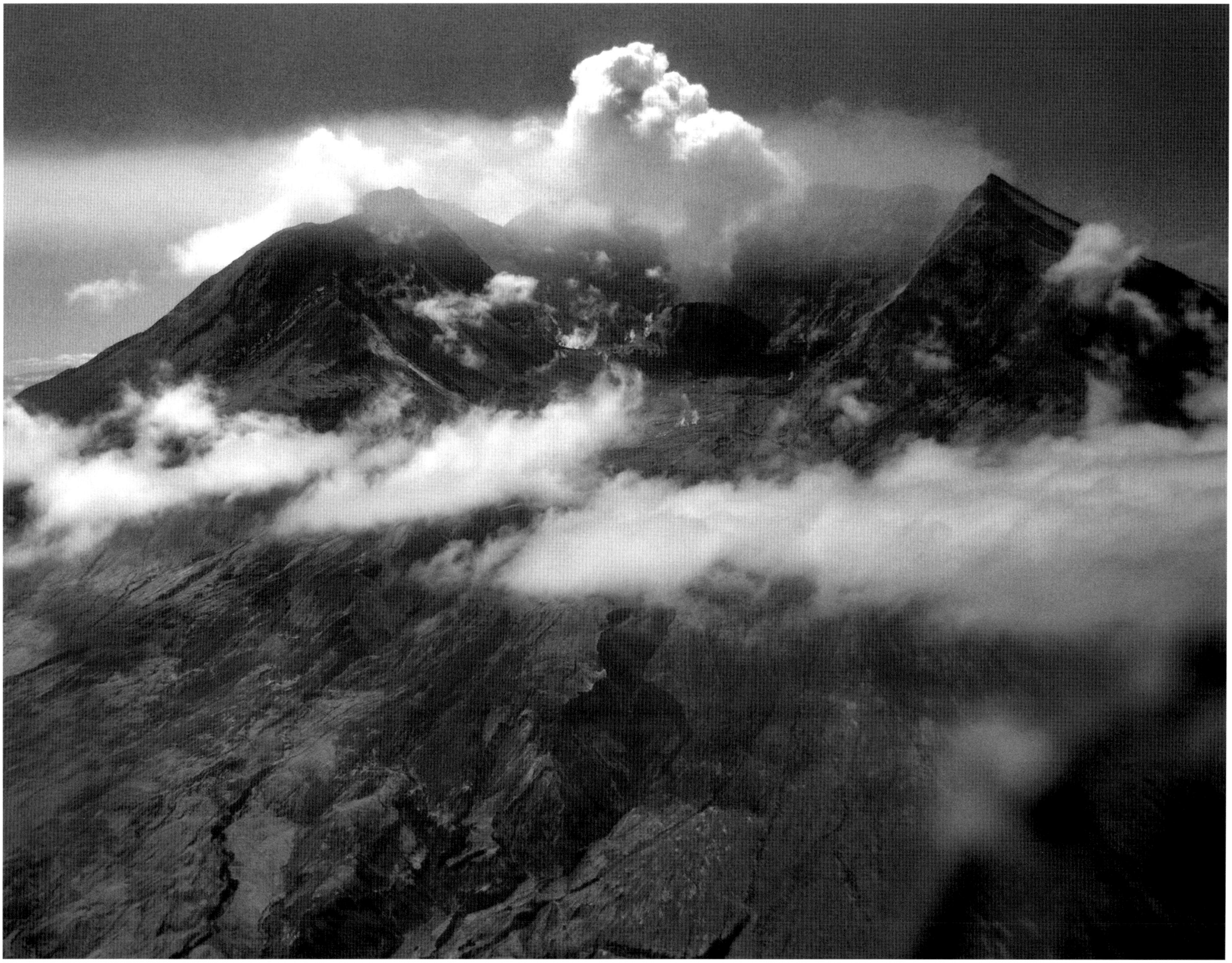

99. Eureka, California. Carson Mansion (1884–86).
100. Redwood National Park. Redwood nördlich des Lady Bird Johnson Grove.

99. Eureka, California. Carson Mansion (1884–86).
100. Redwood National Park. California. Redwood north of the Lady Bird Johnson Grove.

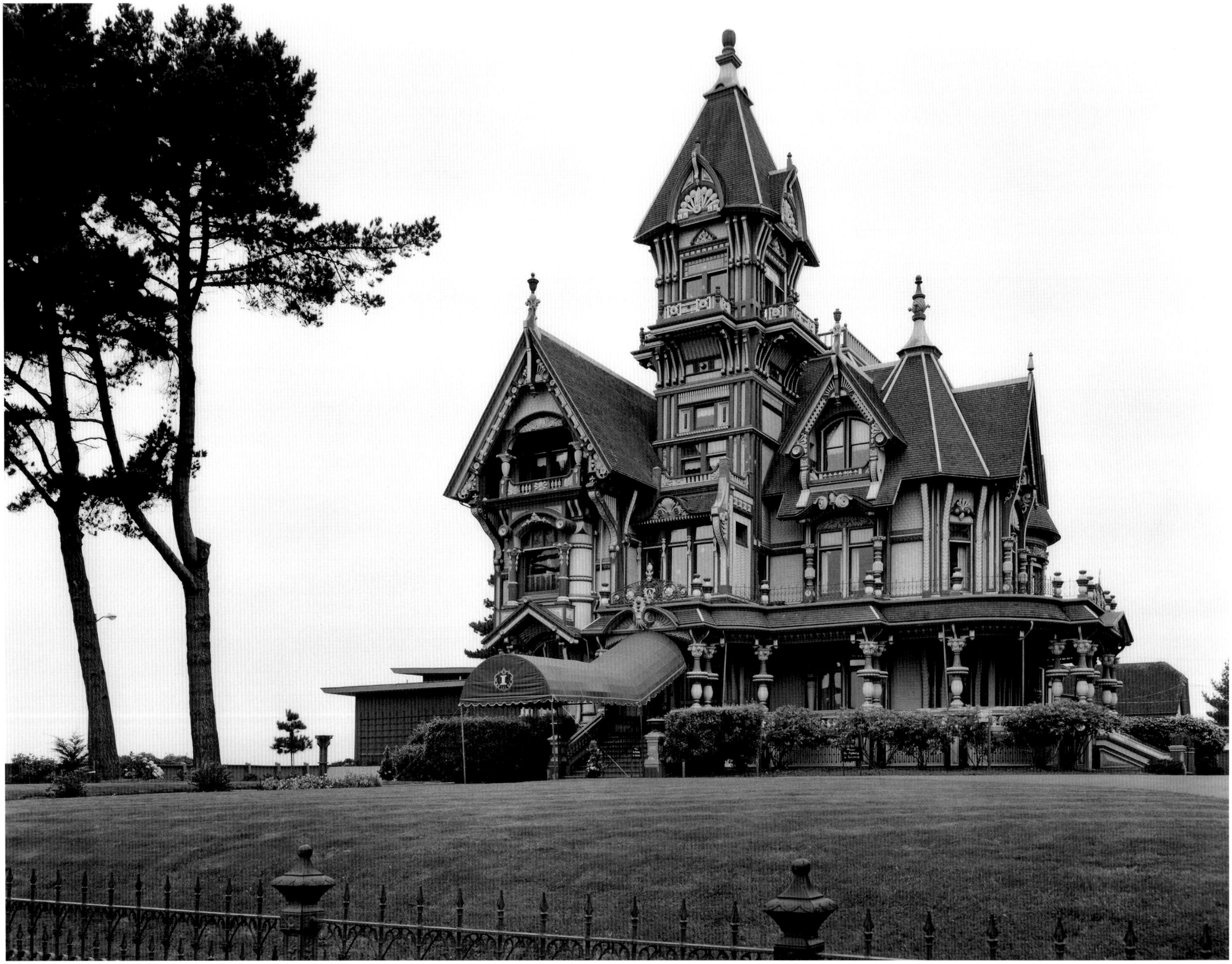

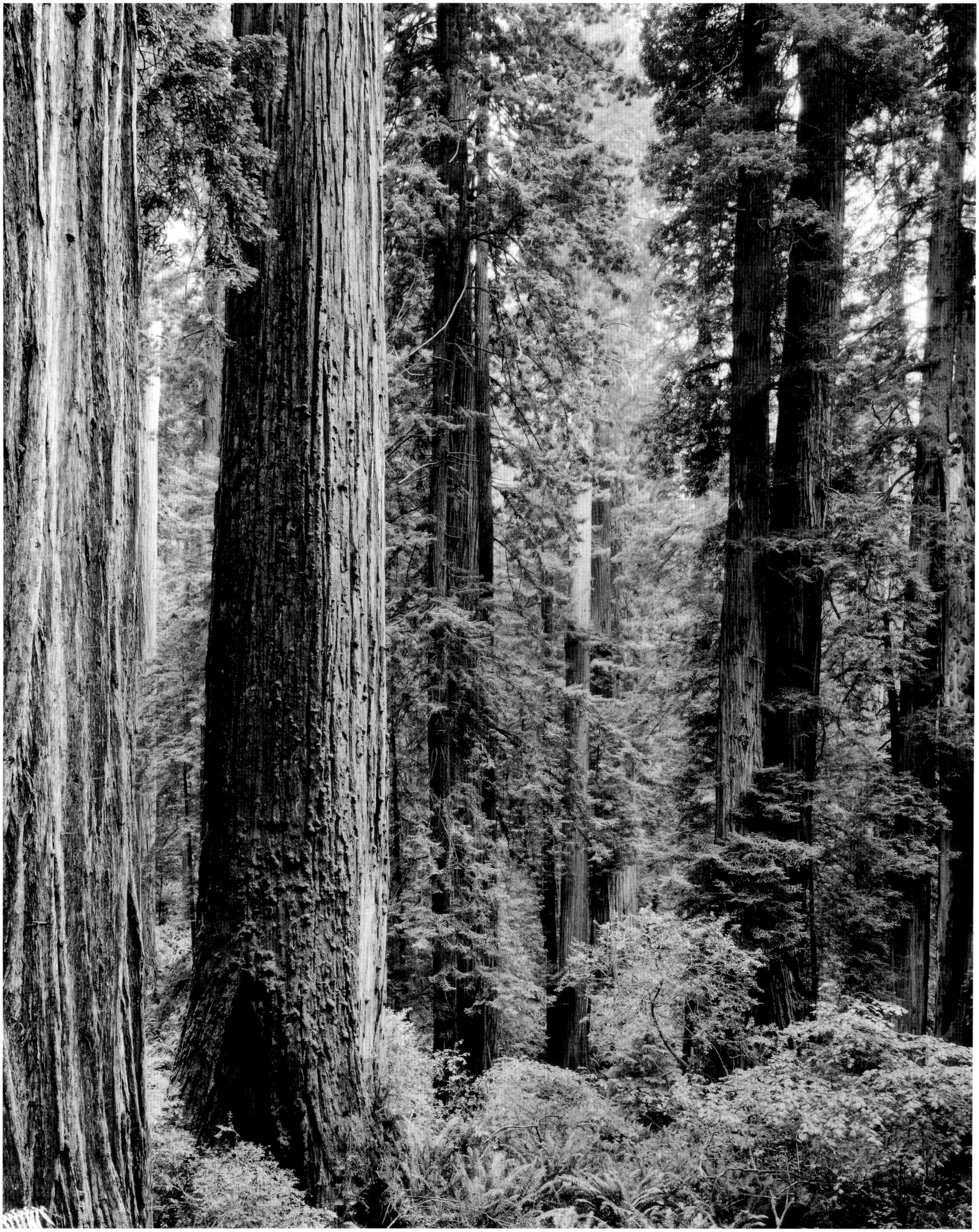

101. Yosemite National Park. Blick vom Glacier Point in das Yosemite Valley, rechts der Half Dome.
102. Yosemite National Park. Half Dome.

101. Yosemite National Park. View of Yosemite Valley, to the right Half Dome.
102. Yosemite National Park. Half Dome.

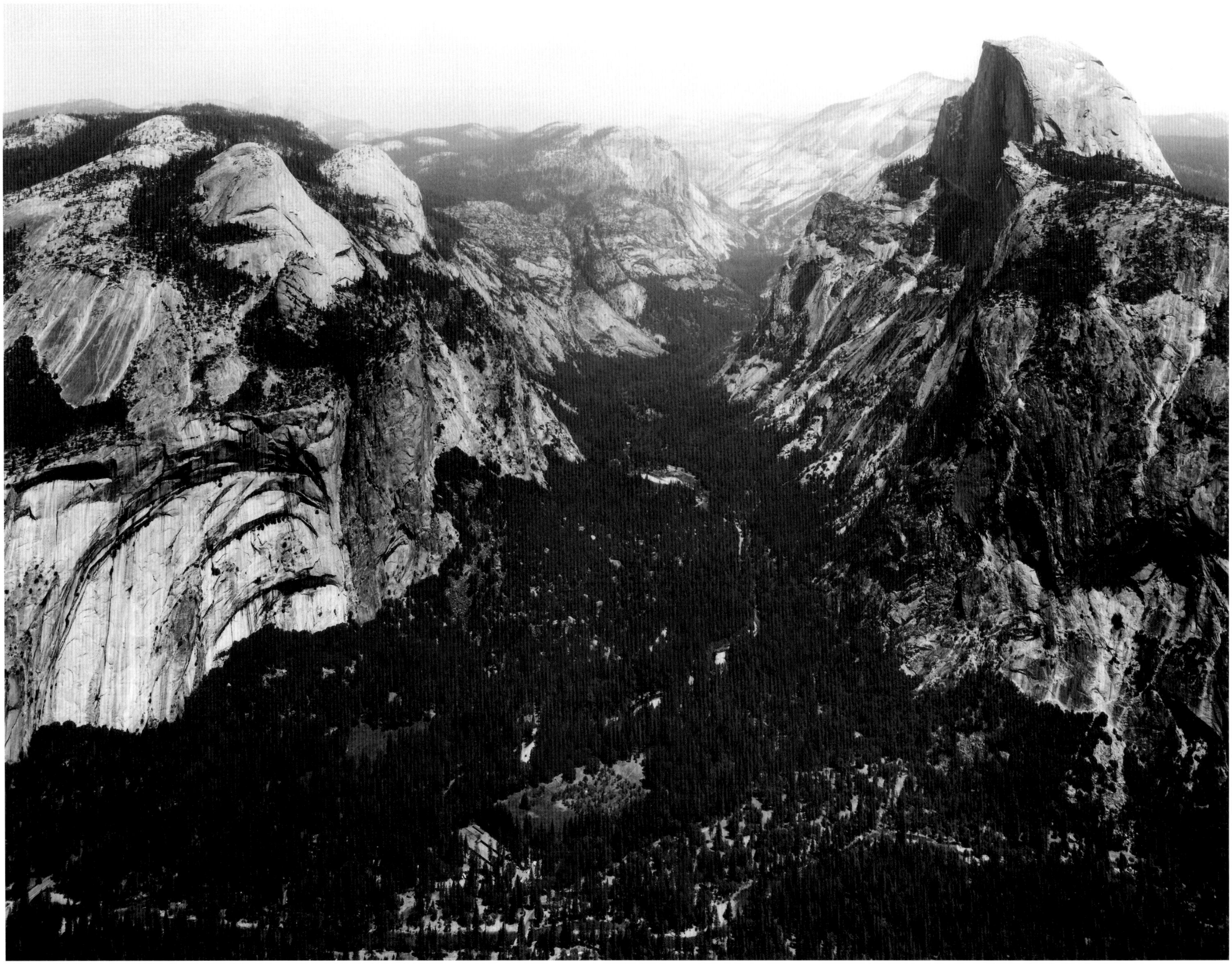

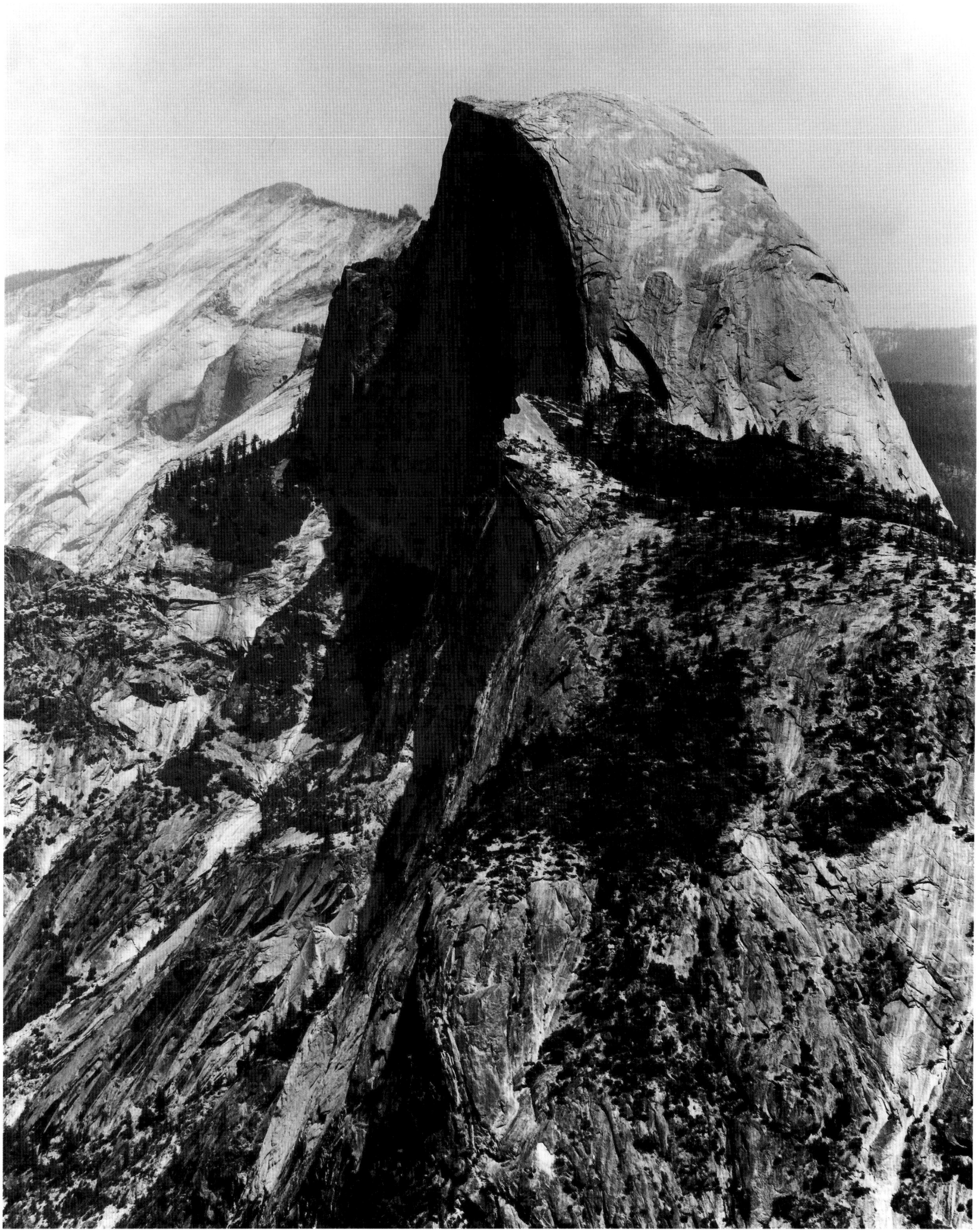

103, 104. Yosemite National Park. Der El Capitan von der El Capitan Meadow aus gesehen.

103, 104. Yosemite National Park. El Capitan seen from El Capitan Meadow.

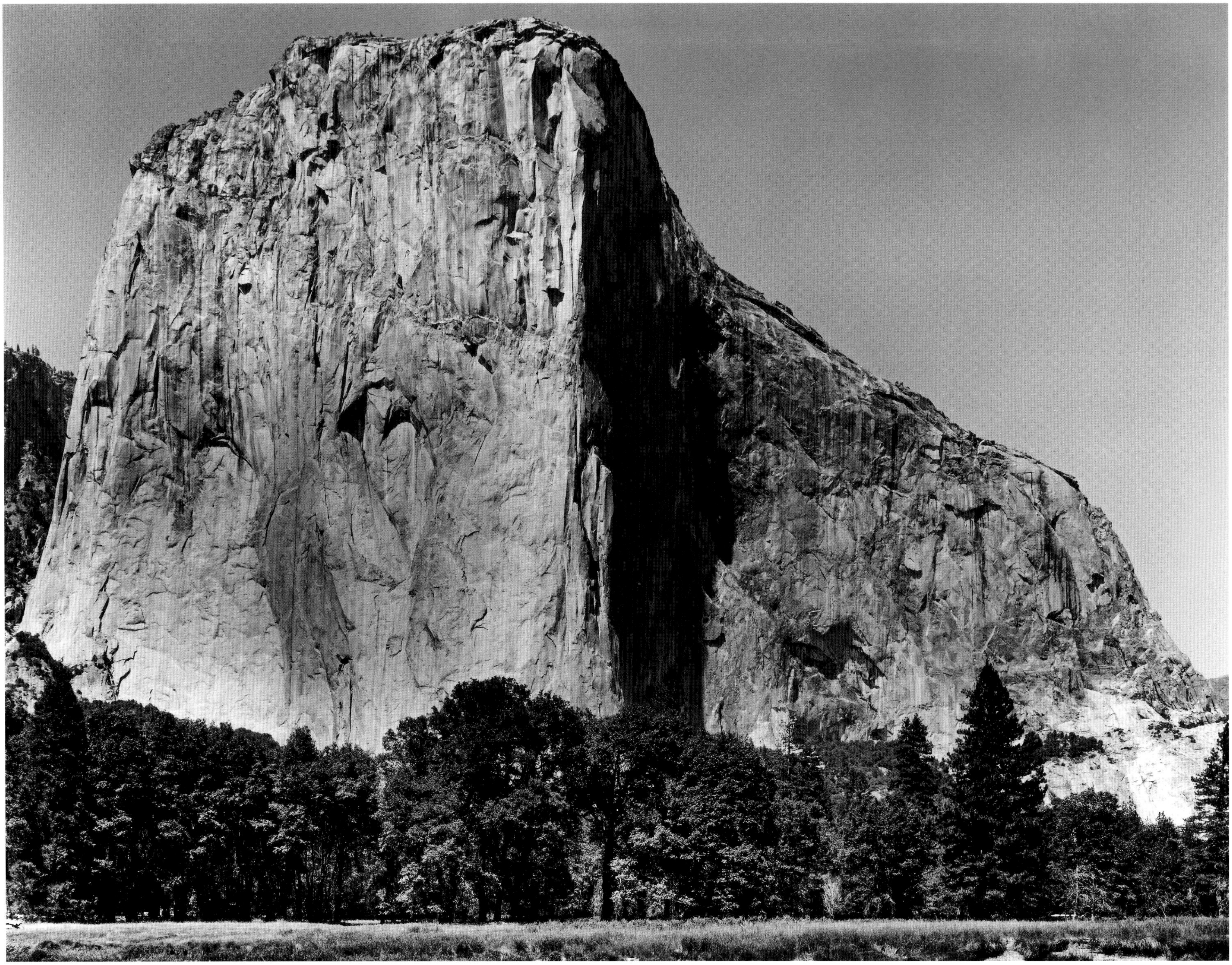

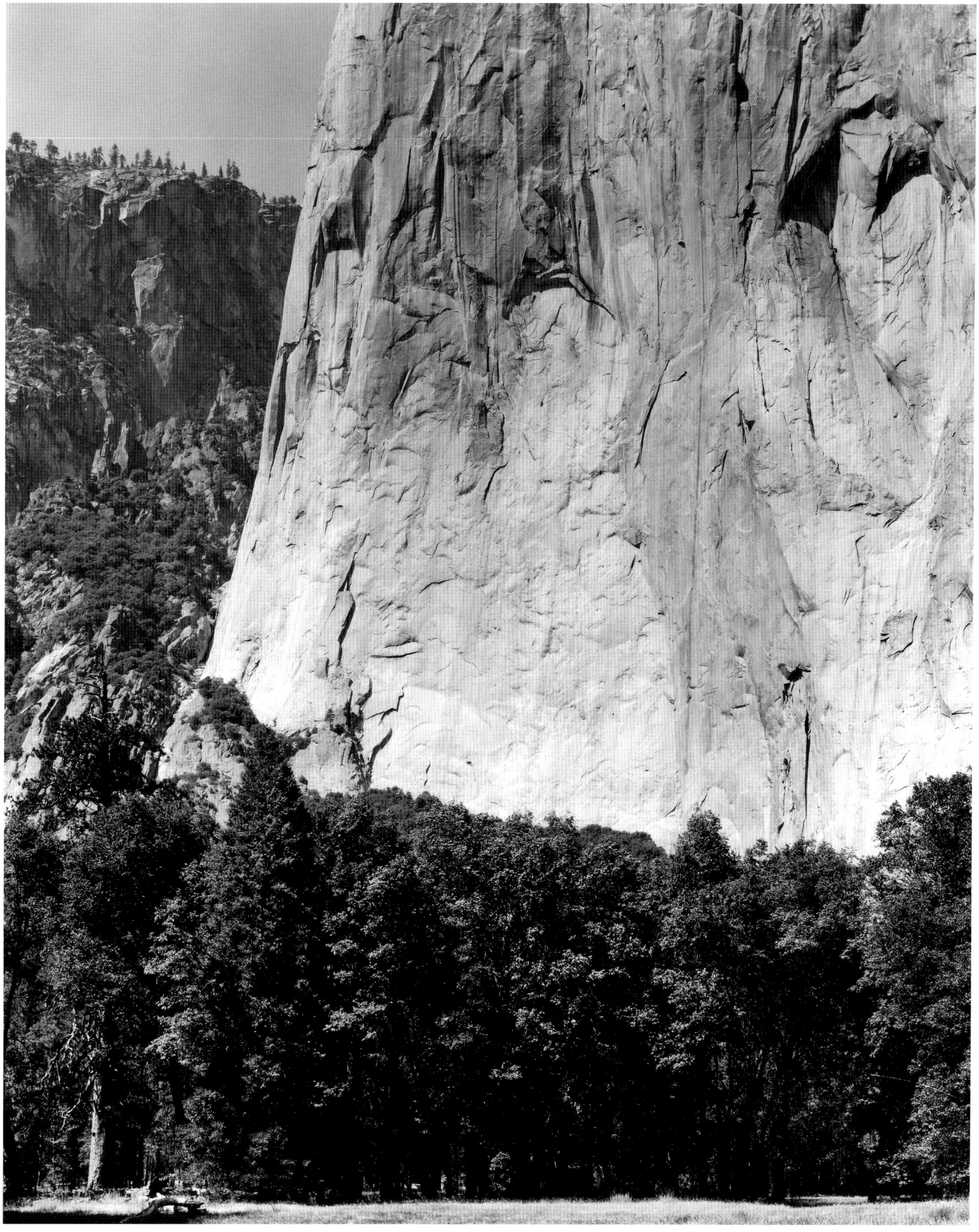

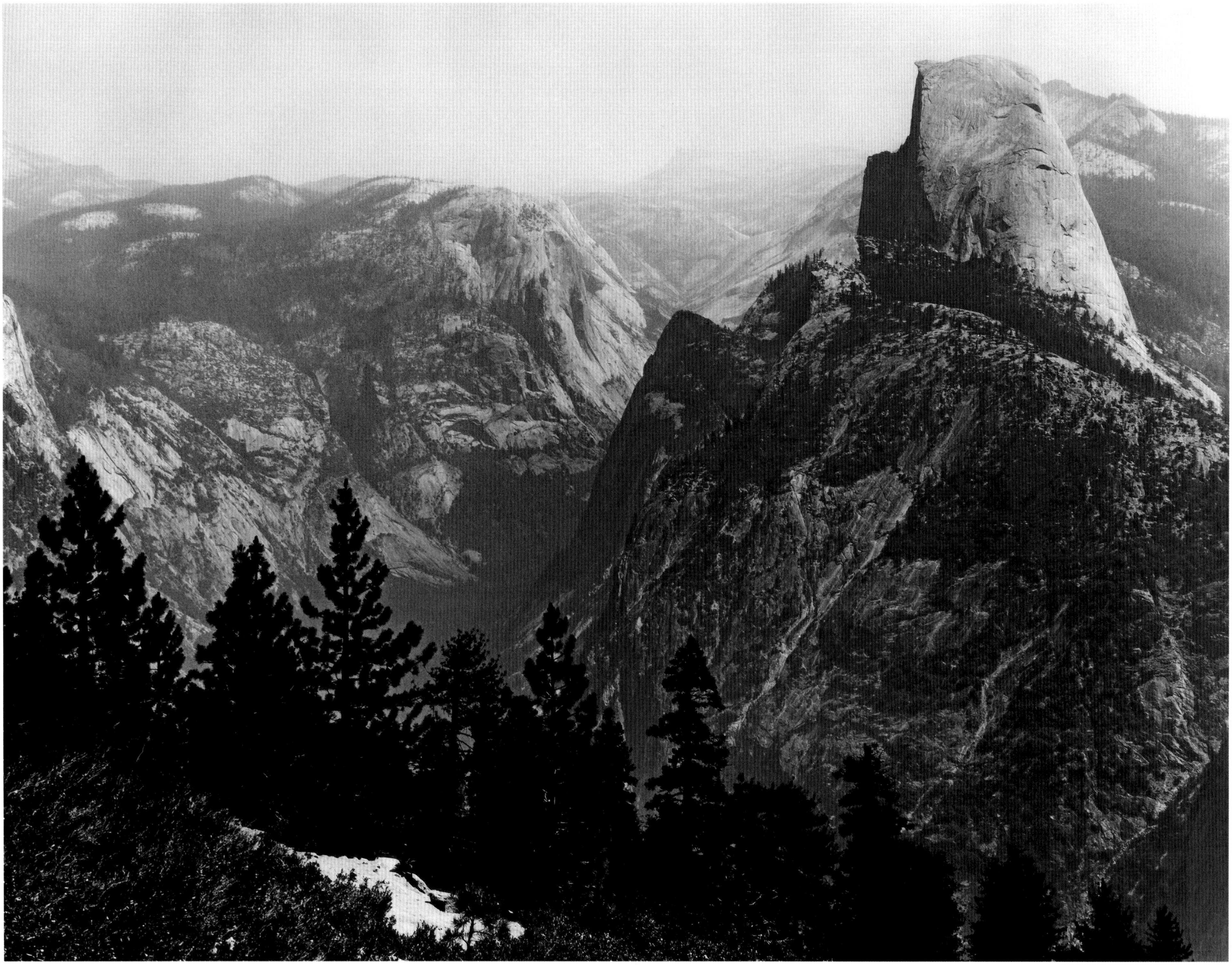

105. Yosemite National Park. Blick vom Washburn Point in das Yosemite Valley, rechts der Half Dome.
106. Yosemite National Park. Blick vom Tunnel View in das Yosemite Valley.

105. Yosemite National Park. View of Yosemite Valley from Washburn Point, to the right Half Dome.
106. Yosemite National Park. View of Yosemite Valley from Tunnel View.

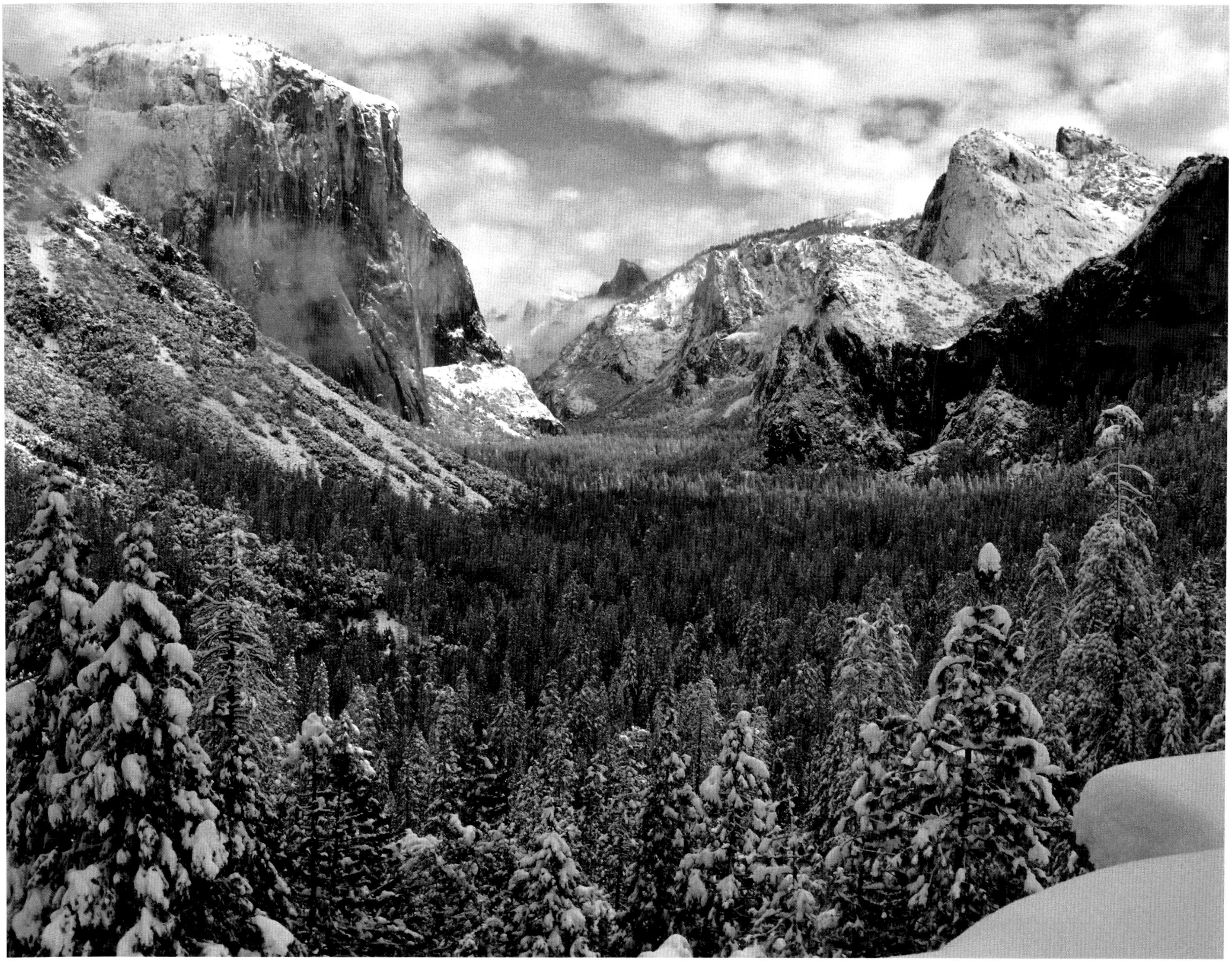